The Comics Form

Also available from Bloomsbury by Chris Gavaler

Superhero Comics: A Critical Guide
Creating Comics: A Writer's and Artist's Guide and Anthology

The Comics Form

The Art of Sequenced Images

Chris Gavaler

BLOOMSBURY ACADEMIC
LONDON • NEW YORK • OXFORD • NEW DELHI • SYDNEY

BLOOMSBURY ACADEMIC
Bloomsbury Publishing Plc
50 Bedford Square, London, WC1B 3DP, UK
1385 Broadway, New York, NY 10018, USA
29 Earlsfort Terrace, Dublin 2, Ireland

BLOOMSBURY, BLOOMSBURY ACADEMIC and the Diana logo are trademarks
of Bloomsbury Publishing Plc

First published in Great Britain 2022

Cover design: Rebecca Heselton
Cover image: 'Autochrome Sequence' by Chris Gavaler

A catalogue record for this book is available from the British Library.

A catalog record for this book is available from the Library of Congress.

ISBN: HB: 978-1-3502-4591-4
        ePDF: 978-1-3502-4592-1
        eBook: 978-1-3502-4593-8

Typeset by RefineCatch Limited, Bungay, Suffolk
Printed and bound in Great Britain

To find out more about our authors and books visit www.bloomsbury.com
and sign up for our newsletters.

Contents

Illustrations

Acknowledgments

Thanks to John Bateman, Carolyn Cocca, Neil Cohn, Nathaniel Goldberg, Simon Grennan, Ann Miller, Andrei Molotiu, Greg Smith, and Barbara Tversky for reading early drafts, and to the following journals for publishing early sections: *International Journal of Comics Art*, "The Meanings of Comics" (18.1, 2016); *European Comic Art*, "Refining the Comics Form" (10.2, 2017); *Journal of Graphic Novels and Comics*, "Clarifying Closure" co-authored with Leigh Ann Beavers (9.3, 2018); *Image [&] Narrative*, "Three of a Perfect Pair: Image, Text, and Image-Text Narrators" (20.1, 2019); and *The Journal for the Philosophy of Language, Mind, and the Arts*, "Perceiving Images" co-authored with Nathaniel Goldberg (2.1, 2021).

Support for the publication of this book was provided by the Class of 1956 Provost's Faculty Development Endowment at Washington and Lee University.

Introduction: Defining Definitions

To analyze the comics form, it may seem necessary first to ask: What is a comic? Answers vary according to whom you ask. García calls a comic a "social object" defined by "its common social usage" (2010: 28), but multiple overlapping and sometimes contradictory usages coexist, producing no single "common" one. Groensteen explains the dilemma: "So great is the diversity of what has been claimed as comics, or what is claimed today under diverse latitudes, that it has become almost impossible to retain any definitive criteria that is universally held to be true" (2007: 14). "The question of definitions and terminology," concludes Earle in a recent introductory text on comics, "is one of the most hotly contested issues in what has come to be called Comics Studies" (2021: 12), a field, adds Hatfield, "defined by the unresolved nature of its very object of study" (2017: xi).

Some scholars accept the lack of definitional consensus as the nature of the object. Comics, argues Cohn, "can only be understood as sociological, literary, and cultural artifacts, independent from the internal structures comprising them" (2005: 9). Beaty offers a similar "functionalist" definition: comics are "objects recognized by the comics world as comics" (2012: 37). The phrase "comics world" makes the social nature of the definition explicit by naming, albeit circularly, a social group. The collective behaviors of creators, publishers, and consumers create a set of objects called "comics." Hague similarly argues that "a comic is what is produced or consumed as a comic" (2014: 27), implying evaluations by individual authors or readers rather than through group consensus. The individuals then might not agree, accepting and rejecting different objects for different and unstated reasons.

Individual scholars sometimes also employ more than one definition or category separated by ambiguous boundaries. Earle identifies "comics" primarily as "an umbrella term for the form as a whole," but she also notes that the same term is used "when discussing the industry, retail networks, and associated institutions," which are not aspects of form (2021: 13). According to Earle, "instructions for flat pack furniture or flight safety leaflets . . . are not strictly comics . . . but they are narratives told primarily via images, positioned in sequence, and, at their heart, this is all comics is" (2021: 1). The instructions and leaflets are not comics in some strict sense, but are comics in some other essential sense. Cohn opens *Who Understands Comics?* with a similar observation about "sequences of images bound by meaningful connections, including the ubiquitous instruction manuals and signage" (2021: 1), which he does not consider comics, yet sequences of images include what Cohn terms "visual narratives," which do include comics—even though abstract comics are a type of comic and a type of image sequence but not a type of narrative. The title of Cohn's *The Visual Language of Comics* and its subtitle, *Introduction to the Structure and Cognition of Sequential Images*, also imply that "comics" and "sequential images" are synonymous (2013).

Rather than asserting definitions, some scholars only imply criteria. Chute includes extended analyses of Jacques Callot's 1633 *The Miseries and Misfortunes of War* and Francisco Goya's 1810–20 *The Disasters of War* alongside chapters on Joe Sacco and Art Spiegelman, functionally categorizing all four as the same type of art since each is illuminated by the same analytical approach (2016). Articulating a similar strategy, Oravetz argues that a formalist approach

> becomes not a mode of definition, but a mode of interpretation. The question of comics becomes not, "What is a comic?", a question that has proven problematic and unanswerable, but "How can we do readings of objects through a comics lens?" Thus, notions of comics definition can be viewed not as exclusive categories, but tools in an analytical toolkit. They are ways in which to view and analyze visual objects, both "comics" and not, freed from the constraints of category and discipline.
>
> 2019: 6

Applying a "comics lens" to an object, however, is to analyze the object formally as a comic. For the lens to be applicable, the object must display a set of relevant formal features. If the set is absent, the formal lens is ineffective.

Beineke might call that set the "comicitous form," coining the adjective "comicitous" to describe works that have comics qualities "without labeling the work as a comic"; while appropriate with film and prose-only literature, Beineke also applies the approach to a "work which is distinguished by its particular use of the comicitous form" (2017: 230). By interpreting several grid-structured works by Andy Warhol as "comicitous," Beineke demonstrates the usefulness of formal comics analysis to works that traditionally are not called "comics," but without defining "the comicitous form" or distinguishing it from the comics form. While avoiding labeling has practical benefits, the strategy does not apply to form because a work that uses a form necessarily belongs to the category of that form. Just as a work in the sonnet form is formally a sonnet, a work in the comics form is formally a comic—though it might simultaneously not be a comic according to other criteria.

The Comics Form does not attempt to define or redefine comics by proposing a single set of criteria, because it is likely that no single set is possible, let alone practical. The initial question is instead: What formal qualities must an object have to be usefully analyzed through a comics lens? Or simply: What is the comics form? The subtitle offers one answer: sequenced images. Though other answers are possible, sequenced images is the most common denominator of comics definitions. Over a dozen comics scholars discussed below directly or indirectly suggest it. Rather than questioning that pervasiveness, I accept it as a directive for further inquiry.

The approach is formal because images and sequence are intrinsic features of perceived objects, and because they are necessary and sufficient to define the form, they are also formalist features. However, since I also retain the term "comics" as an adjective, Horrocks's critique of McCloud may apply here, too: "Essentially, he has taken one term—or concept—(Eisner's 'sequential art') and grafted it on to the old word 'comics.'... The new meaning colonizes the old word" (2001: 31). A reader might similarly object to sequenced images defining the comics form. If so, instead of asking how do comics work, this book's guiding question is: How do sequenced images work? The two questions produce the same answer, which, because I am responding to the scholarly consensus of comics' formal features, is titled *The Comics Form*.

Defining the form is distinct from defining comics generally, which can be sequenced images only when analyzed formally. Some work defined as comics by other criteria are not formally comics, and some works outside those definitions are formally comics. The two features, sequence and images, produce a specific grouping of objects. Other definitions produce other groupings, and though no grouping is inherently superior, it's useful to acknowledge that more than one definition-based grouping is in play and that some apparent disagreements are miscommunications based on unacknowledged differences in definitions and categories. "What is a comic?" is an unsolvable riddle only if it is understood to require a single answer.

Below I map a range of definitions for objects that have been called "comics," before exploring the qualities of sequenced images for the remainder of this book—not because sequenced images is sociologically or historically the most accurate or important definition, but because that pair of formal parameters invites fuller study. Since the pair is considered to be the most common formal quality of comics as defined by other parameters, understanding it better should also produce a better understanding of works across definitions. By defining the form first and then using that form to determine what is or is not formally a comic, I hope to clarify confusions and bridge disagreements.

The remainder of this introduction maps the conflicting reasons an object might be called a "comic." The resulting conceptual terrain may not be comics per se but connotations that the word evokes, each focusing on a different grouping of trees in the larger forest. I begin with an aerial view of what appears to be major definitional or connotational areas. "Comics" has at least four overlapping but competing meanings:

1. comics the publishing history;
2. comics the cartoon style;
3. comics the conventions; and
4. comics the form.

Since applying "comic" to any object that has been called a comic does not produce a tool for analysis (because different speakers may use the word for different unstated reasons), these subdivided categories instead suggest explanations for *why* someone might call an object a comic: *because* of its publication context, *because* it is drawn in a certain style, *because* it shares some qualities with other objects that have been called comics, or *because* it possesses a set of necessary and sufficient physical features. Since all of these approaches can be understood as kinds of social approaches, the category of comics as social objects produces no grouping other than the forest in its entirety. The next four sections explore regions. Though they aren't mutually exclusive, I discuss each independently before considering the Venn diagrams of their overlaps.

1. Publishing History

Barker was one of the first scholars to express this medium-focused approach: "*a comic is what has been produced under the definition of a 'comic'*" (1989: 8). Because publication context is not an intrinsic feature, publishing history is arguably the clearest subcategory of the social approach because it relies on publishers' and purchasers' use of "comic" or related terms rather than on identifying qualities of objects. The approach does not explain why some objects are called "comics" and others not. Defining comics by publishing history requires an overview of that history and the stipulation that all objects and only those objects appearing in the history are comics.

In the nineteenth century a comic was a humor magazine that published prose-only stories and cartoons. What would now be called "comics" were initially called "comic strips": humorous vignettes told in a short sequence of cartoon images. The adjective referred to their genre and the noun to their form. Though there are many forebears, comic strips emerged popularly in the 1890s. The term transferred to newspaper cartoon sections before the end of the decade, becoming synonymous with "funnies" and "funny pages." A comic strip is now considered a kind of comic, but "comic" originally was a truncation of "comic strip" and so referenced the same category. "Comic books" originally referred to collections of newspaper comic strips reprinted in magazine format but later came to refer to individual issues of original-content series, typically published monthly, and each series was called a "comic book" as well. The term was in use by 1904, but the 1934 *Famous Funnies* established the standard size for US publishers. *Action Comics* made the medium massively popular beginning in 1938. The "comic strip" truncation "strip" remained common, too, and referenced any kind of comic, including comic books, until at least 1942 when Wonder Woman was introduced as an "adventure strip character" in *Sensation Comics*. "Graphic novel" emerged in the 1960s and 1970s in an attempt to differentiate book-length works that were also not in the popular children's genres of humor or action. Will Eisner popularized the term with his 1978 *Contract With God*. Although a prose-only novel refers to fiction, a graphic novel may be fiction or nonfiction. "Graphic narrative" emerged to combine graphic fiction and graphic nonfiction, including graphic memoir and graphic journalism. Though not the first example, Art Spiegelman's *Maus* established the category of graphic nonfiction when he wrote to the *New York Times* requesting that it be moved from the fiction to the nonfiction bestseller list in 1991. Though Alison Bechdel's *Fun Home* was called a graphic novel when published in 2006, it is now commonly referred to as a graphic memoir. Though each of the above terms could be used to indicate a distinct category, any work in the above context, according to a general publishing history approach, could be called a "comic."

By not specifying formal characteristics, comics as defined by publishing history prevents the application of "comic" to works created before 1890. Meskin, for example, criticizes "the ahistoricism of McCloud's account" because it accepts "far too many things as comics" (2007: 370). He finds Hayman and Pratt's formal definition similarly "unsatisfactory" because it is "open to plausible counterexamples from the prehistory of comics," which he considers "perverse," dismissing all formal definitions because they suffer from "a trouble that has always faced formalism—its failure to take into account the historical contexts in which works of art are produced" (2007: 369, 373, 374). Miodrag similarly critiques the use of sequentiality in formal definitions because it ignores historical considerations: "It is through reducing the form to this one feature that critics are sometimes led into dubiously categorizing diverse, historically distant artifacts as comics" (2013: 108). These are reasonable objections, and by making them, historically focused scholars acknowledge the larger forest by advocating that some of it be partitioned, including "the Bayeux Tapestry and those troublesome pre-Columbian Manuscripts" because, Meskin argues, they were not intended by their creators to be "comics" (2007: 375).

Reference to authorial intention, however, suggests shortcomings to using publishing history to define comics generally. By Meskin's logic, Jules Verne and H. G. Wells would not be science fiction authors because the term "science fiction" was coined in 1929. According to the *Oxford English Dictionary*, the term "chiaroscuro" dates only to 1686, after the deaths of both its exemplary artists, Rembrandt and Caravaggio, and the technique is also commonly but anachronistically traced to ancient Greece. Ahistoric terminology is a norm of categorization and analysis. Saying a creator did not intend her work to be referred to by a term that did not exist is self-evident and also misleading if it implies that the creator therefore did not understand her work to possess qualities later linked to that term.

Publishing history is also less effective at treating individual features that occur in works published prior to 1890. Whether defined as comics or not, many fifteenth-century illustrations include conventions common to later publishing-defined comics, including panels, caption boxes, and medieval speech scrolls. Because they do not include the pointers (or tails) typical of speech balloons in twentieth-century comics, speakers are indicated by proximity and the curve of a scroll toward a figure's mouth. That a viewer can understand the framed words as the speech of a figure at the moment depicted means a medieval speech scroll and a twentieth-century speech balloon differ in style but little else. Many manuscript pages are also divided into layouts commonly found in the comics medium. As drawn by Maître François, Valerius Maximus's *Facta et dicta memorabilia* features three rows divided into two panels each. Westwell lists the 1470s illustrated manuscript as an example of "Medieval comics" (2014). When discussing a wheel of fortune illustration in the early-fourteenth-century *Psalter of Robert de Lille*, Rust notes that a "circle divided into wedges by means of its 'spokes' depicts a sequence"—a layout also seen in contemporary comics pages (2016: 4). "Thus," concludes Sabin, "the idea that the 'language of comics' was solely the invention of the modern era is manifestly mistaken" (1996: 11).

Because such works are not comics according to publishing-history approaches, their sharing of multiple conventions makes them categorically ambiguous. Such resemblances may be coincidental and so ahistorical, or they may be the result of a history beginning prior to 1890. Sabin begins in the early 1600s with woodblock-printed broadsheets called "comicals" (2016: 12). Tabachnick excludes "hieroglyphics and cave drawing, which are sometimes cited as the origins of comics" but identifies eighteenth-century artists William Hogarth, James Gillray, and Thomas Rowlandson as creating "artworks containing some elements of what would become the comics," including sequential panels, repeating characters, and word balloons (2017: 27).

Smolderen similarly observes that comics "have reactivated a very old tradition that can be definitively located in the work of Hogarth" (2014: 3).

Is it anachronistic then to call Hogarth's works comics? For Meskin presumably yes, because the relevant history begins later:

> The art of comics, which began in the middle of the nineteenth century and developed largely out of eighteenth- and nineteenth-century caricature and mid-nineteenth-century British humor magazines such as *Punch,* can and should be understood on its own terms and by reference to its own history.
>
> 2007: 376

Meskin therefore also implicitly endorses a second definitional approach.

2. Cartoon

According to a comics-as-cartoons approach, an image or a set of images is a comic if drawn in a cartoon style. "Cartoon," however, has its own complex history of meanings.

Beginning in the 1600s, "cartoon" referred to the cardboard-like material artists used for preliminary sketches. After *Punch* published a set of mock architectural sketches for a planned parliamentary building in 1843, "cartoon" came to mean any satirical illustration drawn in the simplified and exaggerated style of caricature—combining publishing history and formal features. "Cartoon" is also sometimes used synonymously with "comics." Vermont's Center for Cartoon Studies offers a two-year M.F.A. in comics, and New Jersey's Kubert School of Cartoon and Graphic Art makes no distinction between the two terms. The University of Oregon has offered an undergraduate minor in Comics and Cartoon Studies since 2012, and the Ohio State University Press publishes a Studies in Comics and Cartoon series focused "exclusively on comics and graphic literature," adding a third ambiguously related term.

Chute asserts that "cartoon denotes a single-panel image" (2010: 12), but Bell and Sinclair instead categorize "single panel" as a kind of comic (2002: 40). Artist Liana Finck offers a possible distinction:

> A cartoon usually consists of a single drawing, often accompanied by a line of text, either in the form of a caption underneath the drawing, or a speech bubble.... A comic, on the other hand, comprises a series of drawings, often in boxes, or, as we like to call them, "panels," which form a narrative.
>
> 2019: n.p.

Finck's adverb "usually" is problematic, since a cartoon that does not consist of a single image then is undefined. Holbo notes that "Using one panel isn't a drawing style, it's a *narrative* style" (2104: 6), but if understood by the qualities of simplification and exaggeration, cartoon is a drawing style regardless of the number of images involved. If a comic consists of multiple images, those images may or may not be cartoons. Though some have multiple panels, political cartoons are typically single images and so are not formally comics if the comics form is defined as sequenced images. One-image cartoons and multi-image strips historically appear together on newspaper pages because they share the genre of humor, the style of cartooning, or both.

Though socially and even institutionally "comics" and "cartoons" are sometimes used synonymously, it may be useful to divide the terms. Rifkind does this by identifying "cartooning" as "the technique used in comics" (2019: 10). Since other image-making techniques, such as the photography used pervasively in Italian fumetto, also appear in the comics medium, the distinction reveals a range of combinations. A "cartoon comic" would be sequenced images drawn in a cartoon style and so distinct from a photocomic. Using cartoon as a definitional approach for comics generally reduces the meaning of "comics" to cartoons and so effectively eliminates comics as its own category. Since many comics—whether defined by publishing history, form, or other criteria—are not drawn in a cartoon style (or not drawn at all), such objects would have no category.

3. Conventions

Cartoon style is a kind of convention, revealing another overlap in definitional approaches. Conventional features, or conventions, differ from essential features according to whether a category requires them. Words, for example, would be an essential feature of comics if a work must include at least one word to be a comic. If a work can be a comic without including words, then words are non-essential, even if they are overwhelmingly common. Some conventions are also formal in the physical sense: reproductions of hand-drawn images produced by ink on bound pieces of paper, for example. Various convention-based definitions combine physical and non-physical features, identifying none as essential.

Inge defines a comic strip as "an open-ended dramatic narrative about a recurring set of characters, told in a series of drawings, often including dialogue in balloons and a narrative text, and published serially in newspapers" (1990: xi). While often accurate, the description does not apply to all comics or even all comic strips. With the exception of "series," Inge's list includes no necessary qualities. Though Inge may have intended his definition to be formal in the essentialist sense, from a common-features approach, it need not be. Groensteen argues that an "essentialist" approach is "doomed to failure" because "comics rests on a group of coordinating mechanisms" that interact in "extremely varied forms from one comic to another" so that any specific work "only actualizes certain potentialities" (2007: 12). If so, comics are a set of works that display a range of conventions that manifest in different combinations but with no requisites. Cataloguing the definitions of thirteen comics scholars, Szawerna identifies twenty-two such optional characteristics (2012: 65). Witek also notes that characteristics are continually changing: "any number of formal conventions that once were commonly used in comics have now nearly disappeared" (2009: 149). Since such features can fall into disuse, they cannot define comics either formally or generally.

A conventions approach allows scholars to select narrower areas of interest, as Carrier does by defining a comic strip as "a narrative sequence with speech balloons" (2000: 4). Since Carrier offers this idiosyncratic subregion as "true comics," his approach is flawed, but understood as "only a question of focus," his analysis is useful (2000: 4). Szawerna's claim that "the panel is without a doubt a fundamental component of comics" (2012: 63) is accurate in terms of conventions (because panels are overwhelmingly common in works that are typically called "comics") but is formally false (because some objects called "comics" do not include panels and so panels are not a necessary feature). Since comics defined as a loose set of conventions has no definitive criteria, the approach is akin to US Supreme Court Justice Potter Stewart's 1964 intuition regarding pornography: "I know it when I see it." Or as Carrier observes: "Comics ... are like pop music—an art form almost all of us understand without any need for theorizing" (2000: 2). However, we understand a musical composition to be or not to be "pop music" by recognizing, consciously or unconsciously, any of a range of possible conventions. Wittgenstein refers to this approach as "family resemblance," and comics defined as a set of conventions is such a family because the category includes many objects with overlapping properties but no property necessarily present in all.

Conventions evolve, and so comics defined by conventions evolve, too. Discussing how Miriam Libicki's graphic nonfiction merges journalism, memoir, and academic essay, Haskett asks whether comics can "really be ... a vehicle for sharing rigorous scholarly research?" (2019: n.p.). She answers yes, demonstrating an expansion in conventions regarding subject matter since "rigorous scholarly research" describes no comic from the first half of the twentieth century. Comics as conventions is so expansive, works that meet no other convention but tone are sometimes referred to as a "comic" or "cartoon." McCloud observes: "Film critics will sometimes describe a live-action film as a 'cartoon' to acknowledge the stripped-down intensity of a simple story or visual style" (31). Schell in his essay "Invitation to a Degraded World" criticizes President George W. Bush for accepting "Bin Laden's invitation to enter into the world of an apocalyptic comic book," dividing "every person and government on earth into two camps—the good, the lovers of freedom, who are 'with us,' and the 'evil-doers' who hate the good ones for their very goodness" (2004: n.p.). Schell is evoking the story conventions of the subgenre of superhero comics, which are sufficient for his application of "comic book" to the post-9/11 world order. Duncan and Smith note the reverse effect, where content conventions can be used to exclude a work, as when Lange opens his *New York Times* review of *Maus* by claiming that "Art Spiegelman does not draw comics" (quoted in 2015: xi).

4. Form

Presumably no comics scholars would exclude Speigelman' work. *Maus* suits comics the publishing history, the cartoon style, and the conventions, as well as comics the form. While many scholars reject a formal definitional approach, it is the most common. Groensteen, despite arguing forcefully against definitions, makes a formal claim: "The necessary, if not sufficient, condition required to speak of comics is that the images will be multiple and correlated in some fashion" (2007: 19). Although Cook suggests it is "unlikely that a precise definition of 'comic,' or even an account of substantial necessary or sufficient conditions for being a comic, will be forthcoming" (2011: 294), excerpts from extant definitions reveal at least two commonalities:

Waugh, 1947: "a sequence of pictures" (1947: 14).
Kunzle, 1973: "a sequence of separate images" (quoted in Carrier 2000: 3).
Harvey, 1979: "a narrative . . . told by a sequence of pictures" (1979: 641).
Eisner, 1985: "sequential art" (2008: 1).
Barker, 1989: "sequences of pictures" (1989).
Inge, 1990: "a series of drawings" (quoted in Beaty 2012: 27).
McCloud, 1993: "images juxtaposed in deliberate sequence" (1993: 9).
Blackbeard, 1995: "sequential narrative in drawn panels" (1995: 10).
Groensteen, 1999: "interdependent images . . . in a series" (2007: 18).
Lefèvre, 2000: "the juxtaposition of fixed (mostly drawn) pictures" (quoted in Harvey 2005: 17).
Carrier, 2000: "a narrative sequence with speech balloons" (2000: 4).
Hayman and Pratt, 2005: "a sequence of discrete, juxtaposed pictures" (2005: 423).
Miller, 2007: "images . . . in a sequential relationship" (2007: 75).
Abel and Madden, 2008: "multiple images . . . intended to be read in a certain order" (2008: 5).
Cohn, 2013: "a sociological context in which [a visual language of sequential images] appear" (2013: 1–2).
Kukkonen, 2013: "images combined into a sequence" (2013: 6).
Cook, 2015: "two or more visually distinct parts" (2015: n.p.).
Duncan and Smith, 2015: "a sequence of juxtaposed panels and pages" (2015: xiii).

Fifteen of the eighteen include "sequence," "sequential," or "series," and Abel and Madden provide an equivalent phrase, "a certain order." Three include "juxtaposed" or "juxtaposition," which is a necessary quality of sequence (and also possibly sufficient as discussed in Chapter 6). All but one includes some variation of "images," "drawings," "pictures," or "panels," with Carrier's idiosyncratic "speech balloons" referring to a specific kind of image, and Cook's "visually distinct parts" moving toward a definition of "images." Only Eisner's "art" is not explicitly subdivided (and Eisner later distinguished comics as a "form of sequential art . . . in which images and text are arranged to tell a story" [2008a: xvii]).

The complete definitions of comics excerpted above include other features which could possibly be included in a definition of the comics form. Text and narrative, for example, are the next most commonly repeated. Both, however, are also commonly contested. Molotiu's 2009 anthology *Abstract Comics* prompted Groensteen to reflect that many experimental works "contest the usual definition of the medium to which they belong," acknowledging that abstract comics were now "labeled and in some sense officially recognized as a category, if not a genre" (2013: 9). The category of wordless comics is significantly longer recognized. Beronä maps a tradition that includes nineteenth-century precedents and early-twentieth-century comic strips and woodblock novels (2012: 17). Images and sequences then are both the most repeated and the least contested features in comics definitions. I therefore limit my focus of study to sequenced images because it reflects a consensus, or near consensus, for formal qualities.

Definition Map

Summarized, the four definitional regions are:

1. publishing history (*c.* 1890s–present, defined by creators, publishers, and consumers);
2. cartoon (image style that simplifies and exaggerates but not necessarily in multiple images);
3. conventions (panels, gutters, reading paths, talk balloons, drawing style, story, genre, etc.); and
4. form (sequenced images).

The metaphor of geographic regions is imperfect, since the overlap may be more complex, but a working map clarifies some miscommunications over the shared term. Represented visually in Illustration 0.1, two Venn diagrams produce thirteen subsections.

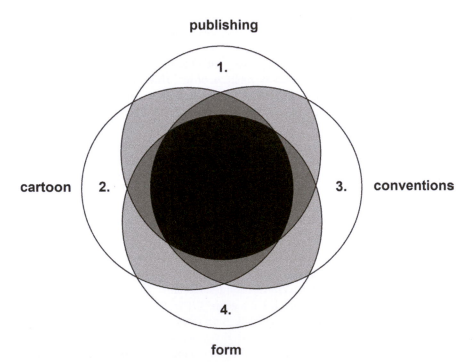

Illustration 0.1 Mapping comics definitions.

The white sections have no overlap, the light gray sections have two, the dark gray three, and the black center four. Every object considered a comic falls somewhere on the diagram. The least controversial fall in the center, which is a source of paradoxical confusion since rationales for inclusion differ without those rationales being apparent. Presumably all scholars would agree that a *Krazy Kat* comic strip by George Herriman is a comic, but each may have a different reason, some of which are shared and some not. *Krazy Kat* is formally a comic because it is a sequence of images, but it is also a comic according to publishing history, cartoon style, and the presence of a wide range of other conventions. If someone favors one of those definitional approaches, then our apparent agreement masks a deeper disagreement—or miscommunication since we are using the same word to mean different things.

Areas of non-overlap are intriguing, too. Schell's use of "comic book" would fall into the white area of circle three because his critique of George W. Bush references only story conventions. Panels and gutters sometimes appear in advertisements, and, if a scholar were working with panels and gutters as defining conventions, those ads would be comics. Alternatively, they may be what Gordon calls "comic-strip-style ads," which "allowed advertisers to create graphic narratives, through the sequential panels that demonstrated visually the supposed benefits of using their products" (1998: 81). Since Gordon includes the synonym "graphic narratives," he appears to use "comic strip" to indicate publishing history and "graphic narrative" to indicate form. Even publishing history includes some apparent non-comics. Though Grant Morrison's *Batman* #663 (April 2007) is "essentially a prose short story," Cook considers it a comic because of context: "it is a proper part of the *Batman* series, which is itself a comic" (2011: 293). If cartoon is defined by publishing history, its subsection may be contained entirely within conventions. However, Pablo Picasso's late period includes a range of line art that satisfies the formal definition of cartoons as simplified and exaggerated representations but that few viewers classify as cartoons. Andy Warhol's *Marilyn Monroe* is potentially a comic in terms of form, but not cartoon and publishing history. Nora Krug's visually diverse *Belonging* prompted Murel to ask whether the memoir employs "comic art as one story-telling device among many, or does its format necessitate expanding the definition of comics as a medium (or does it reveal that such an expansion has already transpired)?" (2019: n.p.). Since Krug's diverse format always includes sequenced images, the expansion would not be of the comics form but of its application within the comics medium.

The Comics Form

The art of sequenced images overlaps overwhelmingly with other approaches and so pertains to a majority of the works contained in them. Though my focus includes some sequenced images that are not comics according to any other approach, it applies essentially to all comics that are. By exploring the most encompassing approach available, I hope to illuminate as much of the forest as possible—and, by some definitions, a few areas outside it.

Though I will discuss works outside comics the publishing history, the category is invaluable, and I refer to it as the comics medium, stipulating that a work is in the comics medium if the work is published and identified as a comic by an entity that identifies itself as a comics publisher. Though the comics medium may be most widely known for what Mag Uidhir terms "mass-market comics" or "mass-art comics" (2010, 2012), the medium is not constrained by method or scope of production and so includes a range of other works, such as digital art appearing in the comics sections of online literary journals and individual artists' self-published mini-comics produced on photocopiers. Since the comics medium is not a formal category, the distinction produces three subcategories: 1) works in the comics form but not the comics medium, which includes all sequenced images not traditionally identified as comics; 2) works in the comics medium but not the comics form, which includes single-image cartoons such Gary Larson's *The Far Side*; and 3) works in both, which includes the vast majority of works in the comics medium.

Adopting a formal approach does not suggest that there is a "traceable lineage" between contemporary works (in either the comics form or medium) and pre-twentieth-century works (in the comics form but not the medium) such as "medieval stained glass windows," an assumption that Miodrag critiques (2013: 3). Yet a lack of lineage is no obstacle to recognizing that stained-glass windows are comprised of sequenced images. Expecting a formal definition to account for lineage reveals a deeper disagreement about not simply the definition of comics but the nature of definitions. Evnine explains the difference in terms of genre. A formal approach treats genres as "regions of conceptual space," where individual works share "certain features," regardless of anything else they may or may not share (2015: 2, 8). Miodrag instead treats comics as "historical particulars," requiring works to be "read and interpreted in the light of previous works" and so understood in terms of "lineage" and "influence" (2015: 4, 16, 20). Many works in the comics medium and stained-glass windows are the equivalent of convergent evolution, producing shared features without shared lineage. Those parallel features also produce shared functions, since the discretely divided, ordered, path-producing visual field of a stained-glass window may be viewed and interpreted in the same manner as other works in the comics form. Holbo offers a similar observation: "the ceiling of the Sistine Chapel and a page from a superhero comic have a lot in common ... at a basic level they *work* the same" (2014: 6).

Since most lineage-defined works also share formally defined features, categories derived by formal definitions contain them, producing a more inclusive and expansive set. Karasik and Newgarden warn that "a definition that attempts a broad inclusion can be so vague as to be meaningless" (2017: 23), but inclusivity is not a goal but a side effect of a strictly formal approach. It presupposes nothing about the nature of the images or the nature of their relationships, including even "interdependent images," an idea that "seems crucial to the recognition of something as comics in our contemporary understanding of this word," but, according to Mikkonen, "is also clearly problematic" (2017: 13).

Mikkonen prizes an "institutional definition" because it "enables us to avoid the formalist trap of focusing on a particular structure or device as the distinguishing factor" (2017: 15). That trap, however, is not "formalist" but a misalignment of approach and category. Most definitions that are considered formalist begin with a body of works grouped according to publishing history and then asks: What are the necessary and sufficient intrinsic features of this group? While it is not impossible for an institutionally determined grouping to have such features, the application of the formalist question presupposes it. The conventions of the comics medium are diverse and include outliers in likely every area of analysis, producing no necessary and sufficient qualities. Expecting the comics medium and the comics form to match misunderstands the nature of both. Instead of attempting to derive a formal definition from a set of works determined by historical and sociological rather than formal principles, adopting a formal definition and allowing it to determine what is or is not formally a comic avoids the misalignment.

I refer to the grouping as "art," though some works in the comics medium, Meskin notes, "can be used nonartistically" (2007: 370). Though I intend this book's subtitle to include such "nonartistic" works as airplane escape hatch diagrams, the term "craft" might better communicate that meaning. Still, the intentions of the graphic designer who creates an airplane diagram include aesthetic considerations. The diagram has a primarily practical function and so is not fine art, but signage and magazine ads include artwork in a general sense and so are arguably art themselves. Because I am primarily concerned with the subcategory of sequenced images called "art," I do draw examples from diverse works, many from the comics medium. I will also refer to many works of art not included in my illustrations. This is due to practical limitations, but I also emphasize that the ideas I discuss originate from a broad range of sequenced images. That range is eclectic, with the expectation that no reader will recognize all or even most, but the hope that all readers will recognize some.

The comics form also highlights the artificial boundaries between the comics medium and other visual art. It does not "distinguish comics from all other visual and verbal forms," the assumption central to Witek's critique of essentialist definitions (2009: 149). Works in the comics medium and fine arts typically but do not necessarily differ. Works in the comics form and fine arts overlap more significantly. Though I agree with García that comics is "an artistic form" and "not a subgenre of literature," the form does not have "its own identity," meaning a set of formal features that distinguishes sequenced images in the comics medium from sequenced images not in the comics medium (2010: 4). Contemporary works in the comics form participate in older and broader artistic traditions of multi-image art. Rather than diminishing the subcategory, I hope to place it in clearer relationship to surrounding fields.

Because aligning prior theorizing reveals gaps, harmonizing requires filling them, either by extending and clarifying others' implicit claims or by developing and applying additional concepts onto pre-existing frameworks. Some of those frameworks also require closer examination, since some of even the most common constituent elements—panels, gutters, sequence, narrative—are ambiguous. Because terms refer to concepts, ambiguity in terminology can also produce conceptual ambiguity, and so harmonizing involves assessing differences between terms and justifying preferences.

Since a work displays its features simultaneously, ordering the analysis of those features is somewhat arbitrary, especially since the understanding of one feature is aided by tools developed through the analysis of other features, and vice versa. Chapter 1 introduces two primary tools of analysis, discourse and diegesis, which are literary and narratological terms that I adopt and adapt to distinguish an essential division between representational content and the physical marks that produce that content. Chapter 2 details further qualities of visual representation, including resemblance, custom norms, style, simplification and exaggeration, style modes, transparency, specification, perspective, framing, focalization and ocularization. Chapter 3 defines kinds of juxtaposition, before analyzing the paradoxical effects of a page as pseudo-formal and detailing the viewer-determined nature of image division independent of panel and gutter conventions. Chapter 4 examines the most fundamental inference produced by multiple images, recurrence, and its supporting effect, erasure. Chapter 5 expands the analysis of inference kinds produced by juxtaposed images. Chapter 6 explores how images trigger order, viewing paths, sequences, and narratives, resulting in a six-part typology, before introducing event inferencing to explain and determine undrawn content. Finally, Chapter 7 defines the roles and features of text-narrators, image-narrators, and image-text narrators in works that include both non-linguistic images and word-images.

1

Discourse and Diegesis

Although comics is a visual art form and comics theory has developed from multiple disciplines, comics scholarship has been largely literarily and narratively focused, a tendency Kukkonen justifies by defining "literature" as "not tied to the written text," since "films can be seen as literature, too" (2013: 2). Even if comics are literary in an expansive sense, the categorical inclusion does not dictate literary methods of analysis. Medley correctly identifies a need "to balance out these literary approaches" (2010: 55), and García warns against "the analytical tendency that makes use of tools proper to narratology," in order to "focus our attention instead on visual and material features" (2010: 4). Miodrag similarly argues "that the practices and methodologies of art criticism are as valuable to the study of comics as the 'literary' readings of theme and narrative that have to some extent dominated critical approaches to the form" (2013: 199).

Many approaches to studying images begin with object-based formal analysis in the tradition established by art historians in the late 1800s: identifying elements of line, shape, light value, space, color, texture, and pattern, as well as such design principles as unity, balance, emphasis, proportion, and implied movement. Iconographic (literally "written image") analysis focuses on subject matter, including the traditions of signs and symbols identified by Panofsky in the mid-twentieth century. Other visual approaches analyze style, historical and cultural context, viewers' perceptual responses, and the history of an image's public reception. Since works in the comics form are a subcategory of the visual arts, all of these approaches are applicable and likely essential to comics analysis. My focus is formal, so reception, cultural context, and iconographic traditions are beyond the scope of this book. While design principles and other elements of visual analysis are essential, I have nothing to add to their theory. Despite García's warning, I do use literary tools, but my focus is not on the narrative qualities that sequenced images may produce, but on the image features that may produce them.

As detailed in the Introduction, *The Comics Form* explores the two most common formal features identified in scholarly definitions: images and sequence. Sequence requires juxtaposition (and possibly nothing else), which I begin to discuss in the third chapter. This chapter and the next focus on the qualities of a comics image. "Image" is an imperfect term because it can be used synonymously with "representation," meaning a simulation of something else. I therefore divide images into two categories: non-representational images are only their physical features; representational images are also understood in relation to what they represent. Adapting terms from literary criticism, these two sets of qualities are diegeses and discourses. A representational image is both the subject matter simulated (diegesis) and the physical substance that simulates (discourse). More simply, a representational image has both form and content, while a non-representational image has form only.

1. Formal Qualities

What are the formal features of an image in the comics form?

I derive "images" from scholarly consensus, but while all scholars understand comics to include them, few specify a meaning. Though "image" can be used to describe multiple senses, when used to describe works that have been called "comics," the term appears to refer to visual images only, ignoring non-visual qualities highlighted by Hague in his accurate description of comics scholarship as ocularcentric. Cohn and Cook also include "visual" and "visually" in their comics definitions (2013: 1–2; 2015: n.p.). Kwa identifies "most significantly, the emphasis on an insistently two-dimensional surface" (2020: xxii). Bateman identifies two qualities, "two-dimensional and static," when stipulating the nature of image-texts (2014: 28), which include most works in the comics medium (defined in the Introduction as works published by an entity that identifies as a comics publisher). "Comics image" then might mean: any visual flat static image juxtaposed with another.

If we accept that inferred definition, works in the comics form do not include three-dimensional art. I suspect most readers would agree that a sculpture garden is not a comic—even when sculptures share prominent features with comics. Siegfried Neuenhausen's 1980 *Small Sequence* consists of five, reproducible bronze statuettes representing a figure dressed in a hat and trench coat who appears to be incrementally sinking from knees to chin into whatever surface the statuettes are resting on. So not only are the statuettes juxtaposed images, they create the impression of a single character repeated in multiple instances that must be viewed in a specific order to experience a unified event. Recurrence and sequence are common qualities discussed later, but despite its possessing such qualities, it seems reasonable to exclude *Small Sequence* only because it is three-dimensional. Similarly, although Nahoko Kojima's 2012 *Cloud Leopard*, *Swimming Polar Bear*, and *Washi* (a bald eagle) are made of paper (the most common comics-medium material), they are suspended from wires to create three-dimensional shapes and so are presumably not comics, despite being juxtaposed images in a thematically unified series. While it's possible to imagine something that could be called a "three-dimensional comic" (perhaps a sequence of dioramas featuring a set of characters that continues an existing comics-medium story), the three-dimensional comic would not be in the comics form.

"Flat" still produces challenges since it is unclear when an object should be considered two- or three-dimensional. Is Lorenzo Ghiberti's 1452 *Gates of Paradise*—which consists of two, five-paneled, bronze doors, containing Old Testament scenes in bas-relief (literally "low raises")—in the comics form? At what point does the discursive depth of an image become definingly three-dimensional? US quarters include bas-relief portraits of George Washington, but their depth is shallower than what a painter employing an impasto technique—as Van Gogh does in his 1890 *Still Life: Vase with Pink Roses*—can produce with layers of oil paint. Technically, any painting or even pencil drawing is three-dimensional. Despite this ambiguous threshold, I accept "flat" as a quality of images in the comics form.

"Static" distinguishes a comic from a film—or at least a projected film. If a film is the celluloid strip of still images that is run through a projector, the strip is a sequence of static images. Even so, the strip not the projection of moving images would formally be a comic. Webcomics offer a further challenge since some include segments of animation. Though segments of webcomics with animation are not in the comics form, if a webcomic contains sequenced static images at least those portions can be analyzed formally as a comic. Conversely, some projected films contain static images—or multiple identical images projected to appear static. Chris Marker's 1962 *La Jetée* consists (almost) entirely of projected stills and so would be in the comics form. Andy Warhol's 1966 *Chelsea Girls*, which features a split screen and so juxtaposed moving images, would not be.

A comics image could include other physical constraints. Kwa assumes a "small format" (2020: xxii). The image might be hand-held and so include both traditionally printed comics and webcomics viewed on a phone, but not framed artboards displayed on a gallery wall. Dividing points could be arbitrary, ambiguous, or both. A laptop is not typically hand-held but can be, while an 80s-era PC cannot, yet both can be used to view a comic on similarly sized screens. Likely any size constraint would eliminate the Nazca Lines, a set of geoglyphs carved in a southern Peru desert roughly two thousand years ago, since some of the images are more than a half mile wide and combined cover 19 square miles. However, the Nazca Lines, which include representations of a dog, whale, spider, hummingbird, and monkey in relatively close proximity, are not formally different from a page of identically drawn and proportionately spaced images. At the opposite extreme, quantum dot technology produces inkjet-printed images the width of human hair and viewable only through microscopes. While excluding such extremes may seem intuitively self-evident, the adjective "small" lacks both clear parameters and formal justification while also adding little to analysis.

Publishing-based definitions require a comics image to be reproduced. If so, artboards used during the printing process are not themselves comics. Comics as defined by their history of publication do not have single originals. Every 1962 copy of *Amazing Fantasy* #15's first run is equally the original comic, but Steve Ditko's *Amazing Fantasy* #15 art housed in the Library of Congress is instead material for manufacturing a comic, which did not include the blotches of white-out and blue guidelines that are elements of the artboards only. The adjective "reproduced" formally distinguishes a work in the comics medium from its artboards, but then the definition applied formally includes all types of reproduction. A PowerPoint projection of a comic scanned into a digital pdf would be a comic, even though the projection is made of light and exists only while projected. If the pdf is printed from a photocopier, its pages of toner-formed images would also be a comic. Meskin explores the issue of multiplicity in greater detail, concluding: "An exact duplicate of a comic does not count as authentic unless it was mechanically copied from the original plate or art or some other genuine copy"

(2014: 41). Attempts to distinguish "authentic" and "genuine" comics reveal the publishing-focused impetus for the stipulation, especially since an "exact duplicate" would be physically indistinguishable from its source. Meskin also ignores "the production, transmission and consumption of unauthorized comic book scans" through a digital culture network involving weekly titles that numbered 28,000 in 2010 (Wershler, Sinervo, and Tien 2013). Regardless, concerns for authenticity and reproduction technologies seem specific to the comics medium, and so I do not adopt "reproduced" or any further stipulated variant as a necessary quality of an image in the comics form.

Other formal requirements are possible. Groensteen and Grennan might include the adjective "drawn," since Groensteen's monstrator is responsible for "*putting into drawing*" (2010: 4), and Grennan's book-length study is *A Theory of Narrative Drawing* (2017). "Drawn," however, would arbitrarily eliminate photographic images and so photocomics, including Italian fumetto, as well as other images produced by creative processes that are not strictly drawing-based. Cook might eliminate *La Jetée* from the comics form because his comics definition requires that the "audience is able to control the pace" (2015). Kwa refers similarly to "the invitation to keep looking" (2020: xxii). The stipulation would separate *La Jetée* from the comics medium, but audience-controlled pace introduces other ambiguities: What if a viewer is watching a film while intermittently pressing pause? Audiences also control pace when viewing galleries and photo albums.

Rather than adopting additional formal parameters in an attempt to exclude works outside the comics medium, I accept the results of the broad formal net. Despite their significant differences, *La Jetée*, Nazca Lines, and many works in the comics medium share a meaningful set of formal features. Because that set is otherwise unnamed, I call it "the comics form," and I understand an image in the comics form to mean any flat, static, visual image juxtaposed with another, leaving "small," "reproduced," "drawn," and other descriptors as common but formally non-essential conventions of the comics medium.

2. Content and Form

Though a work in the comics form includes at minimum a set of the above physical qualities, it often involves something more.

From the Greek word for narrative, "diegesis"—and the adjective "diegetic"—may refer to a story, the elements that comprise a story (including such things as settings, events, actions, characters, and characters' internal experiences), or the larger world in which a story takes place. Since a single representational image may or may not be understood as being, telling, or referring to a story, I understand diegesis to include represented subject matter generally. This visual application is an expansion of diegesis in the literary and narratological sense and may include an entire world represented but only partially pictured. If the image is Kehinde Wiley's 2018 portrait of Barack Obama, its world is understood to be our world. If the image is a still from Fritz Lang's 1927 *Metropolis*, the diegetic world is fictional and therefore a different world. If the image is Frida Kahlo's 1946 *The Wounded Deer*, a self-portrait featuring the artist's head attached to a deer's body, the relationship of the image to our or any other world may be unclear. Regardless, diegesis can be understood generally as all represented content, overt and implied.

"Discourse"—and the adjective "discursive"—refer to an image as a physical object independent of anything it might represent. The discourse of a work in the comics form includes the physical qualities identified in the previous section. In literary approaches, "discourse" may be used to mean or relate to things such as plot, syntax, and other non-physical qualities excluded here, though this stipulated meaning can be applied to a prose-only work, too, "understood in terms of its purely physical properties" (Goldberg and Gavaler 2021: 6). If the discourse is Elizabeth Catlett's 1980 sculpture of Louis Armstrong in New Orleans's Armstrong Park, its discursive qualities are the bronze material's color (gray), height (10.5 feet), and physical shape. Because portions of the bronze's physical shape resemble the physical shape of Louis Armstrong's face, a viewer may experience those discursive qualities diegetically. If the discourse is Deya Muniz's 2015 webcomic *Brutally Honest*, the discursive qualities are the pixels in viewers' variously sized screens. For many works in the comics medium, a discourse is twenty-two, 10 1/8″ × 6 5/8″, pulp-grade, staple-bound pages printed with black and four-color ink. The shapes of the ink marks are discursive and so require a viewer to interpret them and so co-produce their representational content mentally. When viewers interpret physical qualities, they experience a diegesis. Because a diegesis is interpretive, different viewers experience different diegeses triggered by the same discourse, though overlap is presumably significant.

The discourse–diegesis division is common but under-employed in comics theory. Groensteen acknowledges that images in comics "obey criteria that are just as much visual as narrative—or, more precisely, discursive," but he also claims that these "two orders of preoccupation sometimes superimpose themselves to the point of indistinction" (2007: 4). Yet an image's discursive and diegetic qualities, even though simultaneously comprised of and produced by the same marks, are always distinct, and not distinguishing them can confuse analysis. McCloud, for example, describes closure as occurring in the space between images: "Nothing is seen between the two panels, but experience tells you something must be there" (1993: 67). Because panels are discursive, nothing is "between" them but negative space. If something is "between" the two moments that the images represent, that something is diegetic only. If merging the two kinds of "between" is a kind of shorthand, the division should be clearly implied, but others have corrected McCloud, indicating either miscommunication or an accurately communicated error.

Cohn instead poses a question that distinguishes the same two sets of qualities, discourse and diegesis, by similar terms: "what aspects of the *visual surface* allow for inferences to be generated in the *situation model*?" (2019: 4). Cohn also applies a linguistic lens: "Languages are produced in a *modality*" such as "marks on a surface (visual-graphic). These expressions are then decoded by a sense organ (eyes, ears)" (2013: 4). The result of decoding is the diegesis. In semiotics, the division is between discursive signifiers and the diegetic signified. Willats distinguishes diegetic primitives, "the smallest units of meaning available in a representation," and discursive marks, "the actual physical features on the picture surface used to represent the primitives" (2006: 8). Wolheim describes the discourse–diegesis division as "twofoldness," where observers see marks as marks, and they recognize the object represented by the marks: "the two aspects are indistinguishable but also inseparable" (1987: 46). A viewer, however, may attend to discursive qualities alone—noting the length and thickness of individual lines, for instance—without interpreting those qualities diegetically, and so a discourse is always distinguishable and separable. A diegesis is more complicated because representational content is initially dependent on the discourse being interpreted, but once interpreted that content may no longer be directly linked to the physical images because the diegesis continues mentally after viewing stops. Mental images might include a memory of a discursive image and so be partially limited by it, but they might also include inferred content that is not discursive even in the sense of a visually recalled physical image.

The relationship between directly viewing a discourse and mentally visualizing a diegesis is still more complex. Prose-only novels provide a useful contrast because they produce no overlap. The discursive shapes of words are not representational images and so a reader likely does not recall them visually. As Mendelsund explains, prose readers visualize minimally: "even the most … lushly described locales in naturalistic fiction, are, visually: flat" and "characters, in *all* types of fiction, [are] merely visual types, exemplars of particular categories—sizes; body shapes; hair colors"; therefore, since we "don't have pictures in our minds when we read, then it is the interaction of ideas—the intermingling of abstract relationships—that catalyzes feeling in us readers" (2014: 371, 373, 245). Mendelsund describes a different experience when words and images combine:

> I find when I'm reading a book with illustrations, the book's illustrations will shape my mental visions—but only while I am looking at these illustrations. After a period (which varies according to how often the illustrations appear in a text), the particular mental images of that illustration fades. Unless, that is, you are reading a book that has illustrations on every page. In which case there is no escaping the imposition of another's imagination.
>
> 181

While a comics image is not an illustration in Mendulsund's sense and works in the comics form need not include words, those works do have images "on every page" and so the imposed imagination is the author-artist's. The resulting "mental images" or "mental visions" occur not on the pages but in each viewer's mind. No diegesis is exclusively linked to a discourse, but a range of presumably similar diegeses experienced by multiple viewers—including the artist who experiences the representational content during and after the creative process.

While all images are discursive, only images with discursive qualities that represent subject matter are diegetic, too. A work in the comics form, like artworks generally, can instead be called "abstract." Such a non-representational image is not an image *of* anything, and so it produces no diegesis. This presents challenges for terminology. "Non-representational image" is oxymoronic since "image" can be synonymous with "representation," but "abstract image" is also problematic because "abstract" has at least three uses, relating to representational content, narrative sequence, and visual style. Baetens correctly notes how a sequence of "nonfigurative" images can be read narratively and how a sequence of "figurative" images can be read "nonnarratively" (2011: 96). He uses "abstract" in two senses: 1) images that do not represent other subject matter ("nonfigurative"), and 2) images, whether figurative or nonfigurative, that in sequence produce no narrative. Baetens also refers to degrees of abstraction, which is the third meaning. "Abstraction" is often used to describe how individual representational images distort their subject matter. Although all representational images, even photographic ones, distort, "abstraction" in this sense refers to variations on what would appear to be unmediated optic experience.

Because the three meanings are distinct but easily conflated when denoted by the same word, I stipulate the following. First, "non-representational" refers to images with no representational content. Such an image is only its discursive qualities. Jackson Pollock's action paintings and Mark Rothko's field paintings are examples. For the second meaning, I accept the unambiguous term "nonnarrative." For the third, I reserve "abstract" as a description of style. Only representational images can be abstract. A non-representational image cannot have an abstract style because it has no representational content to abstract. I discuss kinds and degrees of abstraction in the next chapter, limiting "abstract" to this third, style-related sense.

Stylistic abstraction can be applied at a micro or macro level. Impressionist works are largely defined by micro-level abstraction, with George Seurat's pointillistic brushwork or Vincent Van Gogh's wide thick strokes combining to represent optically accurate shapes. No viewing distance or squinting, however, will alter the macro-level abstractions of Joan Miro's 1938 *Head of a Woman* or Willem de Kooning's 1952 *Woman* into realistic accuracy. Robert Delaunay's 1927 *Portrait of Madame Heim* appears to resemble a specific individual, but Paul Klee's 1932 *Hat, Lady and Little Table* would likely not convey its subject without its title.

For clarification, consider the three images in Illustration 1.1. The top and middle are both representational, but the middle is stylistically abstract while the top is stylistically realistic. Both represent roughly identical subject matter, and the positions of the figures to each other, the implied viewer, the image frame are identical, too. The top image is a cropped still taken from the 1963 film *Charade*. Though the faces of actors Cary Grant and Audrey Hepburn are partly obscured, they may be recognizable to some viewers. The middle image is a digital adaptation of the same still, and the two actors are almost certainly unrecognizable due to the more abstract lines and shapes that render the content. The more stylistically abstract image is dependent on the photographic image for source material, but its diegesis is not. Different viewers may experience the discursive marks differently. The middle image might suggest a sense of movement (especially if the discursive details are interpreted as blur-related distortions) or possibly passion (if the discursive details are interpreted as indirect representations of the characters' psychological states). The diegeses differ because the perceived emotional relationships of the represented couples differ. The bottom image extends the creative process into even greater abstraction so that, if viewed in isolation, likely distorts the figures beyond recognition and so triggers no diegesis. It is non-representational.

Illustration 1.1 *"Charade* Kisses."

Discourse-diegesis analysis is atypical for visual arts other than film and graphic novels, but it applies equally. The collaborative exhibit "Cumberland Island: Land, Water, Wind, and Light" held in W&L University's Stanier Gallery in January 2020 included photography by Christa Bowden and Emily Goméz, who photographed the barrier island off the southern coast of Georgia during multiple visits. Discourse-diegesis analysis clarifies the distinction between a diegetic world and the actual world when a diegesis is understood to be nonfictional. The discourse "Cumberland Island" are matted and framed sheets produced from a high-resolution printer. The diegesis "Cumberland Island" are viewers' mental impressions of what they imagine to be the actual island. The diegesis is informed by the discourse but is not entirely dependent on it. Bowden's images are black and white, and Gomez's are tinted blue, visual elements understood to be discursive rather than diegetic. Despite never having seen a realistically colored photograph of the island, viewers almost certainly experience a diegesis that is realistically colored. If the exhibit were revealed to be a hoax and the photos to have been taken at some different or several different locations, the exhibit would change from a work of nonfiction to a work of fiction, but the diegesis might be otherwise unaffected, including the expectation of realistic color. The photographs also highlight other formal features including framing, viewpoint, and value contrasts, effects produced in relation to diegetic content but that are also distinct since none exist independently of the images. If the actual place is considered paramount, then the diegesis is treated as though it were the actual Cumberland Island. The discourse "Cumberland Island," because it is a sequence of images, is formally a comic.

3. Representational Qualities

While attention to a representational image's subject is necessary for understanding the image, extended attention to the larger diegetic world implied by an image is not typical of art analysis, especially of single images. Works in the comics medium and film, composed of multiple images typically representing multiple moments in multi-faceted settings, tend to emphasize narrative, character motivation, and other diegetic qualities. However, single images can produce similar qualities.

Consider Johannes Vermeer's 1664 *Woman in Blue Reading a Letter* in Illustration 1.2. When the Getty Museum exhibited the painting on loan from Amsterdam's Rijksmuseum in 2013, curators called it "one of Vermeer's most captivating portrayals of a young woman's private world" and offered detailed descriptions of its diegetic qualities:

Standing motionless at a table before an unseen window, a young woman intently reads the crisp page of a letter—possibly a precious message from a lover. On the table, a second page of the missive partially covers a string of large pearls on a blue ribbon, perhaps just removed from the open jewelry box nearby. . . . Although the content of the correspondence is a mystery, the woman's bent head and parted lips impart a sense of suspense.

If the painting were one in a sequence of images featuring the same figure, many of the curators' implied questions might be answered. Even if the woman remained unnamed, she would become a character—and arguably already is. Though viewers know relatively little about her, the image suggests a range of details about her circumstances, including, at minimum, that she exists spatiotemporally in our world or one essentially like it. The other page of the letter sits on the table in front of her presumably because she set it there moments earlier. Though no window is visible, we know she is standing in front of one and that she likely moved there to read the letter in its light. We know the room extends around her, and a larger building, a private house judging from the furnishings, extends around it. We know time extends, too, that this moment will be followed by another and then another, as she continues to read and then at some point is no longer reading. What will she do next? The curators' experience of suspense is a defining element of plot, and though the plot of *Woman in Blue Reading a Letter* will never be resolved, that diegetic tension is integral to the image.

Viewers familiar with Vermeer will also recognize the setting as a recreation of a corner of the painter's actual studio in his actual house. The implied window is easily merged with the window included in other paintings, but the repetition is not diegetic repetition. Even though they look the same, and are the same in terms of source reference, the rooms are diegetically unrelated. We do not understand the woman to be standing near the same window that figures in *The Milkmaid*, *The Astronomer*, *The Geographer*, *The Music Lesson*, or *Art of Painting* are near. We therefore don't imagine the possibility of the reading woman being interrupted by any of those other characters. Her story, to the degree that she has a story, is limited to a single image. She is limited as a single image, too, to a single set of discursive marks. Rather than encouraging a viewer to imagine her in past or future moments of her life, the singularity of the image isolates her in time. Though Vermeer's realism implies the inevitability of past and future moments, those moments likely seem remote, indeterminate, and arguably irrelevant. This is the single moment of significance. The painting is not primarily an excerpt from a story that indirectly represents that larger story. It is a complete work, not a film still. Though the image implies that the woman is having involved internal experiences of thought and emotion, those experiences are unavailable to viewers. She appears to be caught in the throes of some personal plot, but the particulars are so indeterminate as to exist in only the vaguest, most indirect sense. Were we to learn more through additional images, we might become involved in the content of the letter and the woman's relationship to its writer, but as a single image, the painting might be said to use story as a method to create visual effects, but the effects do not serve any story.

Diegetic attention is often limited even when a painting's larger story is known. After summarizing the biblical passage that inspired Artemisia Gentileschi's 1620 *Judith Beheading Holofernes*, curators of the Uffizi Galleries focused on diegetic qualities specific to the image, noting how Gentileschi

> portrays the moment that Holofernes is killed by the hand of the determined and powerful Judith. The overall effect is both powerful and frightening: the drunk corpulent general is lying on the bed, his head grasped by his hair and the sword plunged into his neck. Furthermore, Artemisia did not shy away from adding the gory detail of blood spurting so profusely as to stain Judith's breast.

Illustration 1.2 Vermeer's *Woman in Blue Reading a Letter* and Gentileschi's *Judith Beheading Holofernes*.

Though the image is explicitly an excerpt from a narrative (Israel is under siege by the Assyrian general, and Judith enters the camp to seduce and kill him), it is more than an illustration designed to convey those events. Like Vermeer, Gentileschi uses narrative to inform and shape her image, but, unlike Vermeer, she presumes her viewers are familiar with both the biblical passage and the tradition of other paintings depicting it, making her rendering a contrasting variant on an established theme. Even understood in isolation, her image does not depict just any moment in an implied sequence of moments but apparently the single most important one that indirectly represents an entire span of multiple, connected actions. Even so, its spatiotemporal concerns are limited. Unlike Vermeer's implied window and house, the setting of *Judith Beheading Holofernes* is comparatively vague. The biblical passage might imply a tent, but the painting does not. Though the figures are crafted as if lit from a specific light source beyond the left frame edge, there is no indication of what that light source would be diegetically. Though the narrative moment could prompt a range of plot questions—Where are the general's soldiers? Has anyone heard the struggle? Will Judith try to escape?—none seem to matter.

Cohn analyzes images in the comics medium in terms of narrative panel types defined by event structure. If Vermeer's and Gentileschi's paintings were images in sequences, they would each likely meet his definition of a Prolongation, "a medial state of extension, often the trajectory of a path" (2013: 79). As reinforced by the titles the paintings are known by, the verb tense of "reading" and "beheading" indicate that an action is in progress. For Judith, the path trajectory is literal as she works her sword through the general's neck. Both images imply the arc of a diegetic event by constructing what appears to be its midpoint, prompting viewers to experience the undrawn but implied content of both its starting point and its conclusion (aspects of event structure detailed in Chapter 6).

Not all single images are so easily or usefully categorized in diegetic terms. Alan Moore describes the content of William Holman Hunt's 1851 *The Hireling Shepherd*:

> The expressions of both the handsome shepherd and the young woman are ambiguous. The shepherd seems lustful while the woman seems coquettish. Seen in another light his expression is slightly more sinister while hers becomes one of suppressed alarm.
>
> 2008: 31

That ambiguity is partly the result of the painting existing as a single image depicting a single moment. Moore continues:

> Now, if we add the dimension of time to that situation, the work of art is completely altered. Instead of having infinite possibilities, if the situation in the painting is to progress through time it must follow only one route. The structuring of events along this route is a plot.
>
> 2008: 31

If *The Hireling Shepherd* suggests a Prolongation, it is unclear what diegetic content is prolonged—a flirtation or a rape? Since that essential question is unanswerable, diegetic analysis of the single image is at best limited.

The comics medium sometimes privileges narrative to the detriment of the images' non-diegetic qualities. "You might be able to draw like Michelangelo," McCloud warns prospective creators, "but if it doesn't communicate, it'll just die on the page—while a cruder but more communicative style will win fans by the hundreds of thousands. Question number one: will readers get the message?" (2006: 29). Mateu-Mestre similarly warns that when drawing a graphic novel, artists "are first of all doing an exercise in storytelling, as opposed to creating pieces of art for a show," and since "the image is the vehicle and the end in itself," artists "cannot afford to get the audience stuck on a particular frame just because the drawing or the scene looks great" (2010: 14). This attitude may largely explain why Fortress assessed newspaper comics as "non-art": "The comic strip artist is not concerned with art problems, problems of form, spatial relationships, and the expressive movement of line. In fact, a concern with such problems would, in all probability, incapacitate the comic strip artist as such" (1963: 112).

McCloud, Mateu-Mestre, and Fortress describe some but not all works in the comics medium and not sequenced images generally. Analysis of such images must extend beyond their diegetic qualities.

4. Intentional Agencies

Clarifying discourse (physical form), diegesis (representational content), and their relationship reveals three broad angles of analysis based on different primary agents within each area: authors, characters, and viewers. The first focuses on the intentional acts of actual creators and so is indirectly discourse-focused. The second is exclusively diegetic and so treats characters as individuals with minds producing observable actions. The last bridges the first two by focusing on the mental processes of viewers.

1. Authorial intentions. McCloud tacitly endorses this approach when he explains that "comics is a vessel which can hold any number of ideas and images. The 'content' of those images and ideas is, of course, up to creators" (1993: 6). He reinforces the authorial approach when he refers to his initial definition of comics, "juxtaposed sequential static images," as arbitrary and revises it to include "in deliberate sequence, intended to convey information and/or an aesthetic response in the viewer" (1993: 9). For something to be "intended" it must have an intender, the author.

Groensteen expresses a similar view. While defending his concept of braiding, Groensteen criticizes Tremblay-Gaudette's assertion that "'elements identified during the elaboration of the braiding process are analysed, contextualised, worked through with theoretical tools that enable us to explain our interpretation of a work,'" asserting instead that "it is not the reader who 'elaborates' braiding, but the author, even if sometimes subconsciously; the work of the reader is to identify it and to respond to it reflectively" (2016: 91). Since braiding involves the meaning–coding relationships between images, Groensteen seems to imply that meaning generally is produced by authors and then received by viewers without requiring interpretive acts. All relevant meaning would be authorial. Groensteen seems inconsistent, since he earlier emphasizes "the active participation of the reader in the construction of meaning" (2013: 3). If construction means identifying and responding to, viewers are only reconstructing authors' pre-existing meanings. If an author can braid subconsciously, the source of authorial intentions is the author's subconscious, removing any conscious individual from meaning production. If so, no one, including the author, can know authorial intention.

Authorial intentions are typically (and perhaps definitively) unavailable, and when an author does state an intention (in an interview or some other format outside the discourse of the work), the author is only a viewer—albeit one with detailed knowledge of the creative process that produced the work. Intentions that may have shaped the creation of a discourse relate ambiguously to the diegetic content experienced by later viewers. Authors working in any form can miscommunicate and otherwise fail to achieve their goals, and so intentions alone determine little. Since authors' interpretations of their own works are uniquely influenced by knowledge of their intentions, an author is arguably the least qualified interpreter.

Still, a viewer need not adopt Barthes's extreme position that "the birth of the reader must be at the cost of the Author" (1977: 148), instead interpreting a work as an attempt at communication by an actual individual. As explained by Baetens, Marion posits that viewers identify with an artist so fully that they have "the ability to redo, to remake, or at least reexperience the enunciative work produced by the author" as though physically drawing the art (2001: 150). Grennan's aetiological approach also focuses attention on an artist's "activities . . . undertaken because they have a tendency to produce a particular result," allowing a viewer to "infer the goal-directedness from the marking and the marking from the intended goal, the drawing" (2017: 7).

Viewers, however, have no direct access to the activities undertaken by artists, and the goals they infer from an image may or may not match the artists' actual goals. So while McCloud might be correct that authorial intention is involved, that fact has limited practical application since those intentions remain unknown. Like any work of art, a work in the comics form involves a perception of authorial intentions which are ambiguously related to any actual intentions.

2. Diegetic intentions. Where authorial intentions privilege a discourse by focusing on the process of its creation, focusing on character intentions achieves the opposite by isolating the diegesis and treating it as if it were peopled by actual individuals whose directly observed behaviors reflect their internal motivations. This is the desired experience of many stories, the illusion of real-world verisimilitude, but its analytical use is problematic, especially when viewers regard characters as sentient agents while excluding the actual sentient agents who create the illusion.

The tendency occurs in comics scholarship. Dubose in his analysis of 1980s superheroes writes:

> Not only does Captain America display awareness of the postmodern nature of morals (by admitting reality does not conform to black and white terms), he also admits that his country has severe problems—no easy feat for someone who is essentially a patriotic superhero.
>
> 2007: 928

While this style of analysis may be a kind of rhetorical shorthand where discussion of a character implicitly references the character's author, Dubose continues:

> Captain America shows awareness of the Government's capacity to throw out the rules of morality as it suits their purpose; the government, after all, is responsible for murdering civilians via the atomic bomb. This is not, however, the first time Captain America realized the government could be wrong—the seventies Nomad stories are credited as starting a trend of questioning "the political underpinning for superhero actions" not just in Captain America but in superhero stories in general (Reynolds 101).
>
> 2007: 933

Dubose references Reynolds's discussion of scripter Steve Englehart's 1975 *Captain America* #180–184 without acknowledging Englehart or analyzing the character's depicted realization as Englehart's construction. Dubose also implies that the character is a single, stable entity across issue runs spanning decades, as if multiple, changing authors were not continually interpreting and re-creating the character but instead reporting Captain America's autonomous behavior. Dubose also does not include any authors of the 1980–9 *Captain America* #241–360 in his works cited, despite their work serving as the primary focus of his analysis.

While Dubose may be an extreme example, his approach illustrates problems with the general tendency of prioritizing diegetic content. The tendency occurs in comics theory, too. Duncan and Smith describe the "process of encapsulation" as "selecting certain moments of prime action from the imagined story and enclosing certain renderings of those moments in panels" (2015: 108). While this likely describes many artists' creative process, a work can be created through a reverse approach where an artist draws an image that creates information about a story world that influences the creation of subsequent images. Elements of both creative approaches likely occur simultaneously. Regardless of process, a comic is not composed of images selected from a diegesis because a diegesis is a mental experience that occurs only after images are created and viewed. A creator might begin with an "imagined story," but that story is distinct from the diegeses of later viewers and likely from the diegesis the creator experiences after the initial and vaguely "imagined story" evolves through the creation of an actual discourse.

Though Cohn understands work in the comics medium to be written in a kind of visual language, and so implicitly as a communicative act between authors and viewers, his analysis sometimes privileges diegesis, too. "Panels," he argues, "act as a 'window' on a visual scene, and thus serve as 'attention units' to highlight parts of a scene in different ways" (2013: 56). The implicit assumption is that representational content, the "scene," is independent of the image rather than a product of it. Though the diegetic world is seemingly independent, a discourse cannot "highlight" certain parts because all of its parts exist mentally through a viewing of the images. Cohn implies that the diegetic world is literal, with panels framing content the way cameras frame real-world subjects.

As with Dubose's reference to characters as seemingly sentient, Cohn may be speaking in shorthand, as suggested by his use of quotation marks around "window" and the phrase "act as" rather than "are." Ault similarly argues that "comics characters are presented as occupying ... an underlying world that exists independent of the panels in which the characters appear," a world that "depends on visual cues that draw attention *away from* the surface gestalt of the page ... and *into* a world constituted not *by* but *through* the drawings" (2004). Ault acknowledges this appearance as an artistic conceit. If panels are treated as actual windows, image content becomes literal representations of diegetic reality. Style either vanishes or is no more relevant than differences in handwriting are to linguistic content.

Cohn's diegetic focus also influences his analysis of "active entities," elements "that repeat across panels by engaging in the actions and events of the sequence" (2013: 56). First, entities are termed "active" as a result of appearing in multiple images, meaning single images can have no active entities. That definition is discursive rather than diegetic, but the entities must also engage in "actions and events" which are diegetic, as are their environments which Cohn understands viewers to build in their "mind" when a sequence does not include a "Macro" panel framing all of the "multiple active entities" (2013: 58). Active entities repeat discursively "by engaging" in diegetic events, while inactive agents also repeat discursively and diegetically but in some non-engaging or "amorphic" manner. Though Cohn's word choice and sentence structure suggests that the entities determine their panel presence, the attribution is determined by the viewer. Cohn provides examples of a comic strip featuring what he identifies as six active entities, including a gunman, victim, and four onlookers, whose "actions need to be followed across panels, and keeping track of it all would require significant attention and effort for a reader" (57). One of the active onlookers is a bird, but the tumbled saloon stool is considered an inactive entity, as are presumably all other non-living elements of the environment (the bar, the bottles, etc.). All of the active entities change position at some point in the strip, but so do many inanimate objects, including characters' clothing and the gunman's gun. Activeness then is not discursive. Image elements are not active by virtue of changing across panels but by a viewer experiencing them as intention-driven.

Cohn's panel types display similar diegetic assumption by focusing on "events" and therefore the characters who enact them (2013: 73). Cohn does not overtly attribute motives to his active entities, but his examples feature sentient characters (boxers, gunmen, human couples, baseball players, jugglers, rope swingers, swordsmen, dancers, drinkers, paper-airplane throwers, dogs, etc.), with a significant exception: a three-panel sequence of a sun setting in the background with an unmoving figure posed in the foreground. In this case the non-sentient sun is the active entity and the sentient human is passive: "the man in this sequence does not affect the syntax, which must deal with the functional relations of panels to the whole. The event in these panels depicts the sun setting. Thus, the syntax is determined wholly by the movement of the sun" (2007: 38). By referencing the event of the sunset, the analysis is still diegetic, but the "relations of panels" could be applied to non-representational images and so without reference to any diegetic element.

Though Cohn's approaches are often effective, they reveal a diegetic bias common in visual interpretation. When a discourse triggers a diegesis in a viewer's mind, the diegesis—or what cognitive science terms "situation model"—can become so mentally prominent that a viewer will in a sense overwrite contradictory elements of the discourse in order to maintain a preferred model mentally (as discussed in Chapter 4). Focusing attention primarily on the diegesis instead of the discourse also privileges the literary approaches of narratology over object-based art analysis of actual images.

3. Interactive intentions. While exclusive attention to either the authorial intentions of creators or to the illusion of intentionality in characters has limited use, much scholarship assumes an intermediary position. Though the intentions of actual writers are typically unavailable, in literary theory a reader infers the intentions of an implied author. Similarly in art analysis, a viewer of a work of art constructs a hypothetical artist who intended the viewer's interpretation of the work. Neither an implied author nor a hypothetical artist is an actual person. They are mental constructs. The diegesis is also a mental construct, and in that sense inferred creators are diegetic, too—but to a different degree or diegetic level since they are constructed to explain features of the actual discourse.

Such levels of intentionality may be understood as narrators. Groensteen adapts Gaudreault's term "monstration," the act of showing, to coin "monstrator," the agency of "putting into drawing" (2010: 4). For reasons detailed in Chapter 7, I replace monstrator with image-narrator. While sometimes seemingly synonymous with the actual artist who creates an image, an image-narrator is the agent that communicates diegetic content through an image's discursive qualities. Although readers may be accustomed to thinking of narration as strictly a verbal act, Baetens and Frey observe that "drawing is . . . a creative operation that produces . . . the very stories themselves" (2015: 164). In the comics form, a diegesis is produced by a discourse of images or image-texts, and so, Baetens and Frey continue, drawn lines "inevitably manifest themselves as narrating agents and vehicles of storytelling. . . . And behind or beyond each line emerges the source of any storytelling whatsoever: the narrator" (165).

Readers are also likely accustomed to thinking of narration as strictly representational content, specifically narrative. Chapter 6 discusses "narrative" as a possible synonym for "sequence," allowing some narratives to be non-representational. "Image-narrator" follows this discourse-based sense. "The narrator," explains Keen, "is the entity from whom the discourse comprising the story emanates" (2003: 34). Though Keen's use of discourse differs, the parallel remains: an entity is understood to produce a discourse that, when viewed and interpreted by a viewer, produces a diegesis. Rather than calling that entity something else, I use the established term "narrator," acknowledging that narrators narrate all content, including but not limited to narrative.

An image-narrator is akin to a character performed by an actor. The character is a set of words performed to evoke the presence of an individual distinct from the actor. Other performed words, such as political speeches, sermons, and lectures, evoke no additional entity and so the qualities of the words and their performance are both attributed to the actual speaker. This is the norm in visual art. The qualities of a painting are typically attributed to the painter, not to an additional entity evoked by the painting, but any visual work involves an image-narrator if its qualities support such an interpretation. Forgeries involve a forger's performance as another painter and so a kind of image-narrator. Journalist Ake Axelsson invented the fictional painter Pierre Brassau in 1964 using paintings created by a chimpanzee. Either the chimp or Axelsson or both might be considered the actual author of the works, but their qualities were understood to be Brassau's.

The relationship is clearer in works of prose-only fiction: the actual individual Margaret Atwood wrote *The Handmaid's Tale*, which is narrated by the character Offred. As readers interpret the language of the novel that is diegetically understood to be Offred's, they also understand that it of course is actually Atwood's, and so the act of interpretation involves hypothesizing what Atwood intends readers to understand about her narrator Offred. Though image-narrators, hypothetical artists, and actual artists follow the same pattern as narrators, implied authors, and actual authors, viewers likely ignore the conceptual apparatus when it does not serve an immediate purpose. Such practical brevity is another kind of shorthand that still indirectly references the underlying structure.

An artist, as interpreted by a viewer, employs an image-narrator that transfers representational content to viewers. Characterizing how that content is transferred is ambiguous. Verbs "depict," "represent," and "show" are commonly applied to an artist, implied artist, image-narrator, or image as the acting agent. If artists "depict," they do so by making images. If images "depict," they do so by existing. Each might also "express," "communicate," or "convey." While these terms suggest an overlap of meanings, they differ in connotation. Samson's use of "enunciation" (or its French equivalent) shares that overlap (1988: 147), but because "enunciate" is synonymous with "pronounce," it connotes a linguistic understanding of images. If an image "tells" or is an artist's "speech," it is in a metaphorical sense since no sounds occur, and then it is unclear if or how such speaking is different from depicting, expressing, etc.

Sterckx presents the comics medium and fine art as mutually exclusive because paintings are regarded as "spatial arrangements" and comics as "telling stories" (1986: 139). While Sterckx understands the dichotomy to be false, no term denotes both being an arrangement and telling a story or the range of possibilities between. Lefèvre differentiates "the expression-part from the representation-part" of an image, meaning expressing and representing would not be synonymous after all (2016: 70). Though "narrate" is the obvious verb for a narrator, the more commonly used verbs listed above are an imprecise but practical shorthand. Image content can also be described with a range of nouns (cues, codes, clues, signs, signifiers, etc.) depending on the interpretive framework (semiotic, structuralist, cognitive, linguistic, narratological, etc.). While most frameworks are applicable, none are form-defining, leaving an image's units of content unnamed. For convenience, I use "marks."

Having established the qualities of discourse and diegesis, I will refer to them for the remainder of *The Comics Form*. The next chapter continues the analysis of images, focusing specifically on the qualities of representational images—ones that evoke diegetic content in a viewer's mind when a viewer observes the physical properties of the image's discourse.

2

Image Narration

Continuing the discourse–diegesis distinction detailed in the previous chapter, this chapter further analyzes qualities of representational images. Style, whether an individual artist's or a set of custom-based norms shared by multiple artists, divides into constituent qualities, most significantly simplification and exaggeration, and then into combinational modes. Style and modes exist ambiguously in the discourse–diegesis divide, displaying semi-representational elements neither clearly diegetic nor entirely discursive. Framing and viewpoints, in both literal and metaphorical senses, share those ambiguities. Such qualities challenge the nature of an image's literalness, or transparency, and so interpretations of its depicted world. Image qualities may be said to be controlled by an image-narrator, a convenient conceit when images produce an impression of person-like features otherwise understood as the actual artist's. Image narration, since it applies to both single-image and multi-image representational works, is common but not unique to the comics form.

1. Representation

Slash a pencil across a sheet of paper and the streak of graphite left by the tip is an image in the discursive sense. In the diegetic sense it may also be the skid mark left by a bicycle tire on a driveway or the water edge along a riverbank or a distant desert horizon. Then it is both a specific and singular graphite streak and also a representation of something else, something embodied by the streak and paradoxically independent of it, something that can be drawn again and so be represented by other entirely different graphite streaks or other marks an unlimited number of times. The discursive image is easy to understand: it is simply itself, a mark on paper. The second image—the skid, riverbank, horizon—presents a puzzle: How does a representational image represent what it represents?

The key may be resemblance. The graphite streak represents a riverbank because the graphite streak in some way looks like a riverbank. Viewers perceive a discursive resemblance between it and a remembered or imagined image of a riverbank. Pierce would call the resemblance-based image a "likeness" or "icon." Wollheim instead describes the "seeing-in" experience of images, which combines the configurational fold, in which the image's marks are grasped, and by the recognitional fold, in which the image's subject is grasped (1987: 46). According to Gombrich, it doesn't matter whether the graphite streak resembles any actual riverbank because the artist and viewer agree that it is a riverbank in a shared game of visual make-believe. Pierce would call the non-resemblance-based image a "symbol." If the symbol game expands to include other graphite streaks made by other artists and understood to be riverbanks by other viewers, Goodman would call that a "custom" and argue that a particular riverbank custom explains the streak's ability to represent a riverbank.

Though both resemblance and custom may be involved in image representation, in a prose work, it is custom only. Discourse and diegesis are instantly distinguished because letter-shaped ink marks bear no resemblance to linguistic content. The words "moving car" look nothing like a moving car. In film, discourse and diegesis are more difficult to divide because every discursive image exactly resembles its diegetic content. A film of a moving car, while only a two-dimensional replica of a three-dimensional event, highly resembles the moving car it represents and is also a historical document of the actual car used to create the image. A photograph of a car has the same discourse–diegesis relationship: the two-dimensional marks produce an optically accurate replica of the subject. Barthes calls a photograph "a mechanical analogue of reality" because, he argues, it transmits or denotes reality without, or with the least possible, transformation (1977: 18). Mitchell disagrees: "it is increasingly hard to find anyone who will defend the view . . . that photographs have a special causal and structural relationship with the reality that they represent" (1994: 282). Chute, however, notes that a "drawing's connection to 'reality' is perceived as immeasurably weaker than the photograph's . . . because it possesses mechanical objectivity" (2016: 20).

Unless a drawing of a car is photorealistic, its discursive qualities differ from its diegetic content. If the image is a minimally detailed gestural drawing or an exaggerated cartoon, its discursive qualities and diegetic content will differ dramatically. If the gestural lines do not bear enough resemblance to the optically perceived lines of an actual car, the representational content may not be experienced at all. The image would be graphite streaks and only graphite streaks. If the streaks resemble other clusters of lines with a history of representing cars, knowledge of that custom could still translate the discourse of graphite streaks into a diegetic car.

Naturalistic images may rely more on resemblances to represent subjects, while caricatural and heavily abstracted images may rely more on custom. A viewer unfamiliar with artistic traditions would likely recognize Chuck Close's 1969 photorealistic *Big Self Portrait* as a representation of a human face. If Close were standing next to the portrait near the time of its creation, a viewer would also likely recognize it as a representation of Close. A viewer who has never seen any drawings may or may not recognize Paul Klee's 1922 *Head of a Man Going Senile* as a representation of a face, especially any single individual's. Since the head is a circle and the mouth is two tiny squares, its resemblance to any actual face is minimal, but its resemblance to other drawings, especially cartoon heads, is significant. A contemporary viewer might notice its similarity to Charles Shultz's *Peanuts* characters or Trey Parker and Matt Stone's *South Park* characters. At a midpoint between Close and Klee, Miriam Libicki, following the norms of comics memoirs, captions an illustration of herself: "This is not Miriam Libicki. You are unlikely to recognize Miriam Libicki on the street, with these drawings to go on" (2016: 48). Libicki is prioritizing a set of drawing customs

Illustration 2.1 Close's *Big Self Portrait*, Klee's *Head of a Man Going Senile*, and "Grids/ Figure."

over capturing a resemblance of her actual face—though her watercolor self-portraits elsewhere in the same collection instead represent her primarily through resemblance (2016: 6, 32, 64, 65, 71, 76, 89).

For Barthes, every reproduction of reality contains "a supplementary message, in addition to the analogical content itself (scene, object, landscape), which is what is commonly called the *style* of the reproduction," something that even photorealism must contain since "there is no drawing, no matter how exact, whose very exactitude is not turned into a style" (1977: 17, 18). Style then is a discursive quality separate from its represented subject and so the quality that distinguishes a representation from a replica. If style were entirely discursive then it would work in opposition to content, producing the kind of optical illusion Gombrich applies to the discourse–diegesis relationship generally:

> is it possible to "see" both the plane surface and [representational content] at the same time? If we have been right so far, the demand is for the impossible. To understand the [representational content] is for a moment to disregard the plane surface. We cannot have it both ways.
>
> 1961: 279

Gombrich offers the analogy of a rabbit-duck illusion, arguing that "instead of playing 'rabbit or duck'" viewers of a representational image play "the game of 'canvas or nature'" (1961: 29).

Gombrich's example is imperfect because both the rabbit and the duck are diegetic as well as discursive. The image "Grids/Figure" in the bottom of Illustration 2.1 instead is discursively a surface of pixels or pixel-shaped ink units that vary in a range of gray gradations and are arranged in layered crisscrossing lines. The pixels also represent the head and shoulders of a human figure. The figure is more easily perceived from a distance; the grid pattern is more easily perceived close-up. Like Gombrich's rabbit-duck, it is likely impossible to attend to both the grid pattern and the figure simultaneously. Rather than a discourse–diegesis relationship, the pattern–figure relationship may be between style and content—with style occupying an ambiguous role as if between discourse and diegesis. The representational content of the figure is produced by the style of layered lines, making the figure diegetic and the line pattern discursive. But the lines are themselves a product of combined pixels, making the lines a kind of representational content, too.

If the content of the figure is understood to be created by the style of the lines, the content–style relationship is akin to metaphor. A subject being described is variously termed "tenor," "target," "ground," or "metaphrand," and the description compares the subject to something else, variously termed "vehicle," "figure," "source," or "metaphier." "Hope is the thing with feathers," writes Emily Dickinson, describing the subject of hope as having qualities of a bird. Unlike a simile, which establishes a difference between a subject and its object of comparison, metaphor synthesizes the two. Hope isn't *like* a bird, it *is* a bird. In Illustration 2.1, the subject of the human figure could be said to exist to the degree that the pattern of lines produces it. The human figure also *is* a pattern of lines. A viewer sees the figure only because the line pattern makes perception of the figure possible.

Alternatively, the representational content could be understood as having independent existence. This understanding is false (because the diegesis is produced by the discourse) and in another sense is true (because once produced the diegesis exists in a viewer's mind without further reference to the discourse and may have separate qualities). If the claim is treated as true, the relationship between content and style may seem antagonistic. Instead of enabling the expression of content, as the vehicle of a bird enables Dickinson to describe the qualities of hope metaphorically, style is an obstacle to diegetic accuracy. The abstract line pattern must be overcome in order to recognize the human figure. Again, style seems neither simply discursive nor simply diegetic.

Fine arts tend to emphasize individual style even when an artist shares the customs of schools or movements (impressionism, cubism, etc.), but in the comics medium, especially the industry-dominating US publishers Marvel and DC, house and genre styles often overshadow individual style. As Mikkonen observes: "visual style of comics can also be a largely genre and format-related issue, shaped by a particular culture and production of the comics in question, with few traces of an individual maker" (2017: 109). Cohn terms the "'mainstream' style of American Visual Language [that] appears most prevalently in superhero comics" as "Kirbyan" (2013: 139). Though sometimes described as relatively realistic, Kirbyan differs from resemblance-defined representation because it involves a set of repeated drawing customs. Cohn notes that "people often critique 'incorrect anatomy'" in superhero comics because of a perception of "attempted realism" and so the "more 'realistic' that authors 'try' to be, the more harshly irregularities may be judged" (2013: 141–2). Kirbyan images then represent their subjects not simply through resemblance to visual perception but through learned customs. Manga and underground comix have customs, too—a face drawn in a Manga style may resemble other drawings of Manga-style faces more than it resembles any actual face—making individual works dependent on a system of symbols shared by many artists and recognized by many viewers.

2. Style Qualities

Though Barthes correctly observes that "there is no drawing without style" (1977: 43), style's constituent elements and effects, whether custom-based, resemblance-based, or non-representational, are difficult to categorize.

Eisner argues that "art style tells the story" through its "emotional charge," producing a "psychic transmission" that expresses "mood," "ambience," and "language value" (2008: 149, 153). Pratt similarly claims that artistic styles "create a mood, give the emotional context of a scene or story, increase or decrease the drama of a moment, and so on" (2009: 110). These are effects produced in viewers, but style can instead be divided into discursive features.

Marion identifies three: lines, contours, and colors (Baetens 2001: 147). Lefèvre lists seven: detail, deformation, line, distribution, depth, light, and color (2016: 75–6). Smith and Duncan's list of "mise-en-scène elements" encoded in panel composition is similar: background detail, color, lighting, distance, angle, movement (2015: 122), but they also include "art style" as an element of composition where "graphic style" is Lefèvre's overarching category, illustrating the potential arbitrariness of categorizing approaches.

The complexities increase with media, since watercolors are different from photographs which are different from computer graphics. Even imitating reality in a set of lines interprets and so alters reality. "In the real world," Sayim and Cavanagh explain, "there are no lines around objects," but "lines trigger a neural response that . . . lets lines stand in for solid edges," giving artists "an economical and powerful method for representing scenes and objects" (2011: 1). The lines themselves are discursive and so have their own physical properties—thick or thin, angular or rounded, straight or jagged, straight or squiggly, continuous or broken, consistent or variable, etc.—that influence a viewer's impression of the content the lines represent.

Lefèvre refers to "line" as a "factor" of graphic style, asking: "What kind of lines dominate the image (rectangular or rather rounded lines; clear, crisp lines or rather vague, 'hesitant' lines)?" (2016: 75). Berger and his co-authors analyze lines as "strokes," categorizing two kinds, "shading strokes" and "contour strokes," with the second category dividing into "complex" or "simple" based on whether the stroke "has more than four maximum curvature points"; they also record length, overlap, pen pressure, and stroke speed, which when combined "reveals a unique signature for different artists" (2013: 55:4). "Style," Berger reports, "is most often described as being composed of two parts: geometry/shape and rendering (texture or strokes)" (55:3). Wolk argues similarly, calling an artist's line

> an interpolation, something the cartoonist adds to his or her idea of the shape of bodies in space. In a cartoon, every object's form is subject to interpretive distortion … A consistent, aestheticized distortion, combined with the line that establishes that distortion, adds up to an artist's visual style …
>
> 2007: 123

Berger's study concludes that the styles of artists who demonstrated higher degrees of "abstraction" drew "fewer, longer, and more complex-shape strokes … instead of many short simple ones" (2013: 55:9).

While length, curve complexity, and overlap are discursive qualities, terms such as "pressure" and "speed" are inexact shorthand since they are actions of an artist who produces lines. "Marks made on paper," writes Chute, "are an index of the body" of the artist (2016: 20), what Marion terms "graphiation" and Baetens summarizes as "a residue of an individual act of creation" (2001: 153). Such strokes are often obscured by an inker finishing a penciller's art in the comics medium, leaving a different set of strokes. Since an image may involve multiple acts of creation by multiple artists, including fingertips on computer keyboards leaving no bodily traces, graphiation is an imperfect approach for analysis.

There is no theory of line quality that provides a consistent method of interpretation. McCloud asserts that "all lines carry with them an expressive potential" (1993: 124), but what is expressed is determined only case by case. Grennan is impressively precise when measuring discursive qualities, observing that the line Mike Mignola uses in *The Right Hand of Doom* "is invariably 5 pixels wide, including the line that outlines panels, speech balloons, thought bubbles and narration" (2017: 185), but the quality produces no clear or consistent diegetic result. Thin straight lines may suggest a range of meanings, even within a single image. When analyzing Lynda Barry's "Red Comb," Chute observes: "The frame is shaded with thin black horizontal lines behind the leaves; this darkening effect appears to indicate evening, or night—or, an alternate temporality, a recollected event" (2011: 284). Khordoc observes that in Albert Uderzo's *Asterix* "the line of certain [speech] balloons is jagged, suggesting a tone of voice which is not steady and calm, but rather, shocked or angry" (2001: 163). Jagged lines do not always communicate shock or anger, and when they do, they often require other details, such as character facial expression and word content, to direct that interpretation. Similarly jagged lines in a non-representational image may produce entirely different effects.

Reviewing David B.'s *Epileptic*, Wilson describes its "quivering, quavering world," claiming that "the tension between David's self and reality charges his sinuous, nervy line," but the causality is reversed: the discursive quality creates that diegetic effect (2005). Tabachnick cites Wilson's description of *Epileptic*'s world, attributing the adjectives to the artist's style: "Beauchard's 'quivering, quavering' drawing line ... captures his shaky psychological world" (2011: 105). The interchangeability reveals how diegetic content influences interpretations of line quality, and vice versa, suggesting no generalized theory of line expression is likely to emerge beyond one core assumption: viewers experience diegetic objects as possessing the psychological effects evoked by the discursive qualities that create them.

While style can include additional elements, Wolk and Berger limit their attention to two, line quality and line shape, leaving a third implied: quantity. Determining an exact number of marks is often impractical if not impossible, and even approximations are hampered by the ambiguity of units. Does a line begin when a previous line changes direction? If so, a square consists of four lines. Does a new line begin when the artist lifts the pencil? If so, lines will be undetectable in areas of significant overlap. The dark portions of many of the panels of Liana Finck's 2018 *Passing for Human* appear to be composed of hundreds if not thousands of individual lines. Julie Maroh employs a similar style for portions of her 2013 *Blue is the Warmest Color* and Rikke Villadsen in her 2018 *The Sea*, contrasting the sparser style Keiler Roberts demonstrates in her 2018 *Chlorine Gardens*. For that reason, line quantity should be understood to mean the accumulative effect of multiple lines in combination. In *99 Ways to Tell a Story*, Matt Madden illustrates such quantity differences by drawing the same one-page scene in "No Line," "Silhouette," "Minimalist," and "Maximalist" styles (2005: 176–83).

When more than one artist is involved in the creation of an image (such as multiple pencillers, inkers, and colorists), style does not correspond with any individual, but viewers may still experience the single, unified style of an image-narrator. Viewers may even experience a single, unified authorial intentionality, justified through Dennett's intentional stance (Gavaler and Goldberg 2019: 187–92). Discursively, style is still a product of actual artists, but if an image is understood to narrate its content, then artists create narrators, bestowing them with aspects of their actual styles. Alternatively, viewers infer narrators, bestowing them with the same aspects. A division between artist and narrator allows viewers to understand image style as revealing qualities of narrators and characters and worlds, particularly psychological experiences. If style were instead only actual artists', image qualities would collapse into the discourse created by the artist's hand and determined by the artist's tendencies. "Style," Postema similarly argues, "in effect ceases to be style, since it is no longer a superficial surface matter," or more simply: "Style signifies" (2013: 122).

3. Modes

Because a work in the comics form may represent a subject through multiple images, the style–subject relationship is not isolated to a single instance but is generalized to a larger representational approach that in the comics medium is often consistent throughout a work, multiple works, or across genres. While style can be analyzed as a range of separate features, features can be combined into patterns that categorize an artist's overall style or a group of artists' shared customs. Witek calls them "modes" and identifies two, naturalism and cartoon, distinguishable by their degrees of simplification and abstraction. The terms "simplify" and "abstract," however, have multiple overlapping usages that require clarification.

Lefèvre refers to line quantity as "detail," meaning "the amount of details versus the degree of simplification" (2016: 75). "Simplified" in this sense refers to a representational image that reduces the amount of detail of its source material. While all but photographic and photorealistic images are simplified, artists in the comics medium tend to simplify much more significantly. The verb "abstract" shares a similar meaning. An abstracted image extracts details from its source and so is therefore simplified. "Abstract image," however, often refers to an image that represents no source material and so cannot abstract details from it. As discussed in the previous chapter, I reserve "non-representational" to describe images without diegeses and "abstract" to describe style, but even when limited to style, "abstraction" is an ambiguous term since it also refers to non-realistic alterations in optic experience that are not simplified in the extracted sense.

Uses of "simplify" are similarly problematic. McCloud draws an "iconic abstraction scale" that illustrates five styles, ranging from a photocopied photograph of a face to a drawn face comprised of an oval, two dots, and a straight line (1993: 29). He claims that all of the faces to the right of the photograph simplify it by "eliminating details" (1993: 30). While largely true of the second "realistic" face and the middle face containing only "outlines and a hint of shading" (1993: 29), the later faces differ in more than line quantity. The qualities of their details change. Though McCloud concludes that the end result is "stripped-down" (1993: 31), each step to the right of his scale illustrates two kinds of changes: each contains fewer lines, and those lines alter the contours derived from the source photograph. McCloud also refers to each face as "more abstract" than the previous, further conflating "extracted" and "altered" (1993: 29). Witek introduces a similar confusion by citing two drawings of Bob Hope to illustrate the cartoon and naturalist modes, even though both are composed of an essentially identical amount of detail (2012: 29). Medley prefers the term "*distillation*" over "simplification," meaning "*some removal of realistic detail*," but also treats "abstraction" and "simplification" interchangeably (2010: 53). For clarity, I will use "simplification" as the reduction of details.

While "abstraction" can refer to the alteration of details, Lefèvre instead describes a drawing's degree of "deformation" as measured against "normal proportions" (2016: 75). The verbs "distort" and "warp" are also applicable, as is the more common term "exaggeration," which refers to lines that magnify or compress the shapes of their source material. McCloud's final face then is both "simplified and exaggerated," what Witek identifies as the two stylistic qualities of the cartoon mode (2012: 31). McCloud also identifies the final face as "the cartoon," differentiating it from the middle face, reflecting the "style of drawing found in many adventure comics" (1993: 29). To further clarify the difference between simplification and exaggeration, consider the horseback-rider icons combined in the top image of Illustration 2.2. All four are composed of

Illustration 2.2 "Horseback Riders" and "Four-Mode Self-Portrait."

exterior-defining contour lines and an undifferentiated interior color and so therefore are simplified to the same degree. They differ only in the qualities of their single counter lines, ranging from a photo-sourced outline to increasing degrees of non-realistic distortion to suggest generic subjects. The far right figure is the least exaggerated, and the far left the most.

Low exaggeration is often associated with naturalism, and high exaggeration with cartooning. Art in the comics medium might be divided into resemblance-based naturalism and custom-based cartoons, but Witek and McCloud both acknowledge overlap. Witek's two modes are "by no means mutually exclusive; comics combining both modes are extremely common" (2012: 28), and McCloud claims that "nearly all comics artists apply at least some small measure of cartooning" (1993: 42). Cohn refers to the same simplified and exaggerated combination as the "Barksian" visual dialect, which he names after Scrooge McDuck artist Carl Barks, though its customs predate Barks (2013: 139). Unlike Witek, who identifies the naturalistic mode as "the preferred approach for stories of adventure and domestic romance" (2012: 32), Cohn does not consider the "Kirbyan" dialect, which he names after Jack Kirby (2021: 139), to be naturalistic and so does not place the Barksian dialect in opposition to it.

Cartoon style may have a biological basis. According to Medley, "realism is not the pictorial ideal" because the human "visual system prefers less-than-realistic images," instead apprehending the world according to "simple propositions" duplicated in how "most comics artists tend to draw and ink their worlds—some degree of abstraction away from realism, clear outlines, flat colours, reliance on closure, a tendency towards caricature" (2010: 67, 56, 68). Despite the possible biological basis, artistic customs are socially constructed and maintained, and so few artists outside the comics medium would term the reduction and alteration of details "cartooning," even though many twentieth-century artists simplify and exaggerate to similar effect. Arr notes that Picasso's 1920 *Portrait of Igor Stravinsky* "would be a cartoon if in a comic book" (1982: 1), and in what formal sense is Picasso's 1955 ink drawing *Don Quixote* not a cartoon? Or Matisse's 1952 cut-out *Blue Nude II*? Or any of Schiele's dozens of drawings from the 1910s? None are called "cartoons" because the term is traditionally understood as specific to a publishing tradition outside fine art.

As mentioned in the Introduction, "cartoon" originates from the French and Italian words for the cardboard-like paper used for preliminary sketches in the 1600s, and it acquired its satirical connotation from *Punch* magazine in 1843. It is often used synonymously with "caricature," which dates to the 1700s and denotes a style of drawing that selectively alters a subject's features for comic effect, what Hamm calls "the art of distorting by exaggeration a person so he still retains his identity" (1967: 33). Referencing the root term "caricare" (literally "to load"), Lynch calls caricature "overloaded representation," akin to Johnson's "exaggerated resemblance" (1927: 1). Lucie-Smith considers "cartoon" and "caricature" synonyms (1981: 9, 13), but caricatures do not necessarily reduce quantity of detail. Contemporary political artist Jason Sieler creates caricatures that are both highly exaggerated and highly detailed, as are many of José Miguel Covarrubias Duclaud's 1930s and 40s magazine illustrations. William Hogarth's 1743 *Characters and Caricaturas* is a visual argument against caricature, then an Italian style newly introduced to England, emphasizing grotesquely detailed exaggeration over Hogarth's equally detailed naturalistic approach. Defining caricature by exaggeration alone would add many artists outside the comics medium to a purely formal understanding of the term. Modigliani's portraits, with their definingly long necks and facial features, are clearly exaggerated but also highly detailed.

Instead of Witek's two modes, the combinations of simplification and exaggeration produce four. Cartoons remain clearly opposed to the detailed, optically accurate style of naturalism, but two additional modes emerge from the crisscrossing spectrums. Some caricatures are exaggerated but not simplified. This combination has no term, but it may be referred to descriptively as "detailed exaggeration." Images that are simplified but not exaggerated are similarly unnamed. Where detailed caricatures often align with cartoons, viewers may regard unexaggerated simplifications as a form of naturalism. Graphic novelist gg works in this mode, and reviewers for *The Globe and Mail* and *Sequential State* describe her 2017 *I'm Not Here* as "photorealist" and "photorealistic" (Rogers, Hoffman). The claim is peculiar considering that gg's images are composed of opaque shapes lacking any interior detail. They are highly simplified, but their contours appear realistic, suggesting photographic source material. This mode also has no name, but may be referred to descriptively as "unexaggerated simplification."

Superhero Comics offers an "Abstraction Grid" that divides exaggeration and simplification each into a five-point scale and then combines the scales into twenty-five subsections (Gavaler 2018: 238). Since the two spectrums can be scaled into any number of subdivisions, only the four defining regions are necessary. The four sections of "Four-Mode Self-Portrait" in Illustration 2.2 corresponds to each: 1) the bottom left corner is an actual photograph, so unsimplified and unexaggerated; 2) the bottom right corner is adapted from the same photo by erasing everything but the minimum lines needed to represent a face, so simplified but not exaggerated; 3) the top left corner is adapted from the same photo by variously expanding and rearranging details, so unsimplified and exaggerated; and 4) the top right corner is drawn using roughly the same number of lines as the image below it and with roughly the same degree of distortion as the image beside it, so simplified and exaggerated.

A mode, according to Witek, relates to a larger ethos. Cartoons tend to create worlds with "a fundamentally unstable and infinitely mutable physical reality, where characters and even objects can move and be transformed according to an associative or emotive logic rather than the laws of physics" (2012: 30), while figures drawn in a naturalistic style tend to "remain stable as physical entities, with any changes in shape and size accounted for by the familiar conventions of visual distance and perspective," and "the world depicted within the panels is presumed to be stable" (2012: 32). "In a humorous drawn comic," Lefèvre similarly argues, "the reader will accept more voluntary inconsistencies in the representation of diegetic space" than "if a comic pretends to be a realistic depiction of our world" (2009: 160). Libicki varies style modes depending on what degree of subjectivity she wishes to evoke:

I found that [naturalistic watercolors] communicated verisimilitude, and was suited to more journalistic pieces (and to more lyrical open-endedness as opposed to rhetoric). Cartooniness, on the other hand, is more immersive (if it's done well), because the reader has to collaborate by translating the "shorthand" of simplified designs back into their real-life referents. Photo-real paintings don't "put pictures in your head" because the picture is already there on paper. I think working in nonfiction means I get to decide whether something is better depicted "subjectively" or "objectively" or a point in between.

2019

Applying a cartoon mode to nonfiction subjects may not produce Witek's cartoon ethos of an actually unstable reality, but the representational style carries those and other connotations. Mather describes early modernist painters similarly: "By moving away from more literal forms of visual reference, vanguard painters mostly attempted to depict phenomena in ways other than they might appear to the unaided or unaffected senses" (2016: 59). Futurist painter Gino Severini similarly explains in his 1913 manifesto: "This is a complex form of realism which *totally* destroys the integrity of matter" (2009: 166).

Though she does not reference Witek, Hyde develops a similar analysis of two sets of illustrations for Chinua Achebe's novel *Things Fall Apart*, linking Dennis Carabine's naturalistic style to literary realism and the "highly simplified, almost abstract gestures" of Uche Okeke to modernism (Okeke-Agula quoted in Hyde 2016: 29). Hyde extends her argument to Picasso, likening his "emphasis on the surface of the picture plane to Achebe's flat style" (2016: 32). Flatness is a product of simplification and so the absence of crosshatched depth that defines many naturalistic drawings. "All of the action," observes Hyde, "occurs at the level of the line as it carves through the blank space of the page. The illustrative power of these drawings gathers at the surface of the image, but this is not the Euro-modernist surface" (2016: 31). Since Okeke's figures both simplify and exaggerate the shapes of their source material, they are formally cartoons that also "suggest a new way of reading Achebe's style" through "Okeke's postcolonial modernism" (2016: 30, 31).

Hyde's analysis aligns with Witek's cartoon ethos, and so she begins to address Medley's call for future research: "An important next step will be to determine how levels of pictorial realism within a comic's world impact upon the way narratives are perceived by the reader" (2010: 68). What ethos might detailed exaggeration or unexaggerated simplification produce? Such questions would have to be analyzed on a case-by-case basis, but in each the overlapping spectrums of simplification and exaggeration extend beyond style to influence the nature of diegetic worlds.

4. Emanata and Blurgits

In addition to simplification and exaggeration, cartooning includes drawing customs shared by comics-medium artists working across a range of subgenres. While the conventions are not unique to cartoons, they are associated with them culturally. *Beetle Bailey* artist Mort Walker coined terms for two of the most prominent, "emanata" and "blurgits," in his 1980 *The Lexicon of Comicana*, though each dates decades if not centuries earlier. Cohn calls them "visual morphemes" and categorizes dozens more. In order to explore style norms further, I focus on the two most common, emphasizing their non-representational qualities in multiple representational contexts.

Emanata, which Walker presumably derived from the verb "emanate," are typically lines radiating from and so directing attention to an implied focal point. Cartoonists often draw emanata around a character's face to "show emotion" and "reveal internal conditions" such as embarrassment or drunkenness, while emanata around non-human objects can suggest physical states including heat, odor, brightness, and "that something is spanking new" (Walker 1980: 28–9). Impact lines are another form of emanata, often drawn in clusters or "bursts." Frans Masereel carved emanata into his 1918 woodcut novel *The Passion of a Man*, but, since halos and aureoles in religious iconography are forms of emanata, the practice dates to at least the Roman Empire with a circle and radiating spokes depicted behind Apollo's head found in a second-century floor tile. Similar sunburst halos appear in Christian art, though later painters replaced flat opaque circles with three-dimensional rings floating above heads (as in Caravaggio's 1605 *Saint Jerome in Meditation*) or with circular bursts of light emanating from behind heads (as in Francesco Podesti's 1864 *Apparition of Jesus to St. Margaret Mary Alacoque*). Emanata may originate from the optical experience of diffracted light around a bright object, and the art term "aureole" denotes whole-body emanata as seen in Frans Masereel's 1920 *Story Without Words* and Keith Haring's 1990 *Radiant Baby* series. Emanata also extend beyond radiant lines to include any drawn element that appears to originate from a subject. Talk balloons are emanata, most overtly when they contain only non-verbal punctuation such as an exclamation mark. Masereel includes a free-standing question mark in *Story Without Words*, a slight variation on the question marks linked to characters with single emanata lines that Bud Fisher draws in his 1918 comic strip *Mutt and Jeff*.

According to Walker, blurgits, or blur units, are "a kind of stroboscopic technique to show movement within a single panel" (1980: 37). A figure wholly or partially repeats along its path of movement embedding multiple brief moments within a single image. The technique dates to at least 1845, when it appears in *The Story of Albert by Simon of Nantua* (quoted in Kunzle 2007: 109). The approach also developed simultaneously in early-twentieth-century newspaper comics strips and the fine arts movement of Futurism, as seen in Giacomo Balla's 1912 *Dynanism of a Dog on a Leash* and Natalia Goncharova's 1913 *Cyclist*. Walker correctly identifies blurgits in Marcel Duchamp's 1912 *Nude Descending a Staircase, No. 2*, which also contains semi-circular motion lines, a related convention for representing movement. Such lines are also called "speed" or "zip lines," presumably after George Herriman whose *Krazy Kat* featured a line and an onomatopoeic "ZIP" behind a thrown brick beginning in 1910. The technique dates to at least Rudolph Dirks's comic strip *The Katzenjammer Kids*, as seen in the December 12, 1897 installment "The Bicyclist's Revenge." Like blurgits, motion lines may be based on an optical effect of afterimages experienced when following a moving object. Cohn and Maher, however, argue instead that "motion lines are conventionalized ... representations understood through experience with a visual vocabulary" (1915: 11). Similarly, Wartenberg classifies speed lines as "not pictorial" even though they are "representational in the sense that they indicate features of the story-world" (2012: 97).

Though these conventions are most associated with cartooning, they are not exclusive to the cartoon mode and often appear in works that are otherwise naturalistic, such as R. Rikuo Johnson's 2005 *Night Fisher* and Jessica Abel's 2006 *La Perdida*. For her

2019 *I Know What I Am*, Gina Siciliano maintains a naturalistic visual tone while impressionistically rendering emanata and blurgits into the patterns of her crosshatching, a technique also seen in Van Gogh's 1889 *The Starry Night*. To the degree that zip lines, blurgits, emanata, and other shared stylistic conventions are conceptual rather than optically inspired, viewers understand them to be paradoxically invisible to characters within a diegesis even though they are intermingled with and often identical to other discursive marks that appear to compose the visually observable physical reality of the story world. Duncan and Smith note that "non-visual sensory experiences have to be suggested by visual imagery" (2015: 141), making the marks synesthetic and so a subcategory of sensory diegetic imagery. They also reveal a more general challenge of interpreting any sensory content from an image's discursive marks.

5. Transparency and Non-transparency

Style mode customs such as emanata and blurgits complicate representation because they further highlight the ambiguous relationship between style and content. Is style— including custom-based techniques shared by multiple artists—an interpretation of an independent diegetic subject, leaving some details unknown, or does it represent the subject by depicting its literal qualities? Drawing norms influence how artists produce the marks of their medium. If those marks are representational, they create information about the diegesis, but unless an image is a perfect replica, it must, according to Gombrich, "involve some degree of "abstraction"" (1963: 1). Abstract qualities may be understood to be qualities of the subject or qualities projected onto it. Recall how "quivering, quavering" may describe either the artist David B's drawn lines or the character David B's psychological experience.

If characters and their worlds are understood to exist as they discursively appear, an image is an "analogue of reality" as Barthes described photographs. According to Cook's similar "panel transparency principle," style defines diegetic reality: "Characters, events, and locations within a fictional world described by a comic appear, within the fictional world, as they are depicted in typical panels within that comic" (2012: 134). Transparency assumes drawn images have the "special causal and structural relationship with the reality that they represent" that Mitchell dismisses for photographs (1994: 282). Though cartoon objects are impossible in our reality, their transparently drawn qualities could accurately depict a cartoon reality. If so, a drawing of Charlie Brown has a round head that is roughly half his height because the diegetic Charlie Brown has a round head roughly half his height. Charlie Brown might then be called a naturalistic cartoon or a naturalistic representation of a non-naturalistic object.

This is only possible if an image is a work of fiction and so set in a world with different natural laws. Fictional worlds with greater resemblance to ours pose a different problem. Consider Julie Maroh's use of color in her 2010 *Blue is the Warmest Color*. While Maroh paints a full range of colors for events that take place in the novel's current time period, past events appear gray except for isolated blue objects, including the main character's diary, her boyfriend's shirt, a child's balloon, her girlfriend's hair, and her girlfriend's dreamt hands. All but the last may be understood as transparently blue, meaning any individual within the story world would see them as blue, too. Even the final example may be understood as literal within the reality of the dream. Everything else, however, must be non-diegetically gray, including potentially other blue objects since Maroh's blue also communicates the main character's emotional interest. The one incidentally blue object, the child's balloon, is blue only because the main character momentarily mistakes it for her lover's actual blue hair in a crowd. Color generally and blue specifically then are sometimes transparent and sometimes not. Similarly in fine arts, Matisse's 1905 *Woman with a Hat* marked the start of Fauvism (literally "wild-beast-ism"), which featured a non-transparent use of color that followed a cartoon ethos of representing reality through "an associative or emotive logic" rather than realistic observation (Witek 2012: 30).

Works of nonfiction pose problems for transparency because, unless photographic or photorealistic, images cannot be literal. Drawings, especially highly stylized, abstract, or otherwise cartoonish ones, do not represent their subject matter through exact visual resemblance. Rather than being transparent, images in nonfiction works are overtly interpretive. When Alison Bechdel draws her and her family members' mouths as single dots in her 2006 *Fun Home*, viewers likely do not imagine that the actual individuals' mouths are so impossibly proportioned. Viewers also don't imagine that Art Spiegelman and his family members have the heads of mice as they appear to in *Maus*. When Joe Sacco's images of the Bosnian War in 2000 *Safe Area Goražde* recall the visual style of underground comix, a viewer may experience two forms of representation: the images represent real-world content through resemblance while also participating in the custom-based representational norms of a specific visual tradition.

Wolheim, Gombrich, Goodman, and Barthes discuss representational images as reproductions of reality—our reality. In literary terms, they theorize visual nonfiction. The comics medium, as suggested by the synonym "graphic novel," include works of fiction. All fiction imitates aspects of our word to create other worlds, but the degree of mimesis varies. Romances, westerns, and mysteries tend to be superficially mimetic, while science fiction and fantasy often contradict fundamental aspects of physics and biology. If the work is prose-only, the visual appearance of the diegetic world is only the hazy, word-evoked images in each reader's head. If the other reality is drawn, it leaves unclear whether images are photo-like replicas, visually independent interpretations, or something between. "Pictures seem more transparent than words," conclude Varnum and Gibbons, "but often their transparency is illusory" (2001: xii).

Cook later rejected his transparency principle, concluding instead that "our access to the physical appearance of drawn characters in general is indirect, partial, inferential, and imperfect" (2015: 25). Lynda Barry playfully coined the term "autobiofictionalography" for her 2002 graphic memoir *One! Hundred! Demons!*, asking: "Is it autobiography if parts of it are not true? Is it fiction if parts of it are?" (2017: 7). The parts that "are not true" include representations of herself, family members, and childhood friends in a cartoon style. Barry draws her mother with anatomically impossible traits, representing her without making any specific claims about her actual appearance (2017: 95). This suggests Gombrich's game of make-believe between artist and viewer. The drawing represents Barry's mother while hardly resembling her. Such indirectly representational images are composed of specific details that are ambiguously related to the actual details of the represented content.

Chute similarly concludes that comics "is not a duplicative form; its drawings may refer to reality, but they constitute their own functioning model" (2016: 21). While the drawings create the diegesis, the style of the drawings is only apparent through distortions of represented content. With caricatural portraits of real-world people, exaggerated details are self-evidently non-literal, especially when outside the range of anatomical possibility. To identify physically plausible exaggerations, viewers need to reference the subject's actual face, which is impossible if the subject is fictional. If the fictional world allows anatomical possibilities impossible in the actual world, style becomes semi-representational, depicting details that appear to be inherent to subjects but that may not be.

Semi-representational qualities may result from the nature of images generally. While it is possible to construct an objectively nonfictional claim in words, a visual claim—even, according to Mitchell, when the image is photographic—may not be possible. In Illustration 2.3, a panel from Marisa Acocella Marchetto's 2006 *Cancer Vixen* includes the following words in a caption box describing the author's experience in a doctor's office: "First he used a roller which was connected to the sonogram. It transmitted the image onscreen" (2006: 4). While the statement isn't necessarily true— Marchetto could have misremembered or knowingly altered the event—all of the verbal qualities are plausible and likely understood to be true by readers. The drawing beneath the caption box, however, is choppily hand-drawn with minimal detail and blocks of color, making it visually impossible even though the event it represents is understood to be nonfictional. If Marchetto had drawn a photorealistic image, its nonfictional content would be plausible, but, since Marchetto is lying on the examination table, at least some of its qualities would still appear to be fabricated unless the event involved a third character who took a photograph that Marchetto later meticulously copied. Regardless, qualities of the diegetic image do not match the implied reality they reference. We know the real-world Marchetto who received an actual sonogram in an actual doctor's office is not made of blocks of undifferentiated colors enclosed by black contour lines in mildly impossible anatomical shapes. Image style is independent of the fully mimetic reality that the image paradoxically produces.

Transparent and non-transparent tensions are common in the comics medium. When Neal Adams introduced the character Havok in *X-Men* #58 (July 1969) as seen in Illustration 2.3, he drew the character's energy discharge as overlapping concentric circles—circles so precise that they foreground their presence as drawn lines and the compass that Adams presumably used to create them. The effect is not cartoonish, but like Witek's cartoon mode, it "disavows any attempt to render the surface appearances of the physical world," focusing attention instead on the surface of the page (2012: 32). Bill Sienkiewicz introduced the character Warlock in *New Mutants* #18 (August 1984), and although the character's shape-shifting abilities are explained by its alien physiology, Sienkiewicz's image in Illustration 2.3 violates typical naturalistic conventions in the superhero comics genre. Warlock's rendering aligns with the cartoon mode in which a character may be drawn non-realistically for slapstick effect. Warlock's hair, for instance, appears to stand on end, and his mouth extends well beyond human proportions.

Illustration 2.3 From Marchetto's *CancerVixen*, Gloeckner's *A Child's Life*, Adams's *X-Men*, and Sienkiewicz's *New Mutants*.

Because Warlock contrasts Sienkiewicz's more traditionally naturalistic renderings of other characters on the same pages, the cartoon qualities are diegetic even though they resist literal interpretation. Rather than embodying exceptions, Warlock and Havok suggest an underlying norm. Because "drawings in comics are static and strongly stylized," Lefèvre notes that "the spectator becomes aware of their hand-drawn quality" (2012: 72). Chabon analyzes superhero costumes similarly: "realism is not, in fact, merely difficult; it is hopeless" because "a superhero's costume is constructed not of fabric, foam rubber, or adamantium but of halftone dots, Pantone color values, inked containment lines, and all the cartoonist's sleight of hand" (2008: 66). Stylistic expressiveness is always in tension with transparent interpretation.

Examples are common in fine arts, too. Childe Hassam's 1917 *Flags in the Rain* include US flags displayed on New York City streets. Though on close inspection, the stripes are gray and orange, a viewer likely understands them to be white and red— rejecting discursive facts (the actual paint on the actual canvas) in favor of knowledge about the diegetic world, which in Hassam's case is our world, where stripes on US flags are white and red. If viewers consciously register experiencing orange as red, they may still understand the color as visually accurate: because of the rain, the distance, or the movement of the fabric, the red stripes looked orange to Hassam and so he accurately produced that visual effect. If so, the painting, including its impressionistic imprecision, could still be understood as transparent. Yet Hassam may have preferred orange for others reasons. Though regarded as an impressionist, Hassam was painting well into the early Modernist period during which color was not necessarily reflective of visual experience. Henri Matisse's 1905 *Woman with a Hat* includes bright unblended swaths of green, yellow, and purple that represent the colors of the figure's face and clothes despite also contradicting them. If Matisse was painting from a model (his wife, who by one account was dressed in black), then the woman and her clothes exist in our world, and so their appearance in the painting is indirect, partial, inferential, and imperfect of their actual appearance: they are non-transparent.

Hassam's orange and Matisse's swaths of color may follow Witek's cartoon mode, where objects can "be transformed according to an associative or emotive logic rather than the laws of physics" (2012: 30). If so, Hassam painted orange stripes because orange stripes produced an effect he preferred over visual transparency. Matisse abandoned transparency in color and detail (his brush strokes are thick and loose) and created an image so non-naturalistic a French critic called it a "wild beast," a term soon adopted for the movement Fauvism. Other early-twentieth-century stylistic challenges to naturalistic norms (Futurism toward movement, Cubism toward perspective, Expressionism toward shared reality) can be understood as non-transparent, cartoon-mode, semi-representational content that indirectly communicates diegetic qualities of subject matter while also largely overwhelming them.

6. Specification

Interpreting an image as representing its subject non-transparently involves assessing degrees of specification. The images in Marchetto's memoir, in addition to being exaggerated, are simplified to a degree impossible for photorealistic images of the same real-world subjects. They are underspecified.

Viewers do not necessarily infer additional visual impressions from underspecified images. Consider the circular and featureless head of the far left horseback rider in Illustration 2.2. Though more realistically proportioned than Charlie Brown, its head appears to balance above its torso with no neck, and it lacks all internal detail. Is it understood naturalistically as the silhouette of a backlit figure? Is the absent neck an illusion of distance? Do the discursive figures produce diegetic counterparts in an implied world? Most likely, the seemingly singular subject represents a conceptual category of multiple potential people in our world. The figure implies no visual information about any individual and so is underspecified.

Drawing from computational linguistics, formal semantics, and psycholinguistics, Sanford and Sturt show that language processing does not necessarily include fully specified interpretations of word meanings either. The referent of the pronoun "it" in the example of the verbal command, "hook up ... engine E2 to the boxcar at Elmira ... and send it to Corning," could be the engine, boxcar, or both, but "because the result of sending it to Corning remains the same, the referent of it may remain underspecified without affecting the key interpretation" (2002: 382). Underspecification is inherent in statements such as "Every kid climbed a tree," which could refer to one or multiple trees while not otherwise affecting the meaning of the sentence (2002: 383). Also, because words "like Vietnam can be interpreted literally (as a country) or metonymically (as a war) ... a precise meaning is not established until needed" (2002: 384). The round featureless head of the horseback rider is underspecified in a similar sense: it refers to all heads without referring to any specific head because its resemblance is underspecified. The same discursive circle when drawn as Charlie Brown's silhouette instead refers to and represents one head only.

The generic head icon is paradoxical because, like all discursive marks, it must be discursively specific and yet it is diegetically non-specific. The visual paradox challenges the norms of representation. Hopkins claims that in order for a picture to represent something "one needs to know what the thing depicted looks like" and that "a picture must depict more" than a word which can "refer to a particular thing ... without saying anything about it" (2005: 145–6). The generic head icon violates those assumptions by indicating all heads, regardless of size, shape, color, or any differentiating quality, while also including all situations, perspectives, and points in time. The lines and shapes of the image then are radically underspecified, creating no spatiotemporal diegesis, instead representing only an idea.

Representational images can also be overspecified. Hopkins observes that "a picture must depict more" than words, sometimes requiring an artist to interpolate or otherwise invent details. For the one-image "Stepfatherly Counsel" from her graphic memoir collection *A Child's Life* (2001: 53) in Illustration 2.3, Phoebe Gloeckner draws her stepfather's sweater in meticulous detail, creating what appears to be the individual threads of the fabric. The patterned weave of the couch is similarly detailed. Are the details reproduced from Gloeckner's photographic memory? Is the moment depicting an exact memory or a conglomerate representing a pattern of recalled events? If the second, then not only is the sweater and couch fabric overspecified, but the figures are, too. Gloeckner must draw them in postures of some kind, but not necessarily as they were ever actually seated in the autobiographical moment or moments they indirectly represent. The overspecified image instead represents generalized content.

7. Framed Viewpoints

Like style, framing and viewpoint pose challenges to the discourse–diegesis divide. When not interpreted representationally, the marks that create framing and viewpoint effects are discursive. When interpreted, the effects relate ambiguously to diegesis because frame edges and the experience of a viewpoint not experienced by a character are not parts of the represented world. Style, framing, and viewpoint are instead qualities of or controlled by an image-narrator.

Hopkins claims that "all depiction is from a point of view" (2005: 145), which may be misleading depending on whether he considers a schematic drawing (which can represent space while de-emphasizing viewpoint) to be a depiction. Subway diagrams simplify and regularize tunnel paths and station intervals in a manner that obscures their actual physical relationships to each other and to the implied (and impossible) position of the viewer. Point of view is only necessary for optically realistic images, with an implied viewer positioned in some physical relationship to the subject, even if the subject is fictional. Even if discursively true, diegetically no character, including the producer of the image, necessarily exists within the scene—and yet angle and proximity establish a diegetic viewpoint experienced by viewers as if present but somehow disembodied. Something else exists diegetically in the location of the perspective. The illusion of a viewer's diegetic presence is, like drawing style, a semi-representational quality, since characters are unaware of the viewer's point of perspective even in instances of extreme proximity created by foreshortening.

Viewpoint can also suggest connotations about subjects, creating qualities that are not independent aspects of a figure. Kress and van Leeuwen employ Hall's "proxemics" for describing the intimacy effects of distances between subjects and implied viewers: close personal, personal, close social, social, and public (1996: 125). They describe vertical effects in terms of power relationships: "if a represented participant is seen from a high angle" then the viewer "has power over the represented participant"; if the participant "is seen from a low angle" it "has power over" the viewer; and if "the picture is at eye level, then the point of view is one of equality and there is no power difference" (1996: 140). They analyze horizontal angles in terms of detachment, with frontal angles of subjects connoting to viewers "something we are involved with" and oblique angles connoting "something *we* are not involved with" (1996: 136).

Viewpoints can also arrange background content in relation to a foregrounded figure for further semi-representational effects. For his 1851 painting *Washington Crossing the Delaware*, Emanuel Leutze isolates Washington's head against the brightening horizon for a radiant emanata effect that would not occur from other angles. Photographer Al Drago's portrait of Donald Trump for the *New York Times* December 14, 2019 editorial "Impeach" arranges the president's profile at the center of the presidential seal on the wall behind him, creating a circular halo intensified by the extreme blurriness of Trump's head. Since Washington's and Trump's heads do not inherently produce emanata, the effects are semi-representational.

Jost coined "ocularization" from the Latin word "oculus" (literally "eye") to name the effect of viewing a film diegesis as if through a character's eyes. Though useful, film terms introduce unacknowledged assumptions. Comics-medium scripters often think and communicate in the language of filmmaking. Percy describes himself as an "aggressive screenwriter . . . some weird combination of director and screenwriter" and artists as "the cinematographer who shoots the picture" (2016: 28). A planned image is often referred to as a "shot," which O'Neil defines as "One picture, but with the content of the picture, the way it is composed, etc. . . . Terms used to describe a shot include closeup, long shot, medium shot, extreme closeup, etc." (2001: 14). Bendis approaches a page in terms of "'camera' angles" and recommends writers "use a screenwriting program called Final Draft" with "the standard screenplay template" (2014: 191, 37). Abel and Madden acknowledge differences of film, but still recommend "film terms for camera placement (shots) and camera angles," adding to O'Neil's list: Establishing shot, Over-the-shoulder shot, Point-of-view shot, Canted angle, Focus, High-angle/low-angle, Iris, Split screen, and Wide screen (2008: 154–5). Of the scripts included in *Panel One: Comic Book Scripts by Top Writers*, most include film terms, with instructions to "pull back" or move in "tight" or in one case: "Camera draws back and now we see that we're in a gym" (Gertler 2002: 93). Mateu-Mestre even differentiates between camera lenses, reproducing long, 50-mm, and wide-angle effects (2010: 28–30).

While film terms are convenient shorthand for verbally describing visual concepts, they limit image analysis by understanding them as framed stills and so maintain spatiotemporal assumptions that impose norms of film. "Most definitions of comics," argues Hatfield, "stress the representation of time, that is, of temporal sequence" (2005: 41), and Lefèvre identifies the parallel expectation "that the diegetic space of a comic is coherent: he expects—in analogy with daily life—a consistent space" (2009: 159). Emphasizing spatiotemporality leads to assumptions of "selecting" discussed in the previous chapter; paralleling how filmmakers literally select from a range of filmed content while editing, Smith and Duncan assert that comics-medium "creators reduce the story to moments on a page by encapsulation" (2015: 112), implying that story and so representational content generally is independent of and pre-exists its rendering. Groensteen asserts that "when a mental image is given birth by a cartoonist, the preconceived parameters of its frame are principally its proportions and its form" (2007: 43), but mental images do not have preconceived parameters. Groensteen conflates discursive images with mental images, ignoring that, as Mendelsund observes, "we cannot advance beyond a vague *sketchiness* in our imaginings" (2014: 192). Artists can conceive ideas for images, but until an artist attempts to execute the idea, there is no actual image and so no parameters.

Many works in the comics medium, including Lynda Barry's 2014 graphic essay *Syllabus*, Anders Nilsen's 2015 sketchbook-like *Poetry is Useless*, and Gareth A. Hopkins and Erik Blagsvedt's non-representational 2017 graphic novel *Found Forest Floor*, proceed without visually representing any clear or consistent diegetic space or time. In addition to viewpoint's effects of "subjective images," Kress and van Leeuwen distinguish "objective images" that do not involve perspective and so "violate the laws of naturalistic depiction or, indeed, the laws of nature" (1996: 130), an underdeveloped area of analysis for the comics medium. Following Marr's account of visual perception, Willats calls such images "anomalous," categorizing Cubists' paintings and many children's drawings as "internal objected-centered descriptions" because "the frames of reference . . . on which they are based are centered on the objects themselves, rather than being determined by the viewer's line of sight or position in space" (1997: 19). Willats rejects the "persistent tradition that pictures are derived … from retinal images—or … internal mental images that correspond more or less directly with possible views" (1997: 18).

Even when diegetic content is spatiotemporal, film terms are misleading. In film, the diegetic world is based on discursive replicas of real-world objects. Actors and locales are selected and altered but not created (except for CGI, a kind of photorealistic animation). The image frame is similarly static and within a range of standard rectangular widths. In a non-photographic image, representational content and framing are infinitely malleable. Consider the filming of a door. The relationships between the tall rectangle of the door and the wide rectangle of the film frame is asymmetrical. A director might include the entire door in the frame and so also areas of the wall left and right of the door. The director might match door width to frame width, cropping the door at the top, bottom, or both. In film terms, the first image is a long shot, the second a medium shot, but neither term addresses the range of possibilities. Since frame shape is malleable, an artist could include the entire door in a door-shaped frame, producing an image that is neither long nor medium because the proximity of the implied viewer is ambiguous. Since the artist controls not only subject–frame ratios but also image size, she could also produce the detail-rich effect of a close-up by drawing the door in a large panel, and yet also produce a medium or long shot effect by including areas to the sides. She could dispose of the frame entirely, leaving image edges ambiguous. In film, an actual camera exists in an actual spatial relationship to the subject it records. While an artist might use an actual door as a reference point while drawing, that door is not directly transformed into the image and so can be as tall or wide as the artist chooses. If the door appears in multiple images, its discursive dimensions may be inconsistent, even as viewers experience it as a stable diegetic object.

Like viewpoint, framing produces a range of semi-representational qualities by placing a subject in relation to the frame which does not exist in the diegesis. Images often follow what Tversky calls "a center–periphery organization," where subjects at or near the center area of an image appear more significant than subjects that are off-centered or cropped (2010: 509). Subjects that appears to break and therefore protrude beyond a drawn frame also gain significance, an effect relatively common in the comics medium but impossible in film since the edge of a film image is an actual edge and not a drawn frame. The relationships between multiple subjects depicted within a single image are similarly affected, since a centered figure will seem significant relative to an off-centered or cropped figure. This is true even of non-representational images. Mitchell describes a 1915 Kasimir Melevich painting as "a small tilted red square below a larger black square," arguing that "the 'hero' of this painting, the protagonist of its one-sentence narrative, is the tilted red square," adding "I take it there's no need for me to specify which square is the father, which the son" (1994: 225–6). In addition to being larger, the black square also dominates the center of the canvas. Based on Melevich's later title, *Boy with Knapsack*, he and Mitchell experience very different diegeses, but the relationship between the shapes is still influenced by framing. Melevich also arranges his 28 × 17 ½ canvas vertically, an option unavailable to most filmmakers.

Groensteen describes "rhetorical layout" in which "the size (and sometimes the shape) of each frame is adapted to the content, to the subject matter of the panel" (2013: 148, 46). Groensteen's term is a misnomer since he is describing the rhetoric of an individual frame and not relationships between frames within a layout. Peeters similarly applies "rhetorical" to "pages" that include images in which "the dimensions of the panel conform to the action being described," citing an example of a figure descending a staircase in a tall rectangular panel which "supports, through its clear verticality, the body of Nestor descending the staircase," followed by a second rectangular panel in which "the framework widens so as to be able to accommodate in its entirety a Nestor who has begun to slant because of his imbalance," concluding with a square panel determined by the character's extended limbs (2007). Both Groensteen and Peeters refer to the same effect which may be more accurately termed "rhetorical framing."

All framed images can be analyzed rhetorically since there is always a relationship between content and frame. Framing rhetoric divides into three categories: "the placement of the subject in relation to the center of the frame (centered or off-centered); the aspect ratios of the frame and the subject (symmetrical and asymmetrical); and the frame and subject size relationship (proportionate, expansive, and cropped or broken)" (Gavaler 2018: 215). Also, frame and subject may align horizontally and vertically, or they may diverge (for example, with the subject filling the frame diagonally because the subject's ground is tilted relative to the rectangle of the frame). Frame and subject also may or may not each align with the horizontal and vertical edges of a rectangular page.

8. Focalization

Despite its origin in film analysis, "ocularization" remains an apt term for analysis because it replaces a literal camera viewpoint with the illusion of a character's viewpoint. A non-ocularized image instead suggests a viewpoint independent of any character. Point of view, however, is a dead metaphor that often indicates not a literal perspective but a mental one, what Pedri defines as "the filtering of knowledge as well as thoughts, feelings, memories and other intellectual processes by fictional agents" (2015: 8). Though Genette identifies viewpoint in the metaphorical sense as "focalization," his analysis is non-visual, leaving ambiguous the relationship between the literal perspective of ocularization (a character's eyes) and the metaphorical perspective of focalization (a character's mind). Mikkonen makes the same distinction between "perceptual and cognitive focalization" (2017: 157), but Jost's earlier terms "ocularization" and "focalization" seem clearer. In a prose-only work, ocularization is generally irrelevant and possibly non-existent since a focalized character's viewpoint is expressed through words that also suggest that character's mental perception of seeing. An image can instead be ocularized but not focalized, conveying the character's literal viewpoint without also conveying the character's mental experience of it.

The term "character" must be clarified since, despite Pedri's summary of focalization as involving "fictional agents," a focalized character need not be fictional. Any

Illustration 2.4 From Ware's *Jimmy Corrigan*, gg's *I'm Not Here*, and Barry's *One! Hundred! Demons!*

spatiotemporal image implies an ocular viewpoint, which can be understood as the image-narrator's. If the image-narrator is also a character within the diegesis, it is a diegetic image-narrator. If the physical viewpoint is diegetically unoccupied, the image is non-ocularized, placing the image-narrator outside the primary diegesis. Mikkonen terms this non-ocularized effect as "impersonal" or "external focalization," presumably a subcategory of perceptual focalization.

Analyzed in combination, ocularization and focalization produce four categories:

1. Non-ocularized and non-focalized. This is a norm of comics-medium images. Unless an image quality suggests otherwise, viewers likely assume an image is a non-subjective, resemblance-based representation of the diegetic world that does not express information about any character's metaphorical or literal perspective. Such an image likely produces an impression of objectivity and so Cook's transparency principle.

2. Ocularized but non-focalized. An individual image can express ocularization by including image content that implies a character's position relative to the content. In Illustration 2.4, gg achieves the effect in two panels from *I'm Not Here*: the first implies a character's ocularization by positioning an object in a character's hands as though viewed from the angle and proximity of the character's head; the second panel includes the focus circles of a camera lens, implying that an ocularized character is looking through the camera (2017). The viewpoints are literal, meaning anyone occupying the same physical positions would experience the visual phenomena depicted, and include no focalized effects.

3. Non-ocularized but focalized. Focalization often involves a change in artistic style that suggests a character's shift in perception away from a previous baseline reality. Seiiche Hayashi's *Red Colored Elegy* includes an image of a contemporary Japanese couple about to embrace followed by an image of Snow White and Prince Charming embracing (2018: 21). Since no character is watching, neither image is ocularized, but the second is focalized (by one, either, or both of the lovers) to suggest the internal experience of idealized romance. In Illustration 2.4, Lynda Barry captures non-ocularized focalization in *One! Hundred! Demons!* without juxtaposition by drawing her younger self and another character with green skin, emanata circling their red eyes, and curving waves of psychedelic colors surrounding them (2017: 118). Even if viewed without the accompanying text and out of sequential context, viewers might glean that the two figures are experiencing the effects of a drug. By splitting ocularization and focalization, Barry's younger self is both the subject being viewed and the internal experience of viewing, which contradicts the diegetic event since young Barry did not view herself.

4. Ocularized and focalized. Viewpoint is both literal and metaphorical, and so the image content is shaped by not only a character's angle and proximity but also an internal experience of the content. In Illustration 2.4, the ocularized and focalized main character from Chris Ware's *Jimmy Corrigan* has been struck by a mail truck and lies on his back looking up at the driver leaning over him. In one panel the driver is wearing a superhero costume—which the viewer understands to be a hallucination or wishful imagining or some other internal experience that represents Jimmy's mental state even though some of the image's qualities, including the driver's body shape and posture, also represent reality as it would be physically viewed from Jimmy's position (1995). The second panel is only ocularized.

Ocularization and focalization are sometimes ambiguous, since it might not be clear whether a viewpoint is from the precise angle of a character's eyes or only roughly near it, lessening but not eliminating the subjective effect. An ocularized image may also not overtly suggest focalization, and yet a viewer may still experience the image in the manner that the character is understood to experience it. This effect is central to Laura Mulvey's analysis of male gaze, where an ocularized heterosexual male character looks at a sexualized female character. Because the female character is also the male character's object of desire, ocularization alone may be sufficient to convey that focalized desire. The desire may also be conveyed without ocularization, since male gaze merges a diegetic character with an implied viewer who experiences the same desire, blurring the distinction between discourse and diegesis. Pornographic images do this prototypically, ocularizing no specific male character but focalizing a generalized heterosexual male audience's desire.

While it is sometimes useful to separate focalization and image-narration, it results in categorical complexities. Focalization, like ocularization, is diegetic and so is an aspect of representational content. Image-narration is non-diegetic to the degree that the image-narrator is not part of the represented world. If the image-narrator is also distinct from the actual artist, which is typical unless the image content is autobiographical, the image-narrator exists ambiguously outside the primary diegesis. Focalization applies only to characters, who only exist within the primary diegesis. A narrator can exist within the primary diegesis as a narrating character or outside the primary diegesis as a non-character narrator. If the narrator is a character, self-focalization and narration are identical.

Duncan and Smith explore a related distinction between "non-sensory diegetic images," those that represent a character's "thoughts, emotions, and psychological experience" (and so focalized images), and "hermeneutic images," ones that interpret or "comment on the story" by "reflecting a particular narrative point of view" (2015: 146, 148). Both are distinct from "sensory diegetic images," images that "represent visual experience" of "what we would see if we lived in the world of the story" (2015: 141). They provide an example of a hermeneutic image from Roberta Gregory's 1997 graphic memoir *Bitchy's College Daze* in which the artist represents herself in the backseat of a car with her parents in the front seat viewed from outside the car and drawn in caricatural styles that express a critical attitude toward each (2015: 147). That attitude could be analyzed either as a product of image-narration (by the memoir's diegetic image-narrator understood to be the actual author looking back at past events) or focalization (of the character of the younger Gregory represented in the image). Even if the two Gregory's attitudes align, focalization and narration are distinct.

An image-narrator is often identified as the actual artist-author, which is likely Duncan and Smith's intent. Though their hermeneutic image examples come from graphic memoirists (Roberta Gregory, Alison Bechdel, and Art Spiegelman), Duncan earlier identifies hermeneutic images in David Mazzucchelli's *Asterios Polyp*: "These images are the author's commentary on the story and are often explicit attempts to influence the interpretation of the story" (2012: 45). According to Duncan, they are "a means for the author to directly address the reader, and they are usually the most purposefully selected images on the page" (2012: 46). Again, images are not "selected," and any image could be likened to a verbal direct address since direct address does not differentiate between kinds of content and so would include the verbal equivalents of Duncan's sensory and non-sensory images. It is unclear why these images should be understood as expressing authorial commentary rather than the focalized experience of the depicted character. Asterios Polyp stands beneath a thought balloon that is raining on him. Duncan argues that Mazzucchelli uses the image to express "bad luck, misery, or despair," which seems true, but since it is the character who is experiencing the despair, the image might be also focalized and so is, in Duncan's terms, a non-sensory diegetic image. Duncan and Smith argue that hermeneutic images "comment on the story itself," while "the vast majority" of images in the comics medium transparently convey diegetic content without a viewer's interpretative attention (2015: 146, 141). Since images produce diegeses, it is ambiguous how producing and commenting on what is simultaneously produced are separable or how some images might perform one task but not the other.

If focalization is the filtering of knowledge as well as thoughts, feelings, memories, and other intellectual processes, there's an additional sense in which the artist is always the filtering agent. While focalization applies only to characters, this larger filtering quality is central to images generally. Arguably, all images convey the mental viewpoint of the image-maker, while a focalized image additionally conveys the mental viewpoint of a character. How artists convey those viewpoints is complexly ambiguous and encompasses the range of topics discussed in this chapter.

While image narration applies to images generally, the next chapter turns to the qualities of multiple images and so to the comics form specifically.

3

Juxtapositions

After the first two chapters explored qualities of individual images, this chapter begins exploring the comics form's second constituent feature, sequence, starting with juxtaposition. For images to be sequenced they must be juxtaposed. If two images are juxtaposed, the arrangement of their physical marks is their shared discourse, and the representational qualities of that arrangement produce their shared diegesis. The juxtaposition, however, is only discursive. Images are not diegetically juxtaposed unless they are juxtaposed within the represented world. Since a potentially infinite number of juxtaposed objects might exist in a diegesis, only discursive juxtaposition involves the comics form.

The chapter first establishes kinds of juxtapositions (contiguous, temporal, and distant) and clarifies their relationship to the comics form. Some image juxtapositions are a product of individual perception and so are a rudimentary quality of a diegesis. If a single physically undivided visual field is interpreted as multiple images, the juxtaposition cannot be defined formally. I offer "pseudo-form" to account for such non-formal visual features treated as if they were formal. Panels, frames, and gutters are prototypical since they are drawn and therefore are representational content not physical parameters shaping content. Though pseudo-formal qualities are a kind of representational content, they are typically distinct from other diegetic elements, suggesting two kinds of diegeses: the primary diegesis of the story world and the secondary diegesis of the pseudo-formal image arrangement. The distinction provides tools for further analysis of image division and image relationships within visual fields and between multiple fields.

1. Types of Juxtapositions

Images may be juxtaposed contiguously, temporally, or distantly.

Two images are contiguously juxtaposed if they appear simultaneously within a single visual field, such as a canvas or page. "Contiguous" is sometimes used ambiguously, as when Hatfield writes: "temporal images in a comic are laid out contiguously on a larger surface" (2005: 48). Strictly defined, images would be contiguous only if they share borders, something that the negative spaces of conventional gutters prevent. Even in a non-strict sense, not all images are contiguous. If a visual field is divided into a 3×3 grid, the far right image in the first row and the far left image in the middle row are not contiguous whether gutters are present or not. I therefore subdivide directly contiguous (images in close proximity within a visual field) and indirectly contiguous (images not in close proximity within a visual field). Leaving the parameters of the field unspecified still allows ambiguity—when does the distance between two images create two fields?—which I acknowledge but won't attempt to resolve.

If contiguous juxtaposition is a necessary quality of the comics form, some works in the comics medium would not formally be comics. *Marvel Fanfare #29* (November 1986) features a story that creator John Byrne intended for *The Incredible Hulk* but was rejected because it consisted of twenty-two full-page images and so violated the dominant convention of multiple images contiguously juxtaposed within single pages. Some of the pages face each other and so are contiguously juxtaposed, but Byrne did not necessarily plan for the placement of full pages of advertisement and other publishing material interspersed between his drawn pages. Juxtaposed images are ubiquitous—flyers on bulletin boards, side-by-side billboards, strips of Friends' photos on Facebook users' homepages—but none are considered art if they lack (the viewer perception of) intentionality. Even found art is art by virtue of someone's selection and repurposing of the found material. Milt Gross's 1930 *He Done Her Wrong: The Great American Novel*, the first graphic novel drawn in a cartoon style, also consists primarily of full-page images, but without the interruption of ads, Gross presumably planned all of the two-page arrangements. Max Ernst's 1934 *Une Semaine De Bonté: A Surrealistic Novel in Collage* follows the same format, as does a range of contemporary works, including Renée French's 2010 *H Day*, Sophia Foster-Dimino's 2017 *Sex Fantasy*, and Eleanor Davis's 2018 *Why Art?*, establishing books of facing full-page images as a significant subcategory of the comics medium. Postema categorizes such works as the second format in her six-part taxonomy of layouts (2014: 31).

Other works involve little or no contiguous juxtaposition. Brain Selznick's 2019 *Wild Oak With Moss* consists entirely of single-image two-page spreads, and Richard McGuire's 2016 *Sequential Drawings* features individual images on each right-hand page, leaving all left pages blank. The early-twentieth-century woodcut novels of Frans Masereel and Lynd Ward follow the same format. Schocken Books 1989 editions of Masereel's *The City*, *The Sun*, *Landscapes and Voices*, and *Hamburg* and The Library of America 2010 two-volume collection of Ward's six novels display one one-page image for each two-page spread, presumably to prevent reverse images appearing through the paper. Although Walker considers Masereel "the grandfather of the graphic novel" (2007: 10), Seth questions whether his romans in beelden (literally "novels in pictures") should be considered part of comics history: "If you look at these wordless novels carefully you'll see that they have almost nothing to do with today's graphic novels," avoiding "the two most basic elements of the comic strip—multiple panels and word balloons" (2007: 416). Spiegelman observes similarly of Ward: "Denied a comic-strip vocabulary, Ward would grow up to help define a whole other syntax for visual storytelling" (2010: x). Despite that "new *narrative* language," Spiegelman still considers him "one of America's most distinguished and accomplished graphic novelists" (2010: xiii, xxii). Whether or not necessary to the comics form, contiguous juxtaposition is the most prominent type of juxtaposition in the comics medium. Miodrag argues that "it is the spatiality of the sequence—the simultaneity of sequential panels on a two-dimensional page—that really separates comics from its nearest comparative medium, film" (2013: 79). If the comics form requires contiguous juxtaposition, then Masereel's and Ward's books are not formally comics.

Though their plates when not published side by side are not juxtaposed contiguously, Masereel's and Ward's images are juxtaposed in a second sense suggested by Miodrag. Juxtaposition in film analysis describes montage. Kolshev demonstrated in 1920 that viewers perceived different emotions in an actor's expressionless face according to other images (a bowl of soup, a child in a casket, a woman resting on a couch) shown immediately before. The Lights Film School website refers to the "Kolshev Effect" as "the power of juxtaposing shots." While such juxtapositions still require a common visual field, they are primarily temporal, with each image viewed discretely. When turning the pages of Masereel's *The City* or Ward's *Wild Pilgrimage*, viewers' eyes remain stationary as one image peels away to reveal the image underneath it. Temporal juxtaposition refers to any two images that immediately follow one after the other in a single visual space. If temporal juxtaposition is sufficient to produce sequenced images, then the comics form includes a range of works outside the comics medium, since images viewed in slide projectors, PowerPoints, and phone apps operate similarly.

Berger encapsulates the comics form as contiguous and temporal juxtaposition when he writes in *Ways of Seeing*: "The meaning of an image is changed according to what one sees immediately beside it or what comes immediately after it" (1971: 29). Juxtaposition, however, may also allow a third sense. The *OED* identifies juxtaposition's first textual appearances in the second half of the seventeenth century, including John Locke's 1690 description of how the mind brings "ideas together, as by their Juxta-position." If a currently viewed image encourages a viewer to recall a previously viewed image, the two images are mentally juxtaposed. Distant juxtaposition refers to any two non-contiguous images that do not immediately follow one another. Because the juxtaposition does not occur physically, distant juxtaposition is possibly juxtaposition in only a metaphorical sense. Since a viewer might experience any two images as distantly juxtaposed, distant juxtaposition is unbound by discourse and therefore may have no formal qualities. Although not a necessary part of a work in the comics form, distant juxtaposition is a common experience when viewing images sequenced over multiple visual fields.

2. Pseudo-Form

A work in the comics form may employ all three kinds of juxtaposition, but contiguous is most common in the comics medium. When constrained to a single visual field (such as the non-scrolling segment of a PC screen) or a portion of a single visual field (such as a comic strip on a newspaper page), sequenced images employ only contiguous juxtaposition. The juxtaposition requires at least two images, but differentiating two contiguously juxtaposed images from an image composed of two parts presents additional challenges to the form. In praising Masereel's 1921 *Reminisces of My Country*, Avermaete remarks, "each plate swarms with little scenes which together form a complete narrative. Never was juxtaposition of scenes used to greater effect" (1976: 28). How can the scenes be juxtaposed, if the plate is a single unified surface? Most pages in the comics medium pose the same challenge, since pages only appear to be physically divided.

In the previous chapter, I offered "semi-representational" to describe image qualities that have an ambiguous relationship to their represented subject, since an image's rendering style, perspective, and framing evoke connotations but do not necessarily reflect a subject's literal qualities. I now suggest "pseudo-formal" to explore similar ambiguities of juxtaposed images. Pseudo-form is an illusion of physical qualities that creates an impression of contiguously juxtaposed images within a single visual field. In the comics medium, the field is a page or two-page spread, which I use interchangeably with "canvas" to include works not printed in books.

While representational images often create an illusion of three dimensions within a story world, works in the comics medium also often rely on an additional illusion of depth produced by images that appear to overlap or rest atop the background of another image or the otherwise unmarked white of a page, with the edges of drawn frames shaping intermediary negative spaces. Kwa identifies the artistic technique as "interposition":

> an object that obscures another one tells the viewer that the former is in the foreground and the latter in the background. Even though both objects are at the same position with respect to the surface of the page, the fact that we see one object fully outlined while we see only portions of the other object causes us to make assumptions about which is in front and which is behind.
>
> 2020: xxvi

The pseudo-depth effect is distinct from the illusion of depth produced by most diegetic images through naturalistic techniques such as vanishing points and light-sourced shadowing because the depth appears to be discursive: it's as if physical card-like images sit atop the actual page.

Not all contiguously juxtaposed images involve pseudo-depth. In Illustration 3.1, Donald Baechler's 2000 *Cone (A Feat of Strength)* includes over a dozen images on separate sheets of paper affixed to a canvas with a painting of an ice-cream cone placed on top of them. The juxtapositions do not create pseudo-depth since the overlap of collaged materials is actual. The ice-cream cone and other images are physically layered and so have actual rather than illusory depth. This differs from artists working in the comics medium who instead draw pseudo-depth effects. In Illustration 3.1, Julie Maroh draws her protagonist as if curled atop an otherwise traditional layout of panels in *Blue is the Warmest Color* (2010: 130), an effect Dianne Kornberg develops further in her and Celia Bland's 2014 *Madonna Comix*, using partially erased *Little Lulu* pages for under-paintings. For his and Chuck Palahniuk's 2015 *Fight Club II*, Cameron Stewart draws realistically sized pills that can be momentarily mistaken for actual objects because they appear to cast shadows on the page surface. The technique is not historically recent. When discussing the early-fourteenth-century manuscript *Psalter of Robert de Lille*, Rust notes the use of circular panels called roundels that appear "to rest on the roll of parchment rather than to inhere in it and thus to have a notional manipulability—as if we could pick them up and move them around" (2016: 16).

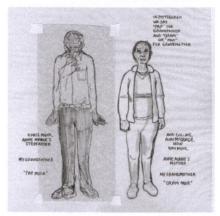

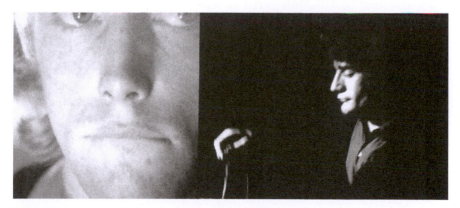

Illustration 3.1 Baechler's *Cone (A Feat of Strength)*, from Maroh's *Blue is the Warmest Color*, Santoro's *Pittsburgh*, and Warhol's *Chelsea Girls*.

The pseudo-formal effect is so pervasive, Chute describes drawn frames as if they were physical boundaries, asserting that "comics claims and uses the space surrounding its material, marked frames in a way that, say, painting cannot" (2010: 8). Painting, however, can claim and use interior space in exactly the same way as works in the comics medium; the only "material" frames are the edges of the page or canvas. Groensteen similarly treats panels as though they were literal, asserting that "the panel is an entity that leads to general manipulations," including enlargement and the reassembly of multiple panels into different configurations (2007: 25). While a traditional comics panel might be reproduced in any number of ways, it leads no more to general manipulations than, say, Mary Cassatt's 1884 *Children Playing on the Beach*, which can be found on framed prints, posters, postcards, T-shirts, and coffee mugs. Unlike a Cassatt painting, a comics panel must first be isolated from the larger artwork of its page, just as an art textbook might isolate a portion of a Cassatt to enlarge and reproduce as a detail.

Pseudo-depth is a drawn effect no different from other drawn effects and so is a diegetic quality. However, pseudo-formal details are typically understood to be distinct from the story world of the representational images in the same work. Unless also metafictional, characters in a story are unaware of the nominal manipulability of a pair of seemingly overlapping images, just as they are unaware of the frame edges of seemingly non-overlapping images. A range of visual elements (frames, gutters, drawn sound effects, word containers, words inside word containers, and the semi-representational qualities of style) exist outside character visual awareness, but such drawn details still represent aspects of the diegesis. Sounds do not exist as drawn letters in the story world, but the discursive letters still represent something that exists diegetically. Similarly, when a memoirist draws herself in a cartoon style, those simplified and exaggerated lines still indirectly represent her actual but dissimilar appearance.

Pseudo-formal qualities, in contrast to semi-representational qualities, do not necessarily have a relationship to the diegesis of the story world or what might be termed the "primary diegesis." A copy of Thomas Hoccleve's 1400s *Regiment of Princes* provides an early and atypically explicit example of pseudo-form producing distinct diegetic effects. Having accidentally omitted a stanza while copying the manuscript, a scribe printed the words in an unused area of the page and then drew a rope around it and a human figure pulling the rope as though to move the stanza to its intended position between two other stanzas. Drimmer explains:

> The rope-tugging man wants, with all his might, to emend the text, but his presence was not summoned by its content. His presence, in this respect, is irrelevant, and word-and-image studies, which encourage us to monitor the conversations that occur between texts and images, would have little to offer by way of elucidation.
>
> 2017: 175

Unlike other representational illustrations, the metafictional figure has no relationship to the diegetic content, yet the figure is still representational, as is the rope, which is no more an actual rope than a conventional comics panel frame is an actual frame.

While most pseudo-formal qualities are similarly "not summoned" by the primary diegesis, Witek categorizes an exception he terms "the 'gestalt' layout, in which the overall shapes of the panels take on narrative or thematic significance," citing an example of "a scene set in a[n] airplane in flight is enclosed in a series of panels shaped like an airplane's fuselage" (2009: 154). Witek describes the relation between the panel shapes and story setting as "connections between the page and its contents," but panel shapes are not qualities of the page—they are contents, too (154). Conflating page and layout is a pseudo-formal effect. Moreover, "the design of a 'gestalt' page echoes or reinforces the story's themes or actions" only if page designs have diegetic qualities generally (154). The rope-tugging man and the fuselage-shaped panels can make those secondary diegetic qualities overt only because such qualities already exist.

Cohn describes a similar division when he separates "depiction into two planes: an inner one of content—the Representational Plane (RP)—and an outer Framing Plane (FP)," in which the "Representational Plane contains all the 'visual content' for the sequence, while the Framing Plane contains devices such as carriers, panel borders, and text" (2013: 50). Pseudo-form, however, may involve more than just conventional devices. Even though they are drawn as if apart from other image content, the seemingly three-dimensional pills in *Fight Club II* are derived from the primary diegesis. Kornberg's Madonna may be metafictionally aware that she is leaping from a ledge of panels, but Maroh's character seems unaware of the panel layout beneath her curled body, presumably because the image embeds her figure from a separate diegetic location, prompting viewers to imagine her curled on some diegetic but undrawn surface, perhaps a bed.

Baechler's *Cone* produces no primary diegesis, and the actually overlapping images create no pseudo-formal diegesis either. Reproductions of such actual features produce further complexity. The pages of Julie Delporte's 2019 *This Woman's Work* appear to include cut-out drawings and strips of typed and handwritten words held to the surface of the white pages with pieces of translucent tape visible at the edges of the cut-outs. Frank Santoro's 2019 *Pittsburgh* pushes the technique further, using thicker tape and overlapping cut-outs affixed to what appears to be yellow sheets of warped and wrinkled paper, as seen in Illustration 3.1. As memoirists, Delporte and Santoro are their own subjects, making not only the content of their images but their emphasis on their image-making process part of their art. Unlike the pseudo-depth illusions drawn by Kornberg, Stewart, and Maroh, Delporte's and Santoro's artboards (like Baechler's *Cone* canvas) have actual depth because they include actual tape and layered paper. The artboards and the book pages created from photographs of the artboards are distinct, since the printed pages have only the illusion of depth. Rather than notional manipulability, Delporte's and Santoro's cut-out panels, tape, and wrinkled paper have actual manipulability. They are three-dimensional objects that rested on a surface (perhaps Santoro's desk or the glass of Delporte's digital scanner) at the moment they were photographed. The pages in their published memoirs are records of those spatiotemporal events. Like drawn pages, their photographic features create the illusion of notional manipulability, but the resulting images of creases in tape and the slightly raised edges of cut-out panels are no more real than if they were drawn. The page of any work in the comics medium is a flat unified surface, even though Delporte's and

Santoro's multi-faceted artboards, like Baechler's similarly constructed *Cone*, have no pseudo-formal qualities.

Illustration 3.1 also features two juxtaposed images taken from a live viewing of Warhol's split-screen film *Chelsea Girls* in The Andy Warhol Museum in Pittsburgh in November 2019. While *Chelsea Girls* is not in the comics form, the segment of Illustration 3.1 is (provided juxtaposition is sufficient for the two images to be sequenced, a question addressed in Chapter 6). The slightly cropped left and right edges are a product of the camera's angle and proximity to the projection screens at the moment the photograph was taken; the slightly cropped top and bottom edges were produced digitally afterwards, as was the conversion from color to black and white; and the surrounding negative space and position on the page were designed during the layout process of this book and then reproduced in its physical and digital copies, including the one you are currently viewing. The original uncropped photograph regarded as a physical object would likely be experienced as a single image regardless of its content and so would not be in the comics form. Without knowledge of the creative process that produced it, that area of Illustration 3.1 would likely be experienced as two discursively juxtaposed images. If the photograph were not cropped to remove the surrounding details, I suspect viewers would understand it to be a single image of two images—that is a single discursive image of two diegetically juxtaposed images— and so not in the comics form.

The nature of the juxtaposition therefore fluctuates according to whether viewers understand images to be juxtaposed on a page or in a diegesis. If the juxtaposition is on the page only, there are two levels: the physical page and the content of each image. If the juxtaposition occurs historically in the actual world, there are three: the physical page, the images' content, and the intermediary space of the original viewing. For the Warhol example, the intermediary space was the museum's viewing room. For the comics medium, there is no intermediary space, only the pseudo-formal illusion of a layered page.

These ambiguities, especially the central yet seemingly unstable nature of the juxtaposition, apply generally to layout. Though panels, frames, and gutters are never formally necessary, when present they and other pseudo-formal elements are representational objects of a secondary diegesis. When the primary and secondary diegeses merge, the work may be metafictional—such as Pascal Jousselin's *Mister Invincible*, in which the titular hero is solely aware of the discursive relationships of framed image content. By reaching through frames and gutters of the secondary diegesis, he disrupts the chronological flow of time in the primary diegesis, often moving recurrently drawn objects as if up or down the rows of panels (2018). To other characters, he appears to be a kind of omniscient time-traveler manipulating invisible portals; to the viewer, he is still constrained by the contiguous juxtapositions of a page (or two-page spread), experiencing the representational content of those images simultaneously while unbound by the pseudo-depth of their framing.

Because its effects are typically not metafictional, Groensteen calls the secondary diegesis "a symbolic structure, a discursive operator—something, in fact, of the order of the concept" (2013: 14). Because that symbolic structure is presented as if it were a physical and so a formal aspect of a page, I term it pseudo-form. Its qualities appear to be but are not simply discursive. Since pseudo-form is a set of non-physical and non-essential conventions, it is not part of the comics form. It is, however, one of the most prevalent conventions of the comics medium and is sometimes used to define comics generally. Groensteen argues that "the apparatus should be recognized as constituting the central element of a definition of comics" because it "is sufficient to establish that [a non-representational] work belongs to the field of comic" (2013: 14). Since sequenced images need not include pseudo-formal conventions, those that do are a subset of comics as formally defined. For Groensteen to be correct and for pseudo-form to be central to a definition of comics, such a definition would be non-formal.

3. Image Division

Since pseudo-form creates only the illusion of contiguously juxtaposed images, it is ambiguous whether such images are in the comics form since they are not actually juxtaposed and may not even be multiple. According to Cook, a comic is composed of "two or more visually distinct parts" (2015). This is a more precise way of saying two or more images, and Cook's precision is useful because it implicitly acknowledges the complexity of dividing a canvas into parts that, since not physically distinct, are experienced as distinct. Mikkonen describes the challenge:

> the notion of a "unique enclosed image" is not always perfectly distinguishable from a series of interdependent images, specifically if a single image depicts several events or an unfolding situation. . . . a sequence may be embedded in a single image; a single-panel image or painting can comprise a series of images.
>
> 2017: 12

Most pages in the comics medium appear to be a set of discrete panels. Lines that form panel edges create the illusion of framing of the kind produced by windows or cameras, but they do so as if from a reality independent of the internal image content since the frame lines do not exist diegetically in the way that a window in the story world exists. What is called a frame on a comics page is not a frame but a drawing of a frame that does not represent a frame in the primary diegesis.

A work's fundamental unit of composition is the physical page it is drawn or reproduced on. If the work is multi-paged and bound, then the two-page spread is also a formal unit. The page fold is a physical boundary, but all other interior divisions are not formally imposed. Eisner calls the page the "super-panel," "meta-panel," "page frame," "full-page frame," or "hard-frame," which "is not the individual panel but the total page'" (2008: 65). When developing machine-learning software to adapt printed comics to web platforms, Rigaud proceeds similarly: "an image is identified as a comic book's page and a region of interest as one piece of content (e.g. a panel)" (8). Hick also acknowledges that "strictly speaking, a comics page is not composed of several drawings, but of one" (2014: 137–8). Molotiu's "iconostasis," "the perception of the layout of a comics page as a unified composition," also rejects the assumption that images are discrete (2012: 91).

Rather than a sequence of drawings, a one-page work in the comics medium may instead be considered a sequenced drawing—that is a single image with areas viewed as ordered units. Is that single drawing composed of separate images? Conventionally, the answer is yes. Abbott claims that a panel "is a fundamental unit of comic art" (1986: 156). Yet such units are not always present and are not always distinct. Arguing similarly against the application of a linguistic model, Miller notes that "an image is not made up of discontinuous elements ... the curves and lines which make up a drawing of a cat, for example, cannot be separated into units in the way that a word can be separated into letters, or a sentence into words" (2007: 77). The separable units of letters and words also produce meaning when read in sequence, further distancing them from the continuous and unordered qualities of images.

What then establishes a drawn element or cluster of drawn elements as an isolated image rather than part or parts of a larger image? What, in other words, is a traditional comics panel? The *OED* lists over thirty definitions for "panel." In addition to its earlier uses in relation to windows, doors, carriages, saddles, fences, photographs, gardens, garments, parachutes, pavement, book spines, and coal mines, a panel is a "drawing in a cartoon or comic strip, typically surrounded by a rectangular border, and usually forming part of a sequence" (1920). This coincides with some of its more general meanings: "A distinct section, typically rectangular in shape, that forms part of the whole surface of something" (1498) or simply "A part, a division" (1450). The comics term may have been imported from other visual arts, such as tapestry: "A section of a tapestry or other ornamental work, usually surrounded by a decorative border" (1856); or painting: "A leaf or section of a folding screen or triptych" (1873); or stained glass: "A compartment of a stained glass window, containing a separate subject" (1873). The *OED* even includes metaphorical panels: "Something resembling a panel in shape and relation to the surrounding space" (1869), which may best describe comics panels since they have no hinges, folds, mullions, muntins, grilles or other physical borders. A traditional comics panel is not a panel; it is a pseudo-formal representation of a panel.

The presence of panels does not necessarily produce separate images. The flags of twenty-eight nations consist of three solidly colored horizontal or vertical panels, but those subdivisions are understood not as separate images but as parts of the single image that is each flag. Many of Rothko's color field paintings, such as his 1954 *No. 9 (Dark over Light Earth)*, create discrete panel-like sections of color on a single canvas, and most of Mondrian's De Still paintings, such as his 1935 *Composition C (No. III) with Red, Yellow and Blue*, resemble traditional layouts with rectangular panels divided by black gutter-like strips. Neither of these paintings are considered multiple images but are single images with subsections producing a unified whole. Psuedo-formal panels occur in representational art, too. Mark Lancaster's 1986 *Cambridge Green* paintings are divided into 4×2 grids, with thin spaces of bare canvas between the rectangles. Viewers might experience each painting as multiple images, because each section is a diegetic unit representing a different viewpoint of the title's location, in a way that viewers of Rothko's and Mondrian's non-representational paintings likely do not. Conversely, a painting's literal division onto actual physically separate panels does not necessarily produce an impression of multiple images. Though the six interior segments of Hubert and Jan van Eyck's 1432 polyptych ("multi-fold") *Ghent Altarpiece* consist of separately framed wood panels, their painted content depicts a continuous landscape.

Holbo argues that a single image with no pseudo-formal divisions can still be understood as multiple images if it represents multiple moments. He provides an example of an unframed image featuring two cartoon figures engaged in a dialogue, each with its own speech balloon. He then presents the same two figures in separate juxtaposed frames, claiming that the first image "might as well be" the second pair of images (2014: 7–8). The claim conflates discourse and diegesis. Diegetically, the two versions represent the same content and to that degree are equivalent, but each is also drawn as though discursively distinct. Diegetic moments and discursive images are not interchangeable. However, if Holbo does experience the two figures in the first version as two images (and the temporal implications of the two speech balloons explains why he might), then they would be in the comics form.

Image division presents an especially practical challenge for the archeological analysis of ancient Roman graffiti scratched into preserved wall plaster. In addition to the thousands of inscriptions, write Benefield and Sypniewski, figural graffiti "can occur in conjunction with text, or they may appear independently as stand-alone drawings" (2015: 29). Because images were omitted from previous archeological records, documenting them now presents a methodological question: "Do we catalog series or clusters of graffiti as a single database entry, or separate them as individual images each with its own entry?" (36). Noting "how obscure the relationships between clusters of graffiti may be," the researchers ask a more fundamental question, "*can we be assured* that certain elements were meant to be understood together?", and default to giving "each element on the wall a unique identifier" (37, 36). They choose to assume division not because division is generally preferably but because images merged into single entries cannot be found individually by the database search engine. That practical solution is necessary only because of the inherently ambiguous nature of the contiguously juxtaposed clusters of marks.

"Units occur when there is a documentable contribution to increasing *discourse coherence*," Bateman and Wildfleuer argue, defining coherence by "*relations* between posited units" and the relations by "*defeasible rules*" linked to "likely interpretations" (2014: 377). Coherence relations combine discursive qualities, such as spatial proximity, to "consequences that may be 'hypothesized' to hold when the identified evidence is found," but the rules remain hypothesized and the consequences interpretive (2014: 378). They later clarify that the "structuring relationships" are not in "*the material being analysed*" but "are always abductive hypotheses that are introduced by the coherence-making process" (2014a: 196). Units are units then only if viewers experience relationships between them.

Ultimately there is no formal criterion that distinguishes an image part from an image whole. The effect is not intrinsic to a discourse but occurs at the level of individual perception. Viewers may understand a visual field to contain multiple images or they may understand the field to be a single image composed of multiple parts. Though a page in the comics medium may present the pseudo-formal conceit of images that are physically divided, that division is performed conceptually by viewers. A canvas is divided only if a viewer perceives it as divided.

4. Image Borders

Though images need not be bordered by gutters to be perceived as discrete images, image division in the comics medium is often indicated through that convention. Since contiguously juxtaposed images do not require negative spaces between them, gutters—which according to McCloud are "host to much of the magic and mystery that are at the very heart of the comics" (1993: 66)—are not a necessary aspect of the comics form. However, contiguously juxtaposed images not surrounded by negative space are sometimes described as having invisible, implied, or, as Postema suggests, "camouflaged" gutters (2013: 29) because "gutter" conflates two distinct meanings, one discursive and one diegetic.

A gutter is a negative space that often but does not always represents a diegetic leap, because not all spaces represent leaps and not all leaps involve negative spaces. When the two aspects are combined, a gutter is a kind of ellipsis. "The narrative process of the medium," Miller asserts, "is founded on ellipsis, the gap in the signifying chain through which temporal and spatial transitions are managed" (2007: 88–9). Nhu-Hoa describes "a significant lack of information" that "expresses itself through the omission of the smallest unit or units of expression"; because an ellipsis is "felt as a particular deprivation," "the elliptical element is explicitly or implicitly signaled by the author and interpreted by the reader" (2006: 284). Negative spaces are only one way to create ellipsis-filling inferences. Although "sign-generating gaps, often called gutters, occur between panels," Bearden-White argues, "these easily-located and discussed areas of referential meaning are far from inclusive. In constructing significance in a graphic novel, a gap can be provoked in the reader's mind with any two or more signs located at any point throughout the book" (200: 348).

The negative space of a discursive gutter is often conflated with the inferences of a conceptual gutter which can be called a gap only in a metaphorical sense. Miodrag correctly observes that the "'filling in,' especially as described by McCloud, is no more than the comics version of the 'intentional sentences correlatives' that Wolfgang Iser describes in prose fiction, which 'disclose subtle connections' between the 'component parts' of the text that together create 'the world of the work'"; however, Miodrag overstates the correlation of discursive negative spaces with diegetic filling-in by also asserting that the "pertinent difference between comics and prose literature is that in the former these narrative gaps are visible, physical spaces on the page" (2013: 67). Spatiotemporal transitions do not require such discursive spaces on the page.

Discursive gutters also do not always produce transitions or other kinds of diegetic inferences. In *Captain America* No. 111, Jim Steranko draws a set of panels that subdivide the title character into segments with the negative spaces between the panels signifying nothing but a seemingly obscured view, making the set of panels a single image that has been divided into distinct parts which are not themselves perceived separately (discussed as continuous inferencing in Chapter 5). The gutters between the parts are still visual ellipses, but not ellipses in the sense meant by Miller and Nhu-Hoa. Illustration 3.2 further demonstrates two kinds of negative spaces. "Strips" either

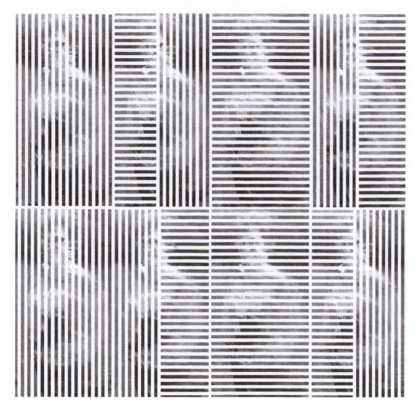

Illustration 3.2 "Strips."

includes four gutters (three vertical and one horizontal) that divide eight repeating images into a 2×4 grid, or it includes 244 gutters (64 vertical and 180 horizontal) that separate 270 strip-shaped images. I suspect most viewers perceive only eight images and so only four gutters, even though those negative spaces are identical in size and shape to the negative spaces within the fragmented images. The single term "gutter" then is ineffective for discussing discursive and diegetic qualities that are distinct and independent.

As a result of a pseudo-form conceit, a gutter is sometimes treated not as negative space but as a semi-literal gutter. In its non-metaphorical sense, nothing runs in a comics gutter. It is a metaphorical gutter because its illusion of pseudo-depth also makes it a kind of representational object: a representation of nothingness, a non-zone, a meta-trough that somehow exists outside of diegetic space and time and yet not simply a discursive quality of drawn images.

Earle notes that "in the actual production of books of any kind, [gutter] refers to the margin between the typed page and the binding" (2019: 8), which is a physical quality that the term superimposes onto other areas of the page. When the page is white, the gutter is white and may be experienced as "empty," even though white areas within diegetic panels are experienced as representational, denoting such things as a cloudless sky, snowy field, or blank page in a character's unlined notebook. Both kinds of white areas are discursively white and so literally identical, and so their difference in meaning results from tension between the primary diegesis and the pseudo-form creating two kinds of white: representational negative space and non-representational negative space. Each corresponds to a different pseudo-formal layer: the plain of the panels and the plain of the background that provides a conceptually non-spatiotemporal space for the arrangement of representational images. The white of gutters may also be experienced as if continuing underneath images placed on top of it, creating the illusion of a partially obscured visual field. That field is not the actual page but a representation of a page, similar to content implied by unmarked areas within representational images.

Illustration 3.3 combines representational and non-representational qualities by repeating a chessboard with one modification in each iteration. No gutters divide them. The representational edge of each image abuts the next image, making the squares within and between each board initially indistinguishable. The boards evolve to produce new black shapes and white negative spaces, eventually producing the impression of a 6×4 grid that divides even the chessboards in the visually undivided first row. Alternatively, viewers may experience the entire canvas as a single undivided image. The absence of traditional gutters is complicated by the impression of representationally white squares along unframed image borders since those negative spaces also resemble and partly serve the function of the non-representational white of gutters. Depending on a viewer's perception, "Chess" may be: 1) a single image composed of hundreds of black and mostly square shapes on a white background, or 2) twenty-four chessboard-like units with implied edges that vacillate with the representational white of the images. The second perception's set of images is sequenced and is in the comics form, while the first is not.

In many cases, images are divided spatiotemporally according to perceived story events. Most mages in the comics medium are diegetic units, whether they also are (or appear to be) physically divided. Panels in a non-representational work are discursive units only and so must appear to be divided visually in order to produce the experience of division. Representational images can trigger division without an illusion of physical division. Consider a page from Kelly Sue DeConnick and Emma Rios's 2014 *Pretty Deadly* in Illustration 3.4. Discursively the page consists of five panels: the top half includes three wide panels, one of which is present in the background between the first two; the bottom half consists of one large panel and a small inset in the bottom right corner (including a frame-breaking paintbrush that appears to be rendering the image, turning the pseudo-form into metafiction). Four of the discursive panels are each a single diegetic image, representing one spatiotemporal moment. The large panel, however, represents multiple moments rendered from multiple angles and proximities and so consists of multiple diegetic images.

Rios draws six full-body figures and one close-up. Three of the figures are the recurrent character Death, three are the recurrent character Fox, and they are paired and angled to suggest three narrative segments, with the close-up of Fox's face

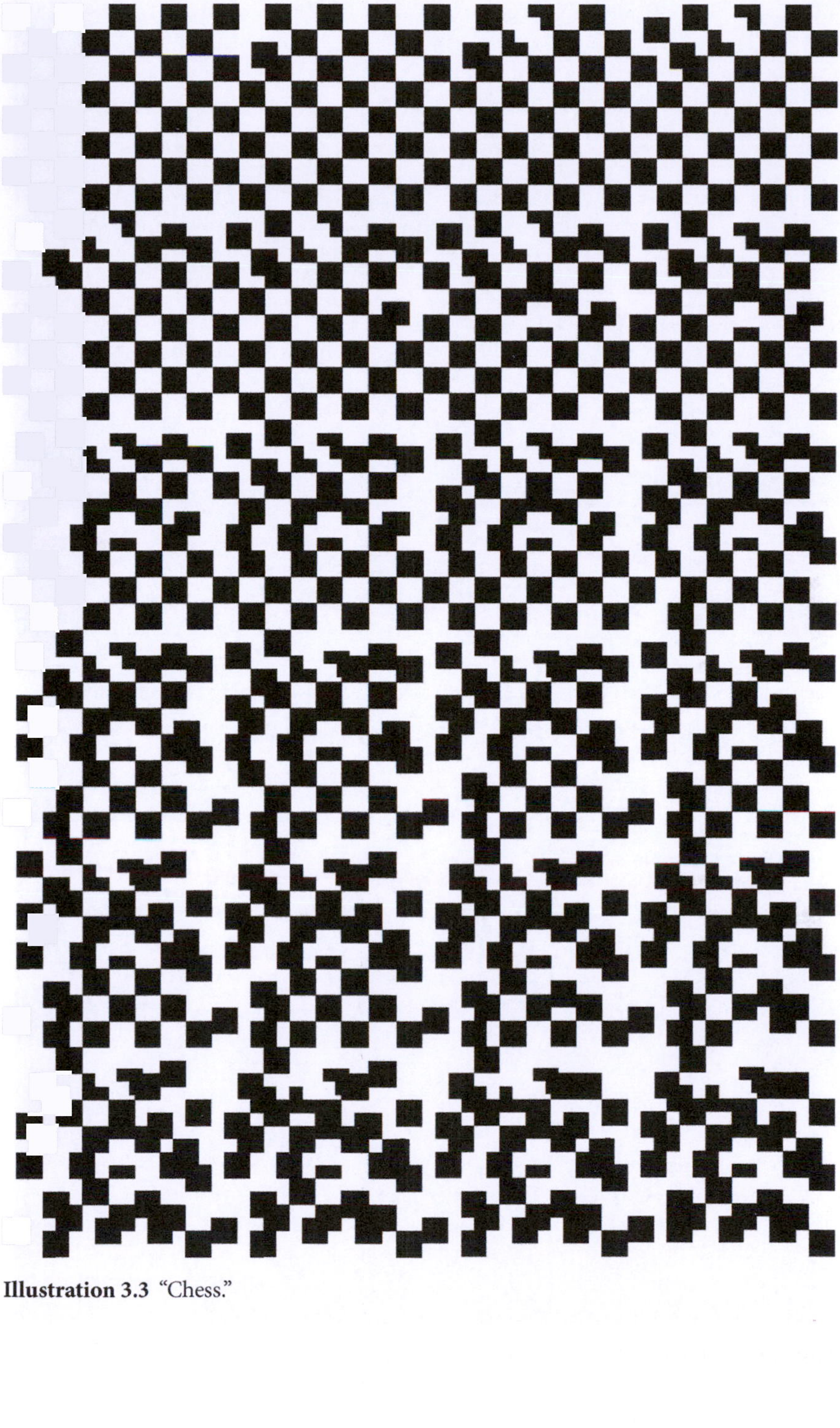

Illustration 3.3 "Chess."

Illustration 3.4 From DeConnick and Rios's *Pretty Deadly*.

establishing a fourth. All four are unframed so that their content overlaps and interpenetrates, likely requiring a reader to scan the shared area multiple times to determine the segments and a path relating them. A viewer might begin in the top left corner with what could be the first blow of Death's sword across Fox's face. The movement lines of the sword, however, violate Z-path norms, requiring the center image to be processed first and so implying that the center image is diegetically first. The content of the two-figure pairings is also chronologically ambiguous, because either could depict the first strike that results in the top right close-up, which is the connecting background image of the first four figures. The close-up could also be a simultaneous moment drawn from a different angle, aligning with either the center or the top left figure pairings, depending on which viewers perceive as chronologically second. The two bottom left figures appear to be the final unit in the implied sequence, though the final Death is largely parallel with and to the right of an earlier Fox.

If we accept, for example, Hayman and Pratt's definition of a comic as "as a sequence of discrete, juxtaposed pictures" where the "visual images are distinct (paradigmatically side-by-side)" (2005: 423), this portion of *Pretty Deadly* is not a comic. Similarly, Rios's example disproves Groensteen's assertion that a comics page "is always a space that has been divided up, compartmentalized, a collection of juxtaposed frames" (2007: 19). Rios's art is segmented, but the segments must be inferred because the figures are elements of a merged visual area. How exactly viewers reach the conclusion that some of the Death and Fox figures are parts of unified images that are distinct from other iterations of the same figures is open to debate, but Tversky, Zacks, and Hard offer some insight: "contours that are continuous and closed, especially under movement, suggest that what is contained by the contour has an existence independent of the background" (2007: 441). Certain contours enclose segments that are perceived as characters, separating them from backgrounds that also contain contour-enclosing segments of the same characters represented at different moments.

Rios's diegetic segments might be analyzed in terms of overlay and interpenetration, with some elements drawn as if stacked above or below or even within other elements. Rather than spaces between images, the relevant element for Rios is an image's perceived edges. Conventional edges are called frames, and, as discussed in Chapter 2, their framing effects are semi-representational because they can create connotations about diegetic content without representing anything as it would be observed within the diegetic world. This may be sufficient for understanding images edges and so image division generally. An image edge is non-representational. An image may be composed of many lines including lines that within the image may represent edges in the diegetic world, including outlines that divide objects from backgrounds and each other. Those edges are representational edges. Rios's panel divides into four representational images through the perception of their non-representational edges. Within three of those images are representational edges that divide the two characters from each other but not from the images of the same two characters surrounding them. An edge then may be simultaneously representational and non-representational. Some of the edges that divide Rios's images also define the outlines of characters and objects, making the lines serve two functions. Though Rios's degree of image overlap within a single panel is rare, two-function edges are relatively common in the comics medium. Most of the pages in Will Eisner's 1980 *Signal from Space* feature two-function image edges. Some of those edges are surrounded by negative space, but most are not, so negative space is not Eisner's primary method for demarking images.

Non-representational edges explain both images with negative spaces between them and images without negative spaces between them. Edge analysis, however, presents one shortcoming. Not all images are divided even by edges, instead overlapping in shared areas. Though relatively rare in the comics medium, the approach is common in photography where two images may be mechanically superimposed. The marketers of the iPhone app Superimpose X call the effects "blending" and "sandwiches," digitally recreating and expanding double exposure techniques originating in the 1860s. By using a pointillistic pencil style in his 1995 *Stuck Rubber Baby*, Howard Cruse overlaps diegetic images by interspersing two sets of representational marks, producing no non-representational edges but still creating a viewer experience of two diegetically distant subjects observed from different angles and proximities rendered in a shared discursive space. Since blending and sandwiches can merge photos into new single images that are experienced as coherent wholes independent of their source materials, the technique itself does not necessarily produce image division. Image division is still determined by viewer experience.

5. Image Arrangement

The discursive arrangement of contiguous images in the comics medium is most often termed "layout." Groensteen refers to the "multiframe" when discussing a multi-page work, and "hyperframe" when discussing a single page, seeing them as "the device upon which the language is founded" (2007: 28). Cohn understands image arrangement as "external compositional structure," which is limited to how a viewer navigates "reading paths" (2013: 91–2). McCloud's interest is on navigation, too, what he terms "flow," meaning "the arrangement of panels on a page or screen, and the arrangement of elements within a panel" that guides "readers between and within panels" by "directing the eye through reader expectations and content" (2006: 37).

Peeters's four layout types (conventional, decorative, rhetorical, and productive) instead display a creator-focus, merging the end results of an artist's creative process with choices that precede it (2007). His conventional layout is similar to Brunetti's "democratic grid" of identically shaped and sized images in a grid (2011: 45), but also includes apparent viewer knowledge that such a grid was selected prior and independently of diegetic content. A decorative layout's irregularity is also understood to precede content, as is a productive layout's choices, though with the distinction that instead of adapting pre-existing content, the layout helps to conceive the content. Only rhetorical layout assumes that diegetic content comes first and literally shapes frames. Since viewers of completed works do not know whether an arrangement structure was determined in advance or in response to content, instead of categorizing layout types, Peeters categorizes artists' creative approaches.

Jesse Cohn considers Peeters to be "a necessary beginning," but one that does not fill the "gap in Anglophone comics theory, an empty space in which *some* coherent and systematic account of the meaning-making properties of the page as designed space needs to be introduced" (2007: 11–12). Miodrag is similarly appreciative of Peeters but notes that "page composition is less widely theorized among Anglophone scholars" (2013: 222), suggesting that the relative lack is due to an overemphasis on sequence. Miodrag's own approach emphasizes what she terms "nesting," which includes image content within frames, frames within pages, pages within spreads, and spreads within books, and "attends to all the various nested layers and the particular relationships that exist between them in a given composition" (2013: 245). Witek divides "spatial arrangements" between "regular grid structure" (noting modifications of "basic building-block panels," as well of slight variations of panel sizes "so that the vertical gutters no longer line up perfectly") and "baroque" (which includes the most extreme variation of "'gestalt' layout," as well as "simple variations of panel size" embellished with baroque "flourishes") (2009: 153–4). Postema's taxonomy of layouts includes six formats: framed panels, one panel per page, several panels per page, frameless panels, panels that are separated by lines only, and insets, with an implied seventh category that combines elements of the first six (2013: 30–46). Comparing Peeters, Groensteen (who refines Peeters), Witek, and Postema, Woo concludes that all four describe and typologize layouts non-exhaustively and without mutual exclusivity since none provide criteria to arbitrate borderline cases (2019: 6–10).

Bateman similarly concludes that, though "layout is one of the most salient features of graphic novels and comics . . . in contrast to this prominence, methods for engaging systematically with the analysis of page design in comics and graphic novels are still in their infancy" (2019: 1). Using 1,260 pages of US superhero comics published from 1940 to 2009, Bateman studied "design strategies" to develop a "differentiating classification scheme made up of over 100 features" that "may be applied to visual composition strategies in other media as well," including newspapers, PowerPoint presentations, instructional texts, and, children's picture books (2019: 4, 6, 32, 3). He combines features into five general approaches:

> dimension 1 is indicative of page irregularity with respect to lack of clear framing; dimension 2 is indicative of strong page regularity in grid shape and sizing; dimension 3 is indicative of strong framing with gaps and irregular spacing between panels; dimension 4 is indicative of tilts and rotations, and with panels that vary in size and shape; and dimension 5 is indicative of regular "waffle-iron" organizations and explicit frames.
>
> 2019: 15

However, Bateman also asserts that the "precise forms and functions" of layout "within the media of comics" will "still need to be determined" (2019: 3).

While Bateman, Miodrag, Woo, and Jesse Cohn all perceive a major gap in theorizing image arrangements, Beatens and Frey instead argue: "Panel structure and page layout are not rigid phenomena that can be described as autonomous forms" and so "the analysis of panel/page layout organization should never be a goal in itself" (2017: 201). Hatfield similarly notes that "there is always the possibility that different protocols will be invoked, different elements stressed" (2005: xiv). Though Hatfield also notes that the experience of viewing a comic may be "decentered, unstable, and unfixable," it is not "always" so, and the form itself should not be described as "unstable" (2005: xiv, xii). As del Rey Cabero, Goodrum, and Mellado instead observe: "panels of various sizes can be arranged in multiple ways along the page, producing an infinite number of different page layouts" (2021: 10). It is possible that Gravett's general observation, that panel content is "important, but so are the proportion, location and relationship of that panel to other panels in its immediate vicinity and as part of the whole page" (2013: 56), is a sufficient principle. The perceived gap in theory may be a pseudo-formal effect. A page has no physical parameters other than its actual edges, providing only evolving conventions to study. Even when artists follow well-established layout norms, each page is an idiosyncratic creation that conforms to conventions only because the artist has chosen to repeat them, not because any formal constraints require it.

There are good reasons why an artist might choose to follow norms, since those norms are patterns of expectations that facilitate communication. Still, they are interactive rules that can be used in sequenced images, but they are not intrinsic qualities. Just as image division is a complex product of perception, the "reading paths" and "flow" of a divided visual field are interpretive, too. No layout automatically produces them. Analyzing that process requires the additional tools of juxtapositional inferences detailed in Chapters 4 and 5, and so I postpone discussion of navigation until Chapter 6.

Analytical emphasis on layout may also partly account for the comics medium's lack of attention within the wider field of visual arts. Layout norms focus on individual panels, de-emphasizing the aesthetic of the larger canvas. Since the medium's creative norms emphasize layout, too, a page sometimes suffers as an artwork because it places its diegetic-focused units above balance, unity, and other wholistic design principles. Even referring to a page as designed implies something other than a rendered work of art.

Whatever its context, a visual field perceived as an arrangement of contiguously juxtaposed images does invite a range of analysis. While a traditional panel can still be defined discursively (any marked-off space within a visual field) and pseudo-formally (any space marked off as if by physical boundaries), image division is often produced diegetically. The interplay between panel and image is often a product of the visual field having both discursive and representational qualities, but a field of non-representational images can divide, too. Molotiu's *Abstract Comics* provides multiple examples of non-representational images divided into traditional panels. Molotiu describes Kandinsky's 1937 *Thirty* (a 5×6 grid of black and white squares containing non-representational lines and shapes and arranged in a chessboard pattern) in pseudo-formal terms: "the subdivision of the canvas into smaller 'panels' . . . seems to parallel the relationship, visible in any comic-book or Sunday strip, between individual panels and overall page layout" (2009: n.p.). Molotiu also describes the 2×2 grid of Willem de Kooning's 1960 *Black and White (San Francisco)* as a "four-panel 'strip'" ending in "a kind of abstract punchline" because the lines in the first three panels are diagonals and the lines in the final panel are nearly vertical.

Neither Kandinsky nor de Kooning paint negative spaces between their panels, but examples of discursive gutters in non-representational image arrangements are not uncommon. Richard Hahn's work in Illustration 3.5 features thirteen irregular rows divided into numerous irregular panels, all divided by thin strips of the same off-white as the margins, suggesting the same pseudo-formal effect of notional manipulability as seen in representational work. The rows of panels also appear to contain continuous shapes and colors that are briefly interrupted by the vertical ellipses. The horizontal

Illustration 3.5 Hahn's untitled work from *Abstract Comics*.

spaces in contrast do not appear to interrupt internal panel marks, further unifying the rows. The page has two kinds of subdivisions: 149 gutter-defined panels, and thirteen non-representational but panel-content-defined images. Each set of related panels may be called a phrase: "Like the words in a line of poetry, the images in a comics phrase are viewed for individual meaning but also together as a sub-unit within the larger compositional unit of the page" (Gavaler and Beavers 2021: 121). Though discursive, phrases can produce diegetic subunits, too. The shapes and colors of the panel content in Hahn's rows could suggest landscapes, perhaps blue shorelines and hills and night skies beyond them. If viewers perceive such landscapes (either idiosyncratically or aided by a representation-indicating title), then the discursive marks also become diegetic and create a represented world. The context of a book titled *Abstract Comics* likely blocks that diegesis, making Hahn's page discursive only.

The repetition of visual similarities can also isolate and so highlight a particular dissimilarity. This can be accomplished with either frames or panel content. Peeters describes the two working in combination. A "conventional" layout, in which "the arrangement of the panels on the page, by repeating itself, tends to become transparent" (meaning unnoticed), and so when an artist repeats panel content, too, "the least modification in the gestures or facial expressions takes on a considerable significance because of the regularity of the units" (2007). Groensteen describes framing and image content working independently, noting that a "regular" layout possesses "the ultimate virtue of handling the possibility of sudden and spectacular ruptures from the initially given norm" (2007: 97).

Groensteen does not name such ruptures, but I have suggested "accent," after Abel and Madden's advice to artists: "Creating panels of uniform shape and size will give your comic a steady rhythm that you can punctuate and accentuate through repetitions and variations from one panel to the next" (2008: 71). Such accenting is a product of contiguous juxtaposition and is possible only if a page features a predictable image frame pattern, such as Ivan Brunetti's "democratic" grid where frames "are all exactly the same size ... from which we can infer their equal weight and value in the 'grand scheme' of the page" (2011: 45). Witek describes a Jack Kirby page similarly: "The panels are identical in size and shape, so that each panel bears a similar narrative emphasis and visual weight" creating "an overall feeling of solidity and methodical movement" (1989: 20). Variations in size and shape then produce unequal weight and value. Abel and Madden describe another type of accent: "When you do break up the strict uniformity of the grid by introducing a tilted panel, to name one variation, the effect is much more powerful because the tilted panel jumps out at the reader to emphasize, a mood, plot point, or dynamic motion" (2008: 71). Plot points and Witek's "narrative emphasis" are diegetic, but dynamic motion and solidity are primarily discursive. In addition to size, shape, and tilts, images can be accented by differences in the pseudo-formal qualities of gutter widths, image overlap, frame style, and image style. Accents also produce diegetic effects if the images are representational, suggesting that objects and moments in an accented image have greater significance than objects and moments represented in surrounding images. Postema describes the effect as a discursive "variation in [a default] format" that "becomes a source of signification" for diegetic "moments of particular significance or tension" (2013: 45).

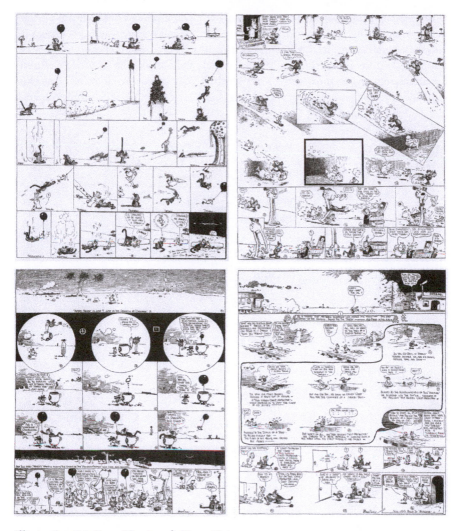

Illustration 3.6 From Herriman's *Krazy Kat*.

Herriman's *Krazy Kat* pages in Illustration 3.6 provides a range of both individual accents and multiple accents that combine as phrases. For the April 30th, 1916, Sunday strip, Herriman separates the final four panels from the preceding eighteen by enclosing them in a thicker, phrase-indicating frame line. July 9th features three phrases: a row of three circular panels, a 2×3 grid of six panels, and a final row of four panels preceded and separated by a thin darkly shaded full-width panel. July 30th accents a centrally framed panel, a tilted panel, and a darkly framed panel within a pace of nine unframed images, before enclosing an ending six-panel phrase in two framed rows. October 22nd encloses a six-image phrase inside a thickly lined talk balloon (2010: 24, 33, 34, 37).

Image arrangements also relate the internal content of images, independent of how each overall image is shaped, framed, or positioned. Rendered subjects within a representational image occupy discursive areas relative to each other and also relative to subjects within other images in the same visual field. Despite the scholarly tradition of emphasizing layout, those subject relationships may be the dominate element of a page. The five contiguously juxtaposed images in Illustration 3.7 depict three diegetic

Illustration 3.7 "Cape Cod, May 2019."

characters, one seated and two moving, plus a mobile implied viewer, producing an evolving set of arrangements that reflect the changing diegetic arrangement of the figures. The juxtapositions also create discursive arrangements not just of the five images as wholes but of the twelve figures within them. Though non-diegetic, the arrangements can influence diegesis through connotation—perhaps suggesting that two subjects are close to each other in a figurative sense because they are discursively near, or that a lone subject is seemingly interacting with himself in paradoxical isolation.

These effects, though arguably some of the most prominent in the comics medium, lack general analysis and terminology. Though layout-related, the visual relationships are not between panels but between elements within panels and so are an effect not typically described through layout analysis. Versaci observes how "creators can play with the design of an entire page by manipulating the visuals within panels and the panels themselves within the page to create additional layers of meaning" (2007: 14–16). Beatens and Frey argue that "a good page layout helps to reveal the functional relationship between panels or elements that are not contiguous," meaning either not sequential, not directly contiguous, or both (2017: 200). To further analyze these juxtapositions in non-layout terms, the next section explores an expanded sense of "braiding."

6. Braiding

Groensteen appears to have something akin to distant juxtaposition in mind when he asserts that a "panel can also be the object of distant semantic determinations," pointing out that even relatively simplistic comics for children can fail "unless the young reader effectuates a reconciliation between distant panels," because "comics should be apprehended as a networked mode that allows each panel to hold privileged relations with any others and at any distance" (2007: 111, 112, 126). Groensteen later describes "diachronic" reading, "which recognizes in each new term of a series a recollection or an echo of an anterior term," and coins "tressage" ("braiding") to describe correspondences between "panels (or pluri-panel sequences) distant by several pages, and that cannot be viewed simultaneously," noting how a repeated image "raises the memory of the first occurrence" in what he calls "a rhyme (distant repetition)" (2007: 147, 148).

Distant juxtaposition is the more general phenomenon of mentally experiencing distant images, some of which constitute braiding by involving visual repetition. Miodrag recognizes distant juxtaposition when she emphasizes that "the reader makes links over a multitude of narrative gaps in constructing the world of the work, significantly in excess of the oft-emphasized panel-to-panel" (2013: 140). Cohn argues that comprehension of distant juxtapositions is a largely unconscious process constrained by hierarchical grouping (2009: 129, 144). Groensteen uses the term "arthrology," which in biology is the study of joints (articulations), extending the term metaphorically to the conceptual connections between images. He defines two kinds: "general arthrology" (non-sequential connections) and "restricted arthrology" (sequential connections); he also identifies spatio-topia (contiguous juxtaposition) as "a part of arthrology," "an arbitrarily detached subgroup, with no other autonomy" (2007: 22). His general arthrology seems to apply to both distant juxtapositions (when the non-sequential connections occur on different non-facing pages and so in a viewer's memory) and to contiguous juxtapositions (when the non-sequential connections occur on a single page). His restricted arthrology describes sequence, which is linear in only a conceptual sense and so paradoxically independent of the physical juxtapositions that produce it. Since he does not classify spatio-topia as a kind of arthrology, spatio-topic connections between contiguously juxtaposed images are not connections in themselves but are aspects of the linear and non-linear connections categorized as restricted and general arthrology.

The adjectives "general" and "restricted" may be counterintuitive since "general" can imply a superordinate category containing various restricted subordinate subcategories, where Groensteen's categories are instead parallel and mutually exclusive. Application of his terms can produce further ambiguities. Miller writes: "Groensteen has introduced the term 'arthrology' for the codes which govern the articulation of the medium, of which he enumerates three": "the 'spatio-topical' code," "the code of 'restricted arthrology,'" and "the code of 'general arthrology'" (2007: 73, 82). The section is titled "Articulation: the three codes," further indicating that arthrology divides into three kinds of connections, despite Groensteen's claiming only two. Also, the subsequent section explaining general arthrology is titled "tressage," and only parenthetically subtitled "Groensteen's 'general arthrology' code," indicating that braiding is a preferred synonym for and not a subordinate quality of general arthrology. Rather than attempting to resolve these ambiguities, I set them aside.

Though Groensteen does "not attempt to sketch a typology of the specific diverse procedures of braiding" because he considers them "impossible to enumerate," he indirectly suggests two when he refers to locations in a work as either "contiguous or distant" (2007: 148). Since braiding applies to each distinct kind of juxtapositions, I suggest dividing it into three corresponding types: contiguous braiding (repetitions on a page or two-page spread); temporal braiding (repetitions synced to a page-turn); and distant braiding (repetitions on non-consecutive pages). If the subject repetitions in Illustration 3.7 are discursive repetitions (because the subject is rendered in a roughly identical set of marks), then the interplay of the diegetic and discursive spaces involves contiguous braiding. If the repetitions are primarily diegetic (because more than one visually distinct sets of marks represent a repeating subject) it is unclear whether Groensteen would categorize the effect as braiding.

Braiding need not include the content of an entire image. One of Groensteen's primary examples is a set of moons and windows from Yslaire and Balac's 1986 *Sambre*. As seen in Illustration 3.8, the circles are relatively small elements within panels. Groensteen writes: "The Z path that the eye must accomplish to sweep over the seven panels that compose this page is highlighted entirely by the succession of circular motifs" (2007: 156), but the panel-defined path is primarily column-based, with much smaller row-based panels only at the start and end. The three moons move the eye from right to left, a direction that only occurs between whole panels in Z-path viewing and then only with saccades, the rapid eye movements between fixed points. The succession of circles contrasts rather than

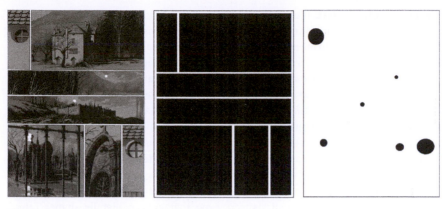

Illustration 3.8 From Yslaire and Balac's *Sambre*.

highlights the succession of panels. If the moons are the braided images, then panels are not the most significant units, contradicting Groensteen's earlier assertion that "the most important codes concern larger units ... that we call 'panels'" (2007: 4).

Since Groensteen's braiding involves repetition, the next chapter addresses it further in terms of recurrence. He does, however, refer to braiding as "structuring elements beneath the surface of the story" (2016: 94), which could be accepted as a general definition of the term, though Groensteen himself attends only to instances of visual repetition. Used in this suggested general sense, contiguous braiding describes the discursive relationships of image parts in a shared visual field, independent of panels or other image divisions.

7. Multiple Visual Fields

While image arrangement is most used to analyze contiguous juxtaposition, it is also involved in the non-contiguous juxtapositions of multi-canvas works.

Regarding distant and temporal juxtapositions, Groensteen differentiates between a "site" (an area on a particular page) and a "place" (the same area on multiple pages), asserting that "braiding brings them to our particular attention" through repeated images (2007: 148). Temporal braiding especially highlights visual repetitions and page positions, because the previous image's afterimage may be momentarily superimposed on the new image. Contiguous braiding does not involve places because they require multiple overlapping sites. Groensteen does not offer "place braiding" or "place rhymes," but the terms would identify similar images placed in the same areas of separate pages. Groensteen implies that visual repetition is necessary for braiding, but two dissimilar images occupying the same place on two different pages could still bring themselves to a viewer's attention and therefore comprise a place rhyme through position only. Groensteen does not treat similarities between panels (whether on the same or distant pages) and layouts as a form of braiding, but all similarly sized and shaped frames visually rhyme, linking their enclosed representational content. Miller and Sienkiewicz distantly rhyme similarly rendered frames in *Elektra: Assassin*, linking the diegetically distant event of an attempted suicide to present events set in an asylum (2012: 12). If all or most frames are similar, the rhyme effect dissipates into a norm of undifferentiated units.

Layouts, when they describe the arrangement of images on separate pages, are temporally and distantly juxtaposed. Viewed temporally, canvasses can be perceived as a cascade of transforming non-representational shapes. Literally flip through the pages of Moore and Gibbons' *Watchmen*, and the omnipresent 3×3 grid and its symmetrical divisions and implied combinations are the defining element of the art. Though too repetitious to produce specific visual rhymes, the unfluctuating base pattern has metaphorical significance in a novel that includes a character with fatalistic knowledge of an unchangeable future in which all of existence follows a predetermined pattern.

When analyzing multi-canvas juxtaposition, viewers may note whether the canvasses reproduce a consistent pattern, how that pattern literally shapes other content, and how the pattern might relate thematically. Bryan Talbot's 2008 *Metronome* (published under the problematic pseudonym Veronique Tanaka) follows an unvarying 4×4 grid of square panels that suggest the time-dividing precision of the title. If the canvasses do not repeat a consistent pattern, is there a semi-consistent pattern recognizable through variations? Like *Watchmen*, Paul Karasik and David Mazzucchelli's 2004 adaption of Paul Auster's prose novel *City of Glass* creates or implies a 3×3 grid on every page, a base pattern that again is potentially significant in the context of the postmodern mystery novel. Tillie Walden demonstrates distantly rhymed layouts in her 2017 memoir *Spinning*, when the unusual 6×4 grid featured in the first chapter repeats for the first time over three hundred pages later, linking two otherwise unrelated diegetic events (2017: 9, 331). Charles Burns's 2005 *Black Hole* links and so relates a range of pages through repetitions of layout, creating "page schemes" to evoke the similar rhyming patterns of poetry (Gavaler and Beavers 2021: 177).

Alternatively, a multi-canvas work may repeat few or no patterns, emphasizing each page as an independent arrangement related diegetically but not through wholistic discursive repetitions. Groensteen calls the approach "neo-baroque," evoking a seventeenth- and eighteenth-century artistic style known for ornate detail, because it "deploys a whole arsenal of unsystematic effects" (2013: 47). Though Groensteen attributes the approach to contemporary 1990s French creators, in the US Jim Steranko beginning in *Strange Tales* #154 (March 1967) and Neal Adams beginning in *X-Men* #56 (May 1969) popularized many of the same elements and combinations, largely replacing the lightly varying rectangular patterns conventionalized by Jack Kirby and Steve Ditko earlier that decade. Neo-baroque has arguably been the norm of US mainstream comic books since, with contemporary artists outside Marvel and DC, such as Adrian Tomine, Julie Doucet, Seth, Leela Corman, Daniel Clowes, and Jessica Abel, echoing the comparative regularities of Kirby and Ditko, which are too regular to produce layout rhyming effects.

These and other layout approaches are noteworthy conventions in the comics medium, but none reveal theoretical principles for the comics form. Having explored the discursive qualities of juxtaposition in this chapter, the next two chapters focus on how juxtapositions interact with image content, the next building block of sequenced images.

4

Recurrence and Erasure

Sequenced images can trigger a wide range of inferences. Before an exploration of that range in the next chapter, this chapter analyzes what is perhaps the form's most common inference, recurrence, and its supporting effect, erasure. Recurrence is specific to the comics form because it is a quality of multiple images that represent the same subject, but recurrence is not a requirement of the form, just one of its most pervasive conventions. In terms of discourse, images may be completely, partially, or not at all similar, and in terms of diegesis, the recurrent subject may be represented at the same or different moments. Recurrence occurs in the three types of juxtapositions discussed in the previous chapter (contiguous, temporal, and distant), and recurrence is also a common effect for experiencing a spatial field as multiple images contiguously juxtaposed. If a canvas includes more than one representation of the same subject, viewers likely experience that canvas as including more than one image, even if the canvas is treated as otherwise unified.

Though I do not identify recurrence as a necessary element of the comics form, some early definers do. Variations on diegetic recurrence appear in the criteria of Waugh's "a continuing character" (1947: 14), Barker's "recurring characters" (1989: 8), Inge's "a recurring set of characters" (1990: xi), and Blackbeard's "recurrent identified characters" (1995: 10). Such a requirement, according to Beaty, "is self-evidently inadequate in terms of a formal definition as it substitutes a common element of the form developed to address marketing concerns for an absolute rule" (2012: 27). Beaty is correct, but Waugh, Barker, Inge, and Blackbeard aren't entirely incorrect. According to Saraceni, the "principal element of repetition" binds "panels together," and "a recognisably and objectively repeated element ... guarantees connectivity between one panel and the next" (2016: 120). Saraceni calls that connectivity "cohesion," noting that one "fundamental way in which two or more panels are linked together is by having elements in common. These can be the same characters, objects, background, or even very small details" (2003: 36–7). Cohesion and repetition describe larger phenomena, while recurrence names the specific cohesion-producing repetition of subjects.

Recurrence is an overwhelming norm of the comics medium because the impression of a single character or a single setting appearing in multiple images cannot occur without it. As Davies observes: "(re)identifiable figures arrayed across the space of a page can be seen as a single persistent entity moving and transforming through time" (2013: 268). If viewers do not decode a repeating set of similar marks—the circular head of Schultz's Charlie Brown, for instance—as a single subject represented multiple times rather than as a series of marks representing different subjects, then those viewers may not experience the images as sequenced. If viewers also do not recognize the circles as heads, they may experience no diegesis at all, just a set of discursive circles. The circles could still be experienced as independent images and so in the comics form, but if the circles are experienced as multiple circles in a single image, they are not recurrent and the image is not in the comics form.

The experience of a single subject also often involves erasure, a diegetically driven coherence effect that blocks perception of discursive elements that do not suit viewers' mental models. If the discursive circles of Charlie Brown's head vary in ways that are not understood to represent changes taking place to the character in the diegetic environment, viewers may ignore those differences. Even if the circles are understood to be nothing more than a repeating circle, the same discursive differences may not be perceived; otherwise the circles would not be experienced as multiple representations of the same diegetically recurrent circle but as a single image of slightly varying circles. Diegetic erasure supports recurrence, and vice versa.

In Illustration 4.1., viewers may register either two individuals who appear three times each or six individuals who appear only once each. The first impression demonstrates recurrence and erasure, requiring a viewer to ignore differences in each iteration in order to experience repeating characters. The second demonstrates neither. The first impression also produces a sequence of images, while the second does not if

Illustration 4.1 "Museum Guards."

the six figures are understood as elements within a single image. The first is in the comics form; the second is not. This chapter analyzes these effects in detail.

1. Types of Recurrence

Like individual images, recurrent representational images have both discursive and diegetic qualities, but recurrent non-representational images have discursive qualities only. Each may be complete or partial.

Complete discursive recurrence repeats an image in its entirety, often by using some form of mechanical duplication (photography, silk screen, digital reproduction, etc.), though hand-drawn images can achieve a similar effect. Groensteen is technically correct that "no panel can be integrally repeated without modification," but he describes viewer perception rather than images' discursive qualities since the "second occurrence of the panel is already different" because "repetition raises the memory of the first occurrence" (2007: 148). He also emphasizes that two images "cannot occupy the same site" (2007: 149), which is not a modification of images but of contexts. While no two images can be made of literally the same set of marks, if the two sets are experienced as identical, the images demonstrate complete discursive recurrence.

Discursive recurrence has no set relationship to diegetic recurrence, and so may produce complete, partial, or no diegetic recurrence at all. The left half of Andy Warhol's 1962 *Marilyn Diptych* in Illustration 4.2 features complete discursive recurrence: twenty-five (essentially) identical reproductions of the same photograph with (essentially) identical silkscreen coloring. The representational content is also completely diegetically recurrent since each image is understood to be diegetically identical: the same subject viewed from the same position and at the same moment. The repetition provides no additional representational content from each face viewed in isolation—except perhaps connotatively. Warhol created this first of his Monroe series the month the actress died, and so the unvarying repetitions might suggest the unchanging permanence of death. Diegetically, however, the images do not represent Monroe frozen in place. Recall "Strips" from the previous chapter for another example of complete diegetic recurrence but only partial discursive recurrence. Like Monroe, the recurrent elements in "Strips" are likely understood to represent one diegetic subject, moment, and perspective, and so do not alter the diegesis.

Complete discursive recurrence does not necessarily produce complete diegetic recurrence. Two identical images may produce the impression of a subject not moving or a setting not changing while time is understood to be passing. Two identical panels from Jillian Tamaki's *SuperMutantMagic Academy* in Illustration 4.2 imply that a seated character has not moved, while the unchanged stars in the night sky behind him imply that the time duration is in a range of minutes (2015: 110). The juxtaposition would allow a shorter period—seconds perhaps—but temporal inferences are more likely to align with the temporal quality of the details that produce them, and movement of stars are gauged in minutes or hours rather than seconds (a temporal effect discussed further in the next chapter). In *Wayward*, Jim Zub and Steve Cummings arrange three identical panels, implying that silent pauses pass while the characters' shocked

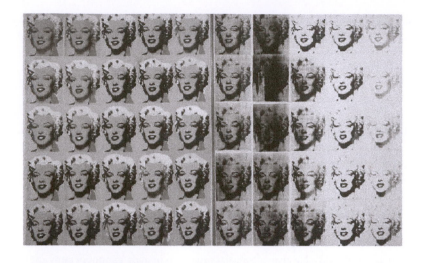

Illustration 4.2 Warhol's *Marilyn Diptych*, from Tamaki's *SuperMutant Magic Academy*, and from Jacob's "37 Difficult Questions From My Mixed-Race Son."

expressions remain frozen (2015: ch. 3, p. 18). Again, the duration of at most seconds is implied because people are not likely to hold shocked expressions for minutes or hours. Whatever duration, some time is experienced as having passed, making the discursively identical images only partially diegetically recurrent because they represent the same characters in the same positions but at different moments.

Complete discursive recurrence is relatively rare in the comics medium. Mira Jacob's 2019 *Good Talk* is an exception because Jacob digitally reuses images of herself and family members, violating the representational norm that different diegetic moments be represented by discursively similar but not identical images. Unlike the Tamaki example in which complete discursive recurrence implies that a character is still but unnoticeably moving, Jacob and her son in Illustration 4.2, based on their animated dialogue, would be noticeably moving, contradicting their drawn appearances. Viewers have difficulty describing the effect. *Publishers Weekly* describes Jacob's memoir as "composed almost entirely of dialogue and static drawings," even though all drawings are necessarily "static" (Klein 2019). *Kirkus Review* instead omits the central feature: "The memoir works well visually, with striking pen-and-ink drawings of Jacob and her family that are collaged onto vibrant found photographs and illustrated backgrounds" (2019), perhaps because the reviewer responds to the diegetic content that paradoxically is not static.

Partial discursive recurrence repeats selective elements. An image may be divided into figure (subject) and ground (setting), either of which can recur independently of the other. If the figure is a representational subject or the ground is a representational setting, discursive and diegetic recurrence overlap. Setting recurrence creates the spatial effect of two images repeating the same perspective of the same area, contradicting the discursive fact of viewers moving their gaze from one image to the next. In "Go Owls," Adrian Tomine repeats an identical figure at an identical position within multiple frames, altering setting elements around her until she is standing alone in an empty parking lot (2016: 70). Because the character is understood to be breathing and making other small movements, the completely discursively recurrent figure is only partially diegetically recurrent. The technique can be used for paradoxical effects, too. In *Jimmy Corrigan*, Chris Ware draws a nearly identical bird at an identically foregrounded position in two panels that, due to changes in surrounding cars and buildings, occur decades apart (2000: n.p.). Diegetically, the bird cannot be the same bird, and yet the discursive recurrence encourages that interpretation.

By repeating some but not all discursive qualities, subjects can also be perceived as partially diegetically recurrent through the Gestalt principle of invariance. Despite differences in framing, scale, rotation, and distortions of shape and shading, two largely dissimilar images may be understood as representing the same subject viewed from different perspectives or viewed after the subject has partially changed. Greater discursive differences require greater diegetic knowledge to produce recurrence. Clark Kent standing beside Superman in Joe Shuster's promotional drawing "ONE AND THE SAME!" diegetically represents the same character even though the two images are discursively dissimilar (quoted in Daniels 1998: 30–1). Diegetic recurrence need not involve any discursive recurrence. A character drawn from different angles and proximities or wearing different clothes may reproduce few or no discursive qualities. Diegetic recurrence without discursive recurrence likely requires text or prior viewer knowledge to link otherwise unrelated images. Tomine's "TRANSLATED, from the JAPANESE" repeats no figures, only aspects of an evolving setting observed from a shifting implied viewer: a train, airport, plane, second airport, highway, dinner, hotel, and cityscape (2016: 75–82), producing partial diegetic recurrence because the images are understood to be spatially linked by a single implied character-viewer within a citywide setting while involving no discursive recurrence. Stainbrook calls this "conceptual repetition" (2003: 90), while Saraceni prefers "collocation" in which images are visually dissimilar but connected by "relatedness of facts," as distinct from "exact repetition" and "visual relexicalization" in which repetition is partial (2016: 120–2).

Partial diegetic recurrence can also be thematic, where the recurrent element is non-discursive and so conceptual only. An antique grandfather clock and a digital watch are discursively dissimilar while still representing objects belonging to the same diegetic category. Looking back to Illustration 2.1, the juxtaposition of Close's and Klee's paintings produces thematic recurrence since viewers are likely to recognize both as representations of human heads, even though their discursive dissimilarities are significantly greater than their similarities. The connecting theme could be discursive instead, with the partial discursive recurrence of diegetically unrelated subjects. The grandfather clock and the Empire State Building have relatively little diegetic resemblance, but framed from similar angles the two tall rectangles might produce partial discursive recurrence. Thematic recurrence can also combine diegetic and discursive similarities and dissimilarities. A round sewer-hole cover and a round space-shuttle hatch have both a thematic resemblance and a discursive resemblance, despite a wide range of greater dissimilarities.

Partial discursive recurrence sometimes produces ambiguous diegetic effects. Like the left half, the right half of Warhol's 1962 *Marilyn Diptych* also features twenty-five reproductions of Monroe's head, only without color and with overt differences as some of the images blur with too much ink and some fade with too little. Out of context, one or two of the images might not be recognizably Monroe. Again, the differences do not represent differences in a diegesis, but the connotations of fading and indecipherable smearing might suggest another element of requiem. Juxtaposing the color and the black-and-white versions of an otherwise identical image is suggestive, too. David Aja employs the technique in *Hawkeye*, repeating an initially color image in black and white to indicate a pause in time as a narrator fills in background information before time and color resume in the next image (Fraction and Aja 2015: n.p.).

A diegesis can also prevent recurrence. In Illustration 4.3, Frida Kahlo's 1939 *The Two Fridas* includes two versions of the artist seated and holding hands. Since recurrence produces an experience of multiple images, the two self-portraits are not recurrent. Instead, the painting is likely perceived as a single image that represents Kahlo as if she existed simultaneously in two identical bodies. Though impossible, the representative content evokes a diegetic situation where such a thing is possible, albeit surreal. The tradition of triple portraits—such as Sir Anthony van Dyck's 1636 *Charles I in Three Positions*—instead presents a recurrent subject at three different angles simultaneously but without surreal results because a viewer likely understands the embedded image to represent not one but three distinct moments and viewpoints (the next chapter discusses this embedded effect further).

Illustration 4.3 Kahlo's *The Two Fridas* and van Dyck's *Charles I in Three Positions*.

Diegetic recurrence usually involves a world in which a represented subject is understood to exist, but a non-representational subject can produce a kind of diegetic recurrence, too. Groensteen describes "Little Line" as a kind of character, one who possess no representational qualities other than the ability to be represented multiple times and so recurrently:

> it is feasible for a line, a shape, a colour, or of any kind of graphic entity, to have "adventures" in its own right, as Menu suggests is the case of Baldi's mini-album *Petit trait* [*Little Line*].
>
> 2013: 12

It is ambiguous whether the recurrent character Little Line may be said to exist in a rudimentary kind of world or if the character is limited to its finite representations on the physical page, but either way a viewer understands each separate discursive line to be the same recurrent subject. The effect is not unique to the comics medium. Curators at the New Orleans of Modern Art describe Mildred Thompson's *Untitled (#111)*, *Untitled (#IV)*, and *Untitled (#VIII)* in terms of recurrence: "In 1973, she created this series of prints in which bright blocks of color move and multiply from print to print in loose and semi-orderly patterns." The blocks of color of course do not literally move from print to print. Each block is a unique mark on a separate canvas, but the blocks' recurrent discursive qualities are sufficient to produce an experience of diegetic recurrence.

Instead of a line or a block, each image in Illustration 4.4 includes a circle or partial circle, which, if experienced as recurrent, becomes a repeating subject in a repeating environment. It is ambiguous whether the circle is growing in the first row or if the implied viewer is moving closer to a stationary circle. The second row could also either depict the movement of the circle or the movement of the implied viewer's gaze away from the circle. Regardless, the circle would be recurrent. Alternatively, a viewer experiences ten distinct circles arranged next to each other and so without diegetic recurrence.

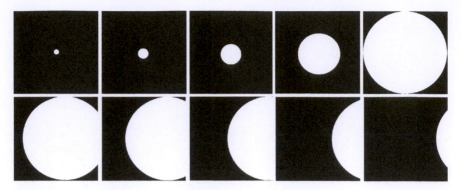

Illustration 4.4 Recurrent subject in ten juxtaposed images.

2. Braiding

Recurrence is essential to Groensteen's braiding discussed in the previous chapter. At minimum braiding involves the repetition of images and so both discursive and diegetic recurrence. Groensteen also identifies "repetition" as "the most frequent type of braiding relation" and even accepts "recurrence" as an alternate term, noting that the braiding repetition may occur "with or without variations" and so includes both partial or complete recurrence (2016: 92). Groensteen, however, clarifies: "Not every type of repetition (such as that of a recurring character) counts as braiding" (2016: 93).

His stipulated meaning may be bound to authorial intention. As discussed in Chapter 1, Groensteen insists that "it is not the reader who 'elaborates' braiding, but the author," and the "reader who has identified it must feel rewarded . . . in the gratification gained from knowing oneself to be an expert reader, a reader capable of uncovering structuring elements beneath the surface of the story" (2016: 91, 94). Consider the museum guards in Illustration 4.1 again. The two figures repeat, but with differences in posture, the implied viewer's angle and proximity, and the discursive effect of bending panels. If Groensteen were correct about authorial intention, I could simply declare my intentions (the images are braided because the discursive arrangement of the recurrent museum guards dominates their diegetic arrangement and so works against narrative continuity), but my unique knowledge of authorial intentions may blind me to the actual features of the completed artwork, making me an ineffective viewer. Braiding may instead be understood as a mental experience of viewers, including artists when they view their own works during and after the process of creating them. It allows a viewer to experience visual repetitions and motifs, which, if perceived as deliberate, would be rhymes in Groensteen's sense.

Groensteen's braiding only applies to a specific subset of repeated images. Though "braiding brings different panels into relation with each other," it "is never necessary to the structuring and intelligibility of the narrative" because "the special (or salient) relationship that we recognise as a braiding effect necessarily produces an enhancement, a layering, a deepening of meaning" (2007: 93, 94). Groensteen considers most image repetition in the comics medium to be "banal and ordinary," and so not braiding, because:

> comics, on account of its sequential and discontinuous nature, is, by its very essence, founded upon the repetition of the same elements—to the point where it has even been called an "art of stammering". From one panel to the next, the same characters, the same background elements are frequently repeated in order to ensure narrative continuity.
>
> 2016: 92

Groensteen does not offer "stammering" as a clearly defined category, and because the term appears to be primarily pejorative, it may carry more connotative than denotative weight. Still, he requires the concept in order to distinguish braiding from other kinds of apparently less meaningful repetition. However, if stammering is discursive repetition required for narrative continuity, it would be at most uncommon since narrative continuity rarely if ever requires discursive repetition. Wally Wood's aptly titled 1980 "24 Panels That Always Work!! Or Some Interesting Ways to Get Some Variety into Those Boring Panels Where Some Dumb Writer Has a Bunch of Lame Characters Sitting Around and Talking for Page after Page!" illustrates a range of drawing techniques (extreme close-up, back of head, part of head, profile, no background, dark foreground, open panel, full figure, down shot, eye level, etc.) that would maintain narrative continuity while producing no discursive recurrence. Stammering then is always a creative choice. The vast majority of the pages in Alan Moore and Eddie Campbell's 1999 *From Hell* maintain narrative continuity while altering angles, proximities, and framing of repeated content—except for three pages that feature the Queen in (nearly) identical images, creating a stammering effect that is neither banal nor ordinary and so therefore presumably braiding even in Groensteen's sense (1999: ch. 2, pp. 18, 19, 28). To the degree that stammering is definable, it may be a subcategory of braiding in which the discursive repetition is judged aesthetically ineffective.

Recall one of Groensteen's primary examples of braiding (specifically contiguous) from the previous chapter: a page from Yslaire and Balac's *Sambre* that features "the succession of circular motifs" across seven panels (2007: 156–8). As diagrammed in Illustration 3.8, the first, penultimate, and last panels include circular windows, and three of the middle panels feature a full moon over landscapes that change as the implied viewer travels between locations. When Groensteen asserts that it "seems that nothing happens," he means diegetically. The braided circles are a discursive arrangement. Though the moon appears three times, it comprises only half of the circles and so is not primarily an element of narrative continuity. For Groensteen, the motif is an example of braiding in part because he believes the circles are intended to be metaphors for eye-like justice, even though that meaning would still be present if the repetitions were stammering instead. It is also unclear in what sense the circle motif can be described as an "enhancement" since it is the commanding element of the page.

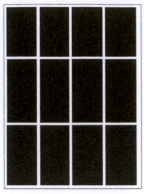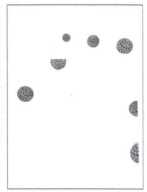

Illustration 4.5 From Sienkiewicz's *Stray Toasters*.

Compare the *Sambre* page to a page from Bill Sienkiewicz's 1991 *Stray Toasters* (also included as an isolated artwork, minus its original words and words containers, in his retrospective *Revolution*) (2019: 24). As in *Sambre*, the *Stray Toasters* page features a circular motif: a ball appears in seven of the twelve panels. Like Yslaire and Balac's motif, Sienkiewicz's circles are the dominating element of the page. The ball can also be interpreted with metaphorical significance relevant to the larger story, but the repetitions presumably would constitute stammering and not braiding since Groensteen asserts that "in general, [braiding repetitions] do not affect the story events, but remain external to them" (2016: 93). This does not describe the *Stray Toasters* page. Unlike in *Sambre*, something does "happen": in the first row, the discursive growth of the ball in relation to the frames is due to the changing proximity of the implied viewer, but in the second row, a robotic hand lifts the child's ball out of frame and then bounces it past the mother's feet after she has removed her shoes in the third row. The movement of the circles in *Sambre* is comparatively inactive because the windows and moon are stationary, so the braiding effect is from a discursive arrangement of implied viewers. Yet the primary effects of Sienkiewicz's page are discursive, too: the seven balls create a dotted curve that does not follow the narrative flow of the panels nor the diegetic path of the ball in the story world. The visual motif is not exclusively diegetic because it draws viewer attention to the surface arrangements of the images.

Much of the artwork in Molotiu's edited collection *Abstract Comics* features braiding, which is arguably the signature technique of non-representational sequenced images. A page coheres through repetition, introducing visual echoes and developing some into patterns. This is equally true of non-representational works outside the comics medium. The fourth panel of de Kooning's 1960 *Black and White (San Francisco)* stands apart only because the first three panels repeat a different kind of brush mark. The non-representational work in Illustration 4.6 braids two kinds of abstract images, creating intertwined columns of identically sized and spaced unframed panels. Further similarities within each image—the size, width, length, density, and seeming direction of movement of smaller units—can be analyzed as braiding, too. According to

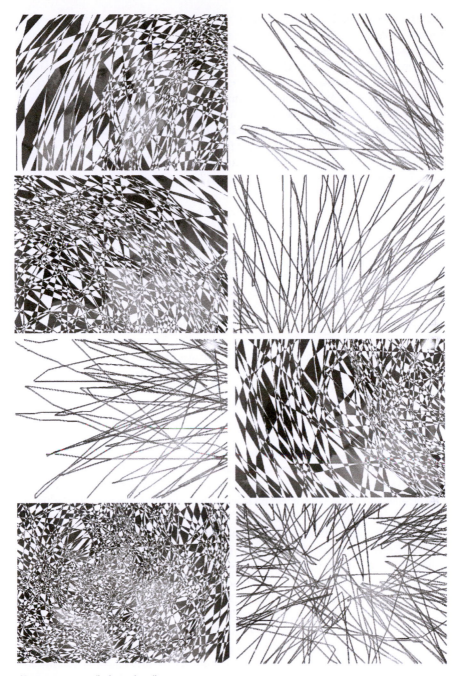

Illustration 4.6 "*Charade* II."

Groensteen, however, these effects might not be braiding because they do not add an additional meaning to the artwork since the artwork produces no diegeses. Rather than excluding non-representational work, I set aside the notion of enhancement.

Postema similarly describes Groensteen's braiding as "a function of the discourse, and not necessarily the narrative," citing an example of clocks and calendars appearing throughout a comic to "create a thematic unity" (2013: 113). Postema's "narrative" may be synonymous with diegesis, but I understand discourse only as marks on surfaces that, when interpreted by viewers, represent diegetic objects such as clocks and calendars. The only thematic unity possible for discursive marks is in shape, size, color, and other non-diegetic qualities. Circular clocks and rectangular calendar could each produce a braided motif, but not together unless the clocks and calendars share some other visual similarity (such as color). If the images are representational, the discursive repetition creates a diegetic repetition, linking the images at two levels. The images may have little or no diegetic resemblance, but discursive similarities in how they are drawn (such as point of view, framing, and style) can still create visual repetition.

It is also possible for discursively dissimilar images to echo diegetically, creating partial diegetic recurrence but without braiding or stammering. While non-representational marks must resemble each other in order to create the experience of a repetition, similar diegetic objects can be rendered dissimilarly but still repeat conceptually. If we adopt Groensteen's term to refer to any discourse-focused repetition, then non-discursive diegetic repetitions are not braiding. The thematic unity of visually dissimilar clocks and calendars is diegetic only. Images of clocks and calendars may be considered a visual motif, but one that is organized by diegetic theme rather than discursive appearance, revealing the primary difference between visual motifs generally and the more specific subcategory of braiding.

Viewers of Robert Kirkman and Tony Moore's *The Walking Dead Vol. 1: Days Gone Bye* might trace two prominent visual motifs: guns and hats. Since guns include visually dissimilar pistols and rifles, and hats include visually dissimilar cowboy hats and baseball caps, neither visual motif is braiding. In contrast, viewers of Victor LaValles and Dietrich Smith's 2018 *Destroyer* may notice the visual rhyme of a seated figure filling the top half of the first and last pages. The repetition is more than diegetic because of similarities in angle, proximity, and the shapes of the two figures. The braiding may include a third, middle iteration, with a third character similarly posed and viewed, but with greater differences since the image is in the lower half of the page and the figure's arms are positioned higher and the implied viewer is slightly lower. The middle iteration is also a visual quotation of material outside the diegesis: the seated statue of Abraham Lincoln in the Lincoln Memorial. The graphic novel includes numerous other images of seated characters, none of which enter the braiding because of their minimal discursive resemblance. The braided images are braided not because they depict seated figures (a diegetic fact), but because the seated figures are rendered similarly (a discursive fact).

Postema also differentiates braiding with what she terms "weaving," which allows "for the retroactive resignification or projection that creates plot out of gaps" as a sequence weaves "individual panels into a sense of temporality and developing action" (2013: 113). Since a non-woven narrative of images does not seem possible, the additional term may have limited use and creates potential confusion since the words "weaving" and "braiding" may seem synonymous. Postema's weaving also appears to be more related to McCloud's closure or Cohn's visual narrative grammar discussed in Chapter 6.

Finally, Groensteen refers to braiding repetitions as "quotations" (2016: 89), though some of his own examples might be more accurately described as paraphrases since they do not involve complete discursive recurrence. Yslaire and Balac's moons, for example, differ not only in size but also in the sharpness of their outer edges and in how other objects partially obscure them. In terms of recurrence, Groensteen's braiding emphasizes discursive recurrence, allowing diegetic recurrence to the degree that the repetition still involves at least partial discursive recurrence. In short, all braiding involves recurrence, but not all recurrence involves braiding.

3. Contradictory Recurrence

Some discursive differences between images could represent diegetic differences in a recurrent subject and yet are not experienced that way. The rest of this chapter explores this recurrence-related phenomenon, beginning with an extended case study.

In *Action Comics* #8 (January 1939), Joe Shuster draws a group of juvenile delinquents facing trial for assault and battery. In their first panels, the four appear

Illustration 4.7 From Siegel and Shuster's *Action Comics* #8.

adult-like: broad-shouldered, square-jawed, and tall in contrast to a chin-high mother; they stand only slightly shorter than Superman in a subsequent panel (2006: 99, 105). Jerry Siegel's dialogue reinforces the impression. In his defense, a delinquent states, "If he had handed over his dough wit' out squawkin' I wouldn't a hit 'im so hard," to which the judge replies, "You speak like a hardened criminal" (2006: 98). After eliminating the corrupting influence of an older criminal, Superman attempts "to throw some fear and humility into" the delinquents by scooping them up and bouncing them on power lines, as they shout: "HA-ALP!—HE'S NUTS!"; "No! We're nuts!—something like this just couldn't happen!"; "But it is!" (2006: 107). However, after Superman threatens to do it again, they respond: "You bet!"; "C'mon! What're ya waitin' fer?"; "It was fun!" (2006: 108). The formerly adult-like delinquents now appear child-like: short, thin-armed, and comparatively round-headed. Superman later bends to speak to them.

How do viewers experience the characters as diegetically recurrent despite the visual contradictions demonstrated in Illustration 4.7?

The most immediate explanation would be a literal interpretation that aligns with Cook's panel transparency principle discussed in Chapter 2: "Characters ... appear ... as they are depicted" (2012: 134). Shuster has drawn a fantastical narrative in which the burly thugs actually shrink in age. While no more or less impossible than a human-looking alien leaping tall buildings, an age-transforming superpower might violate Superman as a character type and his diegetic grounding as a whole. Carney and his co-authors explain that "the figure of the superhero is a stable rendering in the category of 'person,' which is then supplemented with minimally counterintuitive characteristics and abilities," and so superhero narratives feature "supernatural agents who deviate in one, and usually only one, characteristic trait from intuitive ontological categories" (2004: A202–3). *Action Comics* #1 introduces Superman with superhuman strength, and later additions are incremental and adhere to the character's core physicality. A Superman who can transform criminals into children would not be the same minimally counterintuitive character within the same minimally counterintuitive narrative.

Other possible explanations involve a non-transparent understanding of discursive elements. Though an image appears to be literal, it is not but still represents other diegetic qualities. Duncan provides two possibilities.

Shuster's contradictory images could communicate non-transparent but diegetically relevant impressions of the juvenile delinquents' inner experiences. Shuster draws them as thugs in the opening pages because they understand themselves to be thugs. After thrilled by Superman's amusement-park-like ride, they experience themselves as children. As discussed in Chapter 2, Duncan could label these "non-sensory diegetic images" because they "show the internal reality of the characters," not "the physical reality of the world of the story" (2012: 44–5). The interpretive approach is most applicable for images featuring a single character. Do all of the delinquents share the same set of self-images? Or might the psychological perspective be Superman's as he re-evaluates the delinquents?

Rather than psychologically, Shuster's images may instead be interpreted metaphorically. Carroll's pioneering analysis of visual metaphors focuses on single images that superimpose elements from two sources, such as the violin f-holes placed onto a figure's back in Man Ray's 1924 photomontage *Violon d'Ingres*. Shuster's example instead involves two distinct images related by distant juxtaposition (or contiguous juxtaposition in Illustration 4.7), similar to Forceville's analysis of pictorial metaphors that include two pictorially present terms, such as the image of a diver beside an image of dolphin, implying that the diver resembles the dolphin (2002: 10). Shuster's effect, however, would be metaphorical in a different sense. Recall Duncan's "hermeneutic images," which he places outside of the story as an author's interpretive commentary, distinguishable from sensory and non-sensory dietetic images by their non-mimetic qualities (2012: 45). Non-realistic images drawn within naturalistic context may be interpreted as visual metaphors because they resist a naturalistic reading. The delinquents' changing appearances then could be Shuster's "explicit attempts to influence the interpretation of the story" toward "the underlying meaning" (2012: 45, 46), stated overtly by a delinquent's mother: "like all the other boys in our neighborhood ...he might have been a good boy except for his environment. He still might be" (2006: 98). Had Shuster continued to draw the characters in thuggish proportions, other interpretations would be more available, including the possibility that the delinquents have not truly reformed.

The category of hermeneutic images, however, is problematic. If an artist's images "can influence the interpretation of the story," then those images would need to be somehow independent of the story that they also embody. While some images may appear more overtly hermeneutic ("interpretive") than others, even the most seemingly objective image cannot comment independently on the subject it simultaneously represents. All representation is interpretation. Duncan and Smith seem to acknowledge as much, since "Even the pencil lines with which a picture is drawn and brush strokes with which it is inked can have a hermeneutic function" (2015: 148). If lines and strokes have such a function, then an image composed of those lines and strokes presumably does, too.

The remaining possible explanations reject image elements as having representational significance, aligning with Cook's later claim: "the physical appearance of drawn characters in general is indirect, partial, inferential, and imperfect" (2015: 25).

Perhaps Shuster did not intend the later depictions to contradict earlier ones, and therefore the contradiction should be ignored. Though an author's intentions are always unavailable, readers construct an implied author, "the version of the author projected by the text itself and sometimes also conditioned by our knowledge about the actual author's life and career" (Keen 2003: 33). This projection extends to an implied artist and so, in the case of *Action Comics* #8, an implied Shuster who apparently lacks the ability or desire to draw consistent characters.

Alternatively, the inconsistency was not Shuster's, but the formative genre's. Cohn identifies the "'mainstream' style of American Visual Language [that] appears most prevalently in superhero comics" as "'Kirbyan,' in honor of the historical influence of Jack 'King' Kirby in defining the style" (2013: 139). This implies that Shuster was not drawing in the genre's eventual style norms. As a pre-Kirbyan artist, Shuster was exploring forms that had not yet coalesced. In an earlier, high-school collaboration with Siegel, Shuster illustrated "Goober the Mighty" in a parodic, cartoon style, demonstrating his familiarity with stories that "often assume a fundamentally unstable and infinitely mutable physical reality, where characters and even objects can move and be transformed according to an associative or emotive logic rather than the laws of physics" (Witek 2012: 30). Witek argues that superhero comics belong to the naturalistic mode, but the genre did not exist yet. Shuster was free to render his juvenile delinquents in a mutable cartoon mode, despite his overall use of what would later be categorized as a naturalistic approach.

Both accidental inconsistency and proto-genre style instability support the same conclusion: the delinquents don't change diegetically; they just look like they do. A final approach instead avoids both transparent and non-transparent interpretations. In order to resolve discourse–diegesis contradictions, viewers effectively erase what does not align.

4. Diegetic Erasure

When Cook proposed his panel transparency principle, that characters appear as they are depicted, he defended the problematic claim because denying it "would require us to develop a sophisticated account that distinguished those aspects of panels that do depict literal characteristics of the fictional world in question from those aspects that are primarily stylistic" (2012: 135). Cook is correct that sequenced images require further explanation for a range of non-transparent effects, including the contradictory recurrence demonstrated in Shuster's panels. They challenge the relationship between discourse and diegesis, establishing a recurrence-driven effect in which a viewer effectively erases content by not experiencing certain discursive marks as representational or even as discursively present.

The relationship between discourse and diegesis is inherently ambiguous since any representational image may be understood as possessing the semi-representational qualities discussed in Chapter 2. Accepting Barthes's observation that "there is no drawing without style" (1977: 43), no image is simply literal. Neal Adams is known for increasing naturalism in superhero comics in the late 1960s and 70s, reportedly commenting that "If superheroes existed, they'd look like I draw them" (Smith 2011). But even if a superhero image is perceived as realistic, it still does not become a perfect embodiment of its represented reality. Even the near-photorealism of Alex Ross in his 1994 *Marvels* and 1996 *Kingdom Come* works within a range of non-realistic conventions, creating what some reviewers describe as "excessively posed" "product design" (Adams 2009). The most realistic representations—including the photo-recreating drawings of Jon J. Muth's 1992 *M* or the actual photography of Italian fumetti—remain subject to the stylistic effects of framing and of the angles and proximities of implied viewers. Still, for viewers of *Action Comics* #8 to ignore the appearance of a fully diegetic transformation of characters, one or both of the images in Illustration 4.7 must be fundamentally inaccurate.

Chapter 2 introduced specification and the degrees to which discursive and diegetic qualities can be misaligned. Cook rejected his original panel transparency principle after analyzing early 1980s Marvel photographic covers by Eliot Brown, concluding that: "photo-covers don't provide us with reliable information regarding the (fictional) appearance of the characters depicted" (2015: 25). The overspecified photographic details contrast the less detailed drawn representations of the same characters: "Since we are clearly not meant to believe Cap's shield is (or even appears to be) made of plastic, we are not meant to take these photo-covers as particularly reliable or objective representations of the appearance of these characters" (2015: 21, 24). The photographed face of the actor featured in Brown's cover for *Amazing Spider-Man* #262 (March 1985) is far more specified than any of the drawn images inside that or any other issue. While viewers understand that Peter Parker has a mimetically specific face because he exists in a mimetically specific story world, an image with that same level of specificity must be paradoxically inaccurate because it exceeds the accepted range of knowable details.

Images in the comics medium are more typically underspecified. Whatever details an image actually contains, a viewer may experience additional, undrawn ones. Neuroscientists Sayim and Cavanagh explain:

> Scenes in the real world carry large amounts of information about color, texture, shading, illumination, and occlusion giving rise to our perception of a rich and detailed environment. In contrast, line drawings have only a sparse subset of scene contours. Nevertheless, they also trigger vivid three-dimensional impressions . . .
>
> 2011: 1

Those impressions are the viewer's experience of the diegesis, even if they contradict the drawn content of the discursive images. Differences in specification account for viewers assuming greater diegetic detail than is discursively present or rejecting greater discursive detail than is diegetically justified.

Shuster's example occurs within a single, thirteen-page episode, and the juveniles never reappear in subsequent episodes. Superman of course does recur in every issue afterwards, but Shuster only penciled occasional issues after *Action Comics* #24 (May 1940), turning over artwork to new artists including Wayne Boring and Jack Burnley. Curt Swan began drawing the character in 1948, and was a primary artist until 1985, when he was followed by John Byrne in the 1980s, Dan Jurgens and Alex Ross in the 1990s, Ed McGuinness and Frank Quitely in the 2010s. While some incarnations involve reboots or diegetically isolated stories, most of the literally hundreds of Superman artists have depicted the same individual, expanding the dilemma posed by Shuster's juveniles.

If a recurrent character is bound by every detail of a representation, viewers could not perceive the character as a continuous entity when drawn by different artists in distinguishable styles. Because single issues are traditionally drawn by one penciller and one inker, superhero comics tend to avoid immediate contradictions in imagery, but even when multiple stylistic renderings of a character are contained in a single issue, none fully embodies the character. In the 2004 *Avengers Disassembled*, writer Brain Michael Bendis scripted a collage of Scarlet Witch images spanning multiple decades and artists, including Jack Kirby, John Byrne, and George Pérez. Although David Finch is the primary artist in *Avengers Disassembled*, his renderings of Scarlet Witch are no more privileged. Viewers recognize all of the images as manifestations of a single diegetically recurrent character.

Superman, Scarlet Witch, and other recurrent characters exist as a set of repeatable lines, and yet because those lines are not exact duplicates and vary to imply such non-discursive qualities as movement and three-dimensionality, the diegetic character is more than their discursive marks. Cohn calls these sets "*cognitive schemas*": "At their basis, these are patterns in the minds of creators, and need only correspond loosely to 'reality'" (2013: 141). The customs of character patterns are also in the minds of viewers. A fictional world, writes Dolezel, "is constructed by its author," and the author's text "is a set of instructions for the reader, according to which the world reconstruction proceeds" (1998: 21). An artist's images operate similarly, creating a "bridge between actual readers and the universe of fiction" "whose properties, structures, and modes of existence are, in principle, independent of the properties, structures, and existential mode of actuality" (1998: 22, 23). Neither an author's words nor an artist's images are aspects of the world that they enable readers and viewers to experience. Discursive contradictions between images therefore do not necessarily represent contradictions in a diegesis.

Details in Brown's *Spider-Man* cover can be rejected because they surpass the level of specificity indicated by the character's mental model. The photographed actor posed in jeans and a Spider-Man shirt is not Peter Parker but a representation of Peter Parker, one no more definitive—and arguably less definitive—than any other representation, regardless of medium or rendering. Peter Parker exists independently of not only our reality but of the textual fields of the pages that represent him. Differences in execution on the page do not necessarily affect schema and so do not present contradictions in the implied reality. As Oyola observes of the half century of Spider-Man art, though there is

> some shoddy penciling or inking work that made him not look like himself (esp. in the late 90s and early 00s), generally speaking there is some form of continuity across the decades. All the Peter Parkers may not look exactly the same depending on who is drawing him and when, but you can always tell who it is supposed to be at first glance.
>
>   2012

Discursive differences do not affect the previously established mental patterns and so do not present contradictions in the diegetic reality, but mental models are not so vague as to allow any variation. Oyaola finds that Giuseppe Camuncoli's rendering of the character in *Amazing Spider-Man* #689 (September 2012) "looked so little like what I imagine Peter Parker to look like, that until he was identified by name on the next page I thought we might be looking at" a different character (2012). Despite Camuncoli's atypical rendering and the inconsistencies of other artists that produce significant discursive differences, Peter Parker remains a stable mental construct based on an established custom of drawing norms, ones that Oyola and other viewers use to impose meaning onto the page.

Witek argues that the cartoon mode treats "the comic's page not only as a loose representation of physical existence, but also as a textual field for the immediate enactment of overtly symbolic meaning," and so "the cartoon mode is fundamentally a medium of ideas" (2012: 32). This may describe representational imagery generally. Recall Mendelsund's description of prose readers' visualizations from Chapter 1:

characters are "merely visual types, exemplars of particular categories—sizes; body shapes; hair colors" (2014: 373). The same mental schemas apply to recurrent elements in sequenced images. Mendelsund acknowledges that "illustrations will shape my mental visions" (2014: 181), but because he is describing illustrations by the same artist within the same illustrated novel, he does not account for differences between editions. Though the sets of illustrations from two editions of *Things Fall Apart* that Hyde analyzes in Chapter 2 are strikingly different in style, she understands them to be illustrations of the same subjects. Since the subjects are fictional, they exist only as mental models, ones that can be represented by strikingly different sets of discursive marks. The two artists' *Things Fall Apart* illustrations do not appear within the same edition, so any contradictory recurrence is minimal. But the process for resolving contradictions is the same. Viewers understand the accuracy of an image relative to the parameters of the schema in their minds, and those schema may be no more precise than the examplars Mendelsund describes: "we cannot advance beyond a vague *sketchiness* in our imaginings" (2014: 192).

That vagueness explains how viewers can understand multiple and multiply contradictory images on a single page as all representations of the same subject. It also explains Shuster's two sets of juveniles, since both could fall within the characters' vaguely defined schema. It also highlights how a viewer can discount visual information that does not align with diegetic expectations. If viewers accepted the first images of the juveniles as accurate, they may not register the contradictions in the second images because they do not fit their mental model. Responses likely vary. Reviewing over 3,800 change detection studies to assess visual working memory, Balaban, Fukuda, and Luria found that "some items are represented with high fixed resolution and others are not represented at all" (2019: 1). Schema, to the degree that they are initially formed through visual working memory, may vary similarly, with some discursive contradictions going unnoticed because certain details are not maintained in the diegesis and so cannot be contradicted.

This viewer-determined quality of recurrent content also parallels the human visual system. Through the perceptual constancies of size, shape, and color, Medley discusses how the brain is "not merely accepting of what is presented on the retina, but in fact is measuring that presentation against what the brain knows of objects in the world," matching any given "visual presentation of an object upon our retinas … against existing information" that "does not precisely match any 'real' visual version" (2010: 59, 61). Because these mental "faculties are unconcerned with specific information," they will "override purely visual sensation" that does not match pre-existing constructs (2010: 59). Viewers of *Action Comics* # 8 also override the specific information contained in the contradictory visual presentations of Shuster's delinquents. "The image on the retina," writes Medley, "is not taken at face value" (2010: 59), and neither is the image on the page. Details that do not match diegetic expectations may go unnoticed.

"An understanding of the special ways of seeing applied by readers," argues Medley, "is a necessary starting point for a theory of comics' formal properties" (2010: 68). Ironically, the special way of seeing contradictory recurrences involves dismissing some of an image's discursive qualities. The delinquents contain a range of other contradictions, including articles of clothing disappearing or changing color from panel to panel. Even the number of delinquents vacillates between three and four. These are arguably greater challenges to a minimally counterintuitive diegesis than the characters' unstable ages—and yet they likely cause no representational disruption. In relation to the fictional world they presumably represent, contradictory image details may not be literal, hermeneutically non-literal, psychologically non-sensory diegetic, or non-naturalistically cartoonish. They instead have no relationship to the implied reality at all, if viewers treat them as if they do not exist.

Diegetic erasure is not unique to works in the comics form or comics medium. In film, the constituent elements of screen imagery are traditionally dominated by real-world source materials: actors, costumes, props, set locations. The illusion of a stable object or character appearing in multiple shots is a product of the real-world stability of the source materials. Errors in continuity occur, but they are the exception not the norm. The repetition of drawn visual elements, however, typically involves a unique set of lines for each manifestation. Even if images are based on real-world models, they contain discursive differences which viewers ignore in order to understand the content as diegetically stable.

McCloud describes comics as a "dance between the seen and the unseen, the visible and invisible" because of the undrawn content implied as happening between the moments represented in images, but sequenced images can also make the seen unseen (1993: 92). Not only is implied content absent from the page, the drawn content within panels may become invisible, too. Where McCloud's closure describes a viewer's ability to infer physically absent but narratively present content, an opposite and simultaneous process occurs in which the same viewer eliminates present but diegetically incoherent image content. Without diegetic erasure, differences in the renderings of mentally stable schema would prevent diegetic recurrence.

McCloud unintentionally demonstrates diegetic erasure in his first example of panel-to-panel transitions in Illustration 4.8. Asserting that the "first category—which we'll call moment-to-moment—requires very little closure," he draws a recurrent figure, first with her eyes open and then with her eyes closed (1993: 70). Diegetically, the only differences between the images are the eyes represented by the discursive marks of circles and curved lines. The two images, however, also contain a wide range of other discursive differences: the lines representing the clouds above the figure's head, the lines representing the trees and mountains on each side of the figure's head, and the negative spaces representing a pattern in the collar of the figure's clothing. While it is not impossible for the clouds to have shifted, it is implausible for them to have shifted in the "moment" that McCloud intends the juxtaposition to represent. Moreover, it would require weeks if not seasons for the shapes of the trees to change, and even a slight shift in the top edge of a mountain could require decades if not centuries. Most significantly, no time duration could account for the change in the figure's clothing since the collar is understood to be a stable object that might fade or tear with age but not alter patterns that are permanent qualities of the fabric.

Consider Illustration 4.1 again. Each museum guard appears three times. Each appearance varies primarily by body posture and differences in viewpoint as the implied viewer changes positions relative to the paired figures. The bodies of the guards appear blurry and so underspecified in contrast to the presumed level of specificity within their world. Some details—especially the figures' impossibly choppy edges—are

Illustration 4.8 A moment-to-moment example from McCloud's *Understanding Comics*.

likely discounted as semi-representational stylistic effects. The experience of diegetic recurrence then requires rejecting the discursive details of blurriness and choppiness. If viewers experience the images as a temporal sequence, greater erasure occurs. "Museum Guards" could be perceived as three images, each containing the paired guards. Those three images could also be perceived as representing a sequence of chronological events as the two guards converse in a relatively short period of time. If so, discursive differences between recurrent images are the result of the characters changing posture or the implied viewer changing angles. And yet the middle image disrupts this possibility because the guards are standing on opposite sides of each other relative to the first image. If the implied viewer is understood to have rotated 45 degrees relative to the female figure, then the male figure should be in profile, too. If that change violates a viewer's perception of events occurring in a shorter period of time than would allow the guards to change positions and for no diegetically justified reason, the disruptive elements might go unnoticed and so diegetically erased.

As the juvenile delinquents say in *Action Comics* #8, if something like this just couldn't happen, then it just doesn't. Having addressed two primary inferences produced by juxtaposed images, recurrence and erasure, in this chapter, the next chapter moves to a range of additional inferences.

5

Juxtapositional Inferences

Eco may be the first scholar to name the phenomenon of viewers experiencing content implied by paired images:

> The relationship between one frame and the next is governed by a series of *montage rules*. I have used the term "montage," though the reference to the cinema should not make us forget that the montage in a comic is different from a film, which merges a series of stills into a continuous flux. The comic strip, on the other hand, breaks up the story's *continuum* into a few essential components. Obviously the reader welds these parts together in his imagination and then perceives them as a continuous flow.
>
> 1965: 24

Eco presumably borrows "montage" from Eisenstein's film theory, but beginning with the 1993 publication of McCloud's *Understanding Comics*, "closure" replaced it: "If visual iconography is the vocabulary of comics, closure is its grammar. And since our definition of comics hinges on the arrangements of elements—then, in a very real sense, comics is closure" (1993: 67).

Despite its historical significance in comics theory, "closure" remains a problematic term. The *OED* records ten definitions that evolve from enclosing spaces with fences and fortresses to enclosing time by ending specified durations, which then extends to conclusions generally. The final definition references 1924 Gestalt psychology: "the process whereby incomplete forms, situations, etc., are completed subjectively by the viewer or seem to complete themselves; the tendency to create ordered and satisfying wholes." Gestalt psychologists define closure as one of four laws guiding visual perception, accounting for the ability to understand a dotted line as a line and not only as individual dots. McCloud's use of the term for the process of understanding diegetic events synced to the discursive spaces between panels is confusing for at least two reasons. Kukkonen explains:

> "Closure" is perhaps not the most felicitous term here: on the one hand, because it is a term also used to refer to the conclusion of the plot, and on the other hand, because readers do not actually "close the gap" but merely infer connections on the level of the mental model.
>
> 2013: 31

By arguing that viewers do not process "every thing that happens between the images," Kukkonen focuses on the diegesis rather than the discursive marks that trigger the diegesis. Even if viewers did process "every thing," that would not "close the gap" in the discursive Gestalt psychology sense. Perceiving individual dots as a continuous line is a spatial perception with no temporal element. Nothing "happens" between the dots. Viewers do not mentally draw additional images any more than prose readers compose additional sentences.

As discussed in Chapter 3, sequenced images need not include any discursive division between images. The gaps viewers fill are gaps only in a metaphorical sense, even when accompanied by the convention of a gutter's literal gap, "that space between the panels" that McCloud identifies as the site where "human imagination takes two separate images and transforms them into a single idea" (1993: 66). Miller similarly identifies the "inter-frame space" as "a key element in the signifying mechanism of bande dessinée" (2007: 88). McCloud might instead have chosen the term "metonymy," which, Miller notes, some French scholars prefer, describing a bande dessinée as a "metonymic machine" in which parts stand for a whole (2007: 81). Duncan and Smith similarly describe the encapsulation and framing of comics panels as synecdoche because they use "a part to represent the whole" (2015: 112).

Terminology aside, McCloud provides an example of "a four-panel establishing shot of an old-fashioned kitchen scene": "With a high degree of closure, your mind is taking four picture fragments and constructing an entire scene out of those fragments" (1993: 88–9). That "scene," like Kukkonen's "mental model," is diegetic. Because the four panels depict different angles and close-ups of a related but non-continuous diegetic space, viewers do not close the discursive space between the images in the same sense that they close the gaps between dots to perceive a dotted line. Gestalt closure is specific to unconnected visual objects that are perceived as connected but incomplete because a viewer fills in the perceived incomplete elements. Though atypical, a gutter can divide two panels with representational content that is understood to be spatially continuous, so closing the discursive gap and closing the diegetic gap combines the two experiences because they visually overlay. Ironically, none of McCloud's six types of panel transitions accounts for images that produce closure in this original Gestalt sense. Diptychs and triptych routinely produce Gestalt closure, and the technique, which Groensteen dubs "fragmentation" (2013: 17) and Cohn "Divisional" (2003: 31), is also common in the comics medium.

The site of McCloud's closure is a viewer's mind, and it occurs not between two images but only after viewing both. Cohn asks: "If closure occurs 'in the gaps between panels' then how does it work if a reader cannot make such a connection until the second panel is reached?" (2010: 135). The effect then is retroactive. It often implies undepicted diegetic content occurring between depicted moments, but instead of inserting that content between discursive images, the new content is experienced non-discursively through additions in a viewer's mental model. The first image is recalled in memory, though a viewer may also return and view it again. McCloud notes that "we seldom do change direction, except to re-read and review passages" (1993: 105), but a viewer controls not only linear direction, moving forward or moving backwards between images, but also non-linear directions, since juxtaposition is not constrained by the viewing paths prescribed by sequence (as discussed in the next chapter). Most of what McCloud calls closure likely occurs at a subconscious level and is a learned phenomenon that becomes subconscious after multiple experiences.

Rather than a subset of Gestalt psychology, McCloud's closure is a subset of inferences specific to juxtaposed images. Content triggered by visual content is not itself visual. Viewers do not perceive "a continuous flow" as Eco insists. Although readers "connect individual panels through inferences," Kukkonen regards those inferences as no different from other inferences that readers make, whether images are involved or a text is prose-only (2013: 35). Kintsch explains:

> We comprehend a text, understand something, by building a mental model. To do so, we must form connections between things that were previously disparate: the ideas expressed in the text and relevant prior knowledge. Comprehension implies forming coherent wholes with Gestalt-like qualities out of elementary perceptual and conceptual features.
>
> 1998: 93

McCloud's closure is also only "Gestalt-like" and so does not require actual Gestalt visualizing. According to Kintsch, we comprehend by forming "a control structure that regulates comprehension processes" by serving as "a perceptual filter" and "inference machine, in that it fills the gaps that are inevitably found in the actual stimulus material" (1998: 94). Prose-only texts contain similar conceptual gaps, requiring viewers to draw conclusions regarding a range of story-world details, including general facts that define physical setting and plot situations, as well as internal mental processes of individual characters. Inference-producing "gaps" may occur between images, between sets of words, between an image and a set of words, within an image, and within a set of words, and the act of filling them is always conceptual. To construct a mental model, Therriault, Rinck, and Zwaan argue "readers are sensitive to information in the story world at the event level" and so "progress through [a] narrative text indexing each action or event" and store them "in memory on the basis of their dimensional relatedness" (2006: 78).

McCloud identified a subcategory of inferencing specific to juxtaposed images. Though mental modelling is central to both, inferencing in sequenced images and in prose-only texts differs discursively. Unlike words, images are often constrained by pictorial representation, which Hopkins describes through six qualities, including that "all depiction is from a point of view" (2005: 145) and so spatially oriented. For a depiction to have a point of view it must also exist at some moment in time. The image depicts not only the subject but the event of the subject being viewed. The juxtaposition of representational images emphasizes spatiotemporal relationships. Miller explains:

> The temporal and spatial hiatus implied by the inter-frame space is indeterminate, and allows for considerable variations in the rhythm at which a story is narrated. There may be a conspicuous break in time or space within the fictional world, either between sequences or during a sequence, or, conversely, the break may be smoothed over by an impression of continuity.
>
> 2007: 88–9

McCloud's panel transition types, however, do not define the full range of spatiotemporal possibilities.

Moment-to-moment and action-to-action mark a movement in time, but subject-to-subject, scene-to-scene, aspect-to-aspect, and non-sequitur are temporally ambiguous. McCloud also does not account for all spatial relationships. Cohn describes a page from an *X-Force* comic drawn by Rob Liefeld: "there was a large exterior picture of a mountain, and then he provided an interior view of their base inside the mountain … moving from a superordinate space to a subordinate space," a spatial transition outside of McCloud's types (Cohn and Worcester 2015: 4). Cohn went on to devise his own taxonomy of panel transitions (2003), later replacing it with a visual grammar system to reveal panel relationships within multi-panel narratives. Others, including Christiansen, Dean, Saraceni, and Stainbrook, have revised McCloud's initial transition types, too, but such inferencing still requires further analysis.

Previous categorizations, while improving on McCloud's transition types, have also retained a central weakness. Closure types and transition types are separate categories. Closure refers to the inferences a viewer experiences when processing a transition. Since juxtaposed images can produce a range of inferences, they should not be understood as individual transitional types, but as multi-faceted combinations. Though McCloud does not distinguish closure and transitions explicitly, his original presentation of the concepts implies it by categorizing not closure types but transition types that employ closure in his generalized sense of "perceiving the whole." When Cohn revised McCloud he expanded the list of transitions from five to eight (adding View and Cognable) and identified three Transitionally Variant Conditions (Inclusionary, Embedded, Overlay) that can occur in conjunction with the eight transitions (2003: 27–35). I expand that approach by eliminating transition types and instead categorizing inferences entirely in combinational terms.

In addition to recurrence discussed in the previous chapter, juxtaposed images can trigger at least ten inference types. An additional classification of transition types would require mapping every possible combination, producing dozens of subcategories. Such a list would be both ineffectively long and conceptually redundant. Though analyzed most often between contiguously juxtaposed images, the same inferences can be triggered by temporally and distantly juxtaposed images, too. Inferences might also involve more than two images, with information retained from a range of previous images understood in combination when a viewer encounters a new image. Braiding is an example, but inferences are triggered by more than discursive resemblance and so extend beyond visual rhymes and motifs.

1. Discursive and Diegetic

Juxtapositional inferences divide into two general categories: the non-representational relationships between physical marks, and the story-world relationships triggered by the representational qualities of those marks. When images are non-representational, inferences are discursive only. When images are representational, inferences are discursive and diegetic both. Each may be divided into overlapping but non-exclusive subcategories:

Spatial: images share a diegetic space.
Temporal: images share a diegetic timeline.
Causal: undepicted action occurs between depicted moments.
Embedded: one image is perceived as multiple images.
Non-sensory: differences between representational images do not represent
    sensory reality.
Associative: dissimilar images represent a shared subject.
Semi-continuous: discursively continuous but representationally non-continuous
    images are perceived as a single image.

These first seven are diegetic only and so discernible only through recognition of representational content. A non-representational image sequence produces none of these inferences. The next two can occur diegetically, discursively, or discursively only:

Continuous: images are perceived as a single image.
Match: otherwise dissimilar images share matching similarities.

While the subtypes of diegetic inferences are only discernible through analysis of the story world, discursive inferences must be analyzed at the level of the page. Purely discursive inferences involve only discursive marks understood in terms such as shapes and values without reference to representational content. Images that share color or line quality or compositional arrangement may produce a sense of relationship, and so the inferences are through discursive recurrence. A final type is not primarily a quality of image juxtaposition and so arguably is not a type of juxtapostional inferences but a recognition of the absence:

Linguistic: images relate primarily through accompanying text.

All combine for a range of effects.

Analyses of panel transitions typically focus on diegetic effects and so ignore image relationships that do not involve a viewer's mental concepts of objects, actions, settings, and events in a story world. Since the vast majority of works in the comics medium are representational, the diegetic emphasis is not unreasonable. It is even possible to discuss juxtapositional inferences in purely diegetic terms, placing discursive-only inferences in a separate category. Such an approach, however, would privilege diegesis and ignore the discursive qualities that produce it, creating a system of visual analysis that ironically de-emphasizes visual qualities in favor of mental constructs.

The next sections detail each inference type, with combined examples presented in the concluding section.

2. Spatiotemporal

A juxtaposition of representational images leads viewers to evaluate their spatiotemporal relationships, producing both spatial and temporal inferences. It is sometimes difficult to separate the two, since time and space are inextricably connected. The passage of time requires a location in order to be experienced, and for a location to exist, it must in some sense exist in time.

McCloud's closure is exclusively spatiotemporal. Following McCloud's analysis of a comics page as a temporal map of the represented world, Dean details a "tri-partite division" of closure into transitions that are temporal only, spatial only, or both temporal and spatial (2000: 202). Christiansen argues that temporal qualities are more significant than spatial ones and posits three film-derived "forms of connectedness related to temporal continuity" (2000: 116). Cohn, who posits a narrative grammar system of panel types that runs parallel to and helps organize the information involved in mental model construction, categorizes those panels by defining the "interaction" of elements within a story world that includes "setting" and so implicitly assumes diegetic spatiotemporality (2016: 70). As Groensteen observes: "it is the continuity attributed to the fictional world that allows me to effortlessly fill in the gaps of the narration" (2007: 11).

Spatial inferences involve a shared diegetic space, no matter the distance between the depicted locations. Setting typically refers to a single location, but the parameters are undefined since a room, house, city, continent, planet, or solar system might be a setting depending on the spatial scope of the story. At one extreme, two images may depict the same area viewed in the same angle, proximity, and framing, sometimes with virtual if not exact repetition (discussed in the previous chapter as "stammering"). Diegetically nothing may change, but discursively viewers move their gaze to the second image, contradicting the illusion of unbroken viewing.

At the other extreme, a second image has little or no discursive resemblance to the first, requiring viewers to infer that it still represents a spatially related area. That area may be of the same space but from a dissimilar angle or proximity, or it may be of some previously undepicted but nearby area. Alternatively, a second image may be of a distant area but still spatially related, producing what McCloud would likely term scene-to-scene transitions, "which transport us across significant distances of time and space" (1993: 71). Cohn analyzes these kinds of inferences in terms of "spatial structure" (2019: 10). Though a scene change does not have to involve a change in location, it is not necessary to know the spatial and temporal boundaries of a scene to experience spatiotemporal inferences. The spatial relationship between the representational content of two images may also be ambiguous, though typically that ambiguity is resolved after a subsequent juxtaposition. In Marcelo D'Salete's *Angola Janga*, the image of two faces is juxtaposed with an abstract pattern, producing no spatial (or likely any) inference; in the third image, the pattern is revealed to be carved into a tree that the two figures are looking at, producing a retroactive spatial inference connecting the first two images (2019: 34).

Temporal inferences are ingrained into the conventions of panel transitions with a common default assumption articulated paradoxically by McCloud in a three-panel sequence: 1) "This panel and this panel alone represents the present," 2) "Any panel before this one—that last one, for instance—represents the past," 3) "Likewise, all panels still to come—this next panel, for instance—represents the future" (1993: 104). McCloud's claim conflates diegesis and discourse. The viewing of not-yet-viewed images are in the viewer's presumed future and the viewing of the already-viewed images are in the viewer's past, with no necessary relationship to any diegetic time represented in the images. In Richard McGuire's 2014 *Here*, insets and background images present a single and constant diegetic setting depicted from a single and constant viewpoint, altering only the temporal moment of each image as identified by a year placed in the top left corner of each frame. Images represent moments separated by years, decades, centuries, or millennia, and juxtapositions move forward or backward in time, undermining McCloud's assumptions about time.

If provided no contradictory representational content, a viewer familiar with the comics medium will likely assume that a discursive movement between images corresponds with a diegetic movement forward in time, despite differences in corresponding durations or if the image content is temporally ambiguous. McCloud's aspect-to-aspect transitions could contradict that norm, since "time seems to stand still," requiring a viewer "to assemble a single moment using scattered fragments" (1993: 79). Though McCloud's examples show some temporal ambiguity, interpreting each as either aspect-to-aspect or moment-to-moment still requires temporal inferencing since the content of separate images are understood to share some duration. An inference that images are simultaneous is temporal, too. In *The Wicked + The Divine*, Kieron Gillen and Jamie McKelvie establish that four characters are about to snap their fingers at the same instant, before depicting each hand snapping in its own panel (2016: ch. 1, p. 6).

Cohn repeats McCloud's main transition types, distinguishing "Moment Transition" with time as "the dominant factor of change" and "Action Transition" where actions seem to "drive time" (2003: 29–30), reproducing McCloud's categorical ambiguity. In his current work, Cohn considers all instances of time to be inferred qualities. He identifies examples of transitions with "non-temporal relationships" because there is "no apparent time shift" (2010: 139). Spatiotemporal indeterminacy is also separate, since something in the images triggers but does not resolve the expectation of a relationship. In Illustration 5.1, Sophia Foster-Dimino's *Sex Fantasy* includes a one-page image-text of two figures on a bicycle with the words "I'll pick you up from the airport" contiguously juxtaposed with an image-text on the facing page of a repeating figure reading and then crying with the words "I feel like I know you already" (2017: n.p.). The figures on each page appear to represent three different individuals, therefore suggesting that "I" and "you" on each page refer to a different "I" and "you." The textual and visual similarities within a multi-page sequence, however, suggest that the two image-texts are related, presumably sharing a diegetic world. But do they follow chronologically or are they simultaneous moments? Could the three drawn and two or four textually referenced characters interact in a shared but undrawn location, or does each image-text occur in its own isolated world? The indeterminacy suspends spatiotemporal inferencing. Since text is also involved, the effects involve more than juxapostional inferences (a topic discussed in Chapter 7).

3. Causal

Spatiotemporal inferences often include undepicted actions that are understood to take place between depicted moments. Single images can imply actions, too, but when the effect involves two images, the juxtapositional inference is causal. Though he does not designate causality as its own type, Stainbrook uses it to analyze two of McCloud's transitions: "A distinction between Moment-to moment and Action-to-action closures must depend therefore on a reader's ability to perceive a causative element that is not, or not always, depicted directly in the visual medium" (2000: 73).

In two panels from *Aya* in Illustration 5.1, Clément Oubrerie draws an infant playing on a kitchen floor as the mother and grandmother stand at the kitchen table. In the next image, the mother is holding the child (Abouet and Oubrerie 2015: 187). Though more than one inference is possible, the simplest and so most likely is that the mother reached down and lifted the child. Temporal inferences are often a product of causal inferences because time is visually represented through changes in a recurrent subject. In *Anya's Ghost*, after a character has fallen into an empty well, Vera Brosgol draws the character's perspective of the opening twice, first with the sun partially visible on the right and the angle of its light striking the left half of the wall, and next with the sun partially visible on the left and the angle of its light striking the right half of the wall (2011: 24). Viewers likely infer that the sun has moved over the course of several hours. The images would also allow a day and several hours or a week and several hours to have passed, but viewers are most likely to infer the shortest allowable interval unless additional details contradict that interpretation (an effect of event structure discussed in the next chapter).

4. Embedded

Spatiotemporality can also lead viewers to divide a single image according to its diegetic content. McCloud describes this as "one panel, operating as several panels" (1993: 97), but he does not include it among his panel transition types. Hatfield calls the effect "synchronism, in which a single panel represents a sequence of events occurring at a different 'times,'" and also an "*un*divided polyptych," meaning "a single, undivided frame that represents an extended span of time synchronistically" (2005: 52, 53). However, an undivided polyptych is oxymoronic, and embedded images do not necessarily represent different moments. Cohn identifies transitions that occur within "the greater conceptual framework of the single image" and so "without any formal space separating each conceptual element" as "Embedded" (2003: 34). He also distinguishes "Overlay," where "transitions occur both to the linear strand of panels as well as to an overlaid image on top of them" (2003: 35). Since an overlay may be understood as partially embedded, I combine the categories and adopt Cohn's first term. The opposite of Gestalt effects, an embedded inference is the perception and division of a discursively continuous image into multiple diegetic images.

As discussed in Illustration 3.4, Emma Rios's *Pretty Deadly* includes a complexly embedded image. Although the seven overlapping figures are discursively unified, they

Illustration 5.1 From Foster-Dimino's *Sex Fantasy*, Abouet and Oubrerie's *Aya*, and Carroll's "His Face All Red."

diegetically represents only two characters depicted at multiple moments (DeConnick and Rios 2014: ch. 3, p. 19). Because the image is discursively unified, it is also diegetically ambiguous: a different mental model could produce a reading in which sets of identically dressed characters are interacting simultaneously (a scenario no more far-fetched than a man battling a sword-wielding personification of death). In Illustration 5.1, Emily Carroll uses the same technique with a more common effect in "His Face All Red" when a character climbs down a rope into a pit. Although Carrol draws the character three times within a single column-shaped panel—at the top of the rope, at the middle, and at the bottom—viewers likely infer there to be only one recurrent character represented at three different moments (2014: 24). Sir Anthony van Dyck's *Charles I in Three Positions* in Illustration 4.3 also embeds three distinct angles of the same recurrent subject observed presumably at three different moments.

Such diegetic division is in one sense the opposite of McCloud's closure, since instead of "observing the parts but perceiving the whole," viewers observe the whole but perceive the parts. Cohn uses "Divisional" to denote a subset of "Aspect Transition" that produces Gestalt closure inferences (2003: 31), but he also applies it to an "Embedded Transition" where "a figure moves through a single background, but is shown several times in the image" (2003: 29). Embedded inferencing applies to the second case only and typically involves spatiotemporality and recurrent subjects. For Rios, viewers understand the image to be a sequence of chronological events viewed from shifting perspectives. For Carroll, viewers experience similar temporal inferences, while the background setting is spatially continuous as if viewed from a single angle and proximity.

5. Non-sensory

The above subcategories typically imply a diegetic world shared by multiple characters. Images may instead represent the internal experience of a single character. As discussed in the previous chapter, Duncan distinguishes between "sensory diegetic images" that show "the physical reality of the world of the story," and "non-sensory diegetic images" that "show the internal reality of the characters" (2012: 44–5). Juxtapositions between non-sensory images and between sensory and non-sensory images may not follow the same inferential expectations as sensory-to-sensory juxtapositions, allowing for leaps that ignore spatiotemporal logic. Because the subsection "Kisses" in David B.'s *Epileptic* begins with the caption, "Dream from the night of 26 September 1999" (2005: 354), a juxtaposition of images in which a horse inexplicably appears in a bedroom produces no confusion if viewers do not attempt to explain the appearance of the horse through a causal inference. Such non-sensory effects might produce no inferences other than those implied about the consciousness selecting and juxtaposing the image content.

Non-sensory images are not limited to internal experience. Dave McKean changes image style multiple times in *Cages*, often without suggesting anything about a character's mental perspective. In Illustration 5.2, a cat looks through an apartment window, with the interior and exterior spaces rendered in different styles and mediums regardless of viewpoints (2016). Despite their contradictory qualities, all of the images are diegetic, requiring non-sensory inferences to understand their stylistic differences as either discursive only or as expressing connotations through non-literal details.

Non-sensory inferences also occur between sensory and non-sensory images. Lynd Ward's 1932 woodcut novel *Wild Pilgrimage* includes six subsections that appear to depict a character's desires. While the non-sensory nature is suggested by their sometimes fantastical qualities, the transitions between non-sensory and sensory are communicated by contradictory representational content. In one image the male protagonist is shirtless and embracing an unclothed female character, and in the next he and the woman are both fully clothed and she is shoving him away (2010: 101–2). Because the juxtaposition is non-sensory, the differences require no causal inferences; instead, the first image is understood as imagined and the second as actually occurring. The non-sensory images are also printed in orange ink to contrast the black ink of the sensory panels, and by the second or third subsection, the color change alone may trigger a non-sensory inference.

6. Associative

Abel and Madden augment McCloud's six types of panel transitions with a seventh, which they term "symbolic": "a panel that takes place within the storyline is preceded by a panel that depicts something non-literal, in order to make a point about a character's state of mind or situation via a visual metaphor" (2008: 44). Cohn similarly coined "cognable" to describe transitions involving "visual information outside of a mental environment" (2003: 29), but associative inferences are not necessarily non-sensory.

Though a visual metaphor may also occur within a single image, when it involves juxtaposition to establish the relationship between a subject's sensory and non-sensory qualities, the inferences are both non-sensory and associative. In *The Oven*, Sophie Goldstein draws a character seated in the backseat of a car after he has said goodbye to his estranged and pregnant wife; on the facing page shown in Illustration 5.2, his silhouette dissolves into a stream of insects moving toward the horizon (2015: 70–1). The juxtaposition associates two dissolving subjects, the couple's relationship and the insect figure, which could be interpreted as representing the husband's internal experience, or it could be read independently of his consciousness. Associative inferences can also link sensory images. In *Watchmen*, Dave Gibbons draws a smashing pumpkin to imply the damage inflicted to a murder victim's head (1987: ch. 8, p. 28). Unlike Goldstein's dissolving figure, the pumpkin exists within the diegetic world in the same location and moment. A similar sequence in Jim Steranko's *Nick Fury, Agent of S.H.I.E.L.D.* ends with the image of a gun in a holster implying sexual intercourse. Shown as minor background details in an earlier panel, the gun and holster take on metaphorical significance when later juxtaposed with an image of two characters embracing (2014: 267).

If two images produce no inferences, then the juxtaposition is a non-sequitur. This is uncommon both diegetically and discursively because juxtapositions draw attention to similarities. As Abel and Madden explain: "given our basic human desire to make

Illustration 5.2 From McKean's *Cages*, Goldstein's *The Oven*, and Abel's *La Perdida*.

sense of a series of panels, you'll find it's surprisingly difficult to create a true non-sequitur transition. Your reader will perform all kinds of contortions to make sense of it, and before you know it, they'll turn it into a symbolic transition" (2008: 45).

7. Continuous and Semi-continuous

Continuous inferences provide an answer to Mikkonen's question: "when can a group of images be perceived as one image?" (2017: 12). In contrast to embedded inferences creating the perception of a single image as multiple images, continuous inferences create the perception of multiple images as one image. This effect aligns with "closure" as defined in Gestalt psychology, but because McCloud uses "closure" to describe all juxtapositional relationships, using "closure inferences" as a type of juxtapositional inference, while accurate, would further conflate terms. I have previously suggested omitting capitalization and using "gestalt" (Gavaler and Beavers 2018: 20), but "continuous" seems less likely to produce further confusion, in part because its meaning is self-evident.

Discursively, continuous inferencing produces an impression of a visual element partly obscured by a visual ellipsis. Though two lines are separated by an undrawn space, a viewer perceives them as a single line. Hatfield refers to the effect as a subset of "split panels" that "are a means of parsing simultaneous action into successive frames—effectively turning one moment, one panel, into a sequence of two or more," which he distinguishes from "split panels" that are "true polyptychs, showing a single figure moving across a continuous background" (2005: 56). Both involve continuous inferences. In the first, all elements are continuous, also producing the temporal inference of simultaneity. In the second, viewers experience continuous effects for only the setting, as the recurrent subject moves through it. Because juxtapostional inferences do not require panels, "split panels" is an imperfect term. As mentioned, Cohn terms a juxtaposition that involves continuous inferences a "Divisional Aspect Transition" because the image is divided—though continuous operates oppositely, allowing a viewer to comprehend divided parts as a unified whole (2003: 31, 36). Molotiu's "sequential dynamism" with its panel-to-panel visual rhythms is also a form of continuous inferencing (2012). Diegetically, continuous effects produce spatial inferences in which two representational images appear to be viewed from a continuous perspective that corresponds with the actually continuous perspective of a viewer scanning across directly contiguous images. Though the inference is unification, Groensteen terms the effect "fragmentation," where "the page would consist of a single large image occupying the whole surface artificially divided up by the superimposition of the grid" (2013: 17). Artist Stuart McMillen calls "the 'broken into panels' technique" a kind of "punctuation" that creates an "extra 'beat'" and "encourages the reader to linger a little longer on each" portion (2019).

When a visual field is partially subdivided, with some elements appearing to continue between images and some not, attention to the continuous elements will create the effect of a single, subdivided image, while attention to the discontinuous elements will create the effect of separate images juxtaposed. Both may be present simultaneously, and visual elements may be categorized by figure and ground or other dividing principles. In Illustration 5.2, Jessica Abel draws a three-panel column dividing a figure standing in front of department store mirrors in *La Perdida*. While the setting and a partial foregrounded figure positioned at the edge of the frames produce a continuous inference, the centered, middle-ground figure wears different clothes and stands in different poses in each frame, producing the temporal and causal inferences that the character has changed clothes between panels and returned to pose before the mirrors again (2006: 126). Creating a temporal inference between two images inferred as continuous without a recurrent subject appearing in both requires additional temporal markers. In *Panther*, Brecht Evens draws the left half of a house with a moon in the dark sky above it and then the right half of the same house with a sun in the pink sky above it (2016: ch. 1, p. 2).

The continuous impression of an interrupted line is a discursive effect. When the line is representational, continuous inferences create the appearance of interrupted diegetic content, but the interruption may be understood at only the discursive level if the diegetic content of the two images is not continuous. Semi-continuous inferences create discursive connections between discontinuous diegetic content. If the trajectory of a line within one image visually aligns with the trajectory of a line in a contiguous image, a viewer may experience the two lines as a single line–even though representationally the two lines are unrelated. At the discursive level, continuous and semi-continuous inferences are indistinguishable, but semi-continuous create discursive shapes across images that appear to share diegetic qualities even though the images do not exist in a story world together.

Semi-continuous inferences can produce a unifying effect at the diegetic level. The cover of Kevin C. Pyle's *Take What You Can Carry* features half of each of its two main characters' faces arranged side by side and divided by a vertical strip containing the book title. The single discursive face represents no single diegetic face, but the discursive relationship between the two halves suggests a diegetic relationship between the two characters, who, despite the time and distance dividing them, are understood to be unified in a psychological or thematic sense. In Illustration 5.3, Charles Burns applies the technique in *Black Hole* as two characters are diegetically understood to be facing each other, but discursively their juxtaposed half-faces form a single face, creating a paradoxical visual connection at the moment the characters experience estrangement (2005: ch. 4, p. 14). "This conjoining," observes Miodrag, "disturbs our reading, momentarily bewildering our conceptualization of these panels as traditional (or realist) progressive moments and contributing to the creeping uncertainty and unearthliness that the entire text inspires" (2013: 211).

8. Match

Hayward explains the film term: "Match cuts link two shots . . . related in form, subject or action," creating "a spatial–visual logic between" them (2000: 67, 78). Orson Welles makes extensive use of the technique in the opening of his 1941 *Citizen Kane*, first dissolving from a chain-link fence to a similarly angled ornate gate, and then maintaining the bright rectangle of a lit window in the same screen position during a succession of dissolves. Stanley Kubrick's 1968 *2001: A Space Odyssey* features a centuries-leaping match cut between a bone thrown by a human ancestor and an orbiting spaceship, connecting the two similarly shaped and similarly framed objects and implying that the spaceship is the culmination of the first action.

Works in the comics form can employ no cuts, so the inference type is distinct, requiring viewers to recognize a repeated subject–frame relationship between two static images. Unlike in film, where the effect is "seamless continuity (we do not 'see' the cut)" (Hayward 2000: 67), contiguously juxtaposed images require eye movement instead of the transformation of a fixed spatial field. Temporal juxtaposition combined with partial discursive recurrence can produce film-like match inferences. The effect is rare in books since images must be printed on only one side of each two-page spread, as they are in Lynd Ward's 1937 *Vertigo*. An image of a train crossing a bridge is followed by an image of palm trees and a figure reclining on a beach lounge chair. While through spatial, temporal, and causal inferences a viewer may conclude that the figure has traveled by train to a beach resort, the initial relationship between the two images is the discursive resemblance of the bridge arch in the first image and the pair of curving trees in the second. Diegetically, the two are unrelated, but the discursive match links them.

Mikkonen may be the first to apply the cinematic technique to comics, identifying:

an analogous technique to the cinematic match cut to indicate a simultaneous change of scene and/or temporal frame: transitional panels that lead from one scene or temporal frame to another through some visual detail in the image (a spot on the floor, a tile on the wall, hands holding a tool/weapon, fragment of a paintings, and so on), or the effect of zooming into a detail that "connects" somewhere else, thereby establishing a *graphic match* between the panels.

2017: 41

The technique is not limited to changes in locations and time frames and can occur between any two images regardless of representational content. When a match does not involve a change of subjects, Groensteen calls the effect "stammering." The same subject repeats both diegetically and discursively, maintaining the same relationships to the frame and the implied viewer. Images require a change in subject to create match inferences since a repeated subject and setting would simply produce recurrence. A match inference also implies an associative relationship between the two subjects, connotationally linking them. In Illustration 5.3, Yeon-sik Hong's 2020 *Umma's Table* produces match inferences between two successive two-page spreads, the first of the narrator as a child breastfeeding, the second of the adult narrator leaning over his elderly mother in her hospital bed. Looking ahead to Chapter 7, "Mourning Science" in Illustration 7.1 is composed of six images, each with a figure's head at its center, producing match inferences for each juxtaposition.

Illustration 5.3 From Burns's *Black Hole*, Hong's *Umma's Table*, and Shapton's *Was She Pretty?*

9. Linguistic

Two images may relate primarily at a linguistic level if the text supersedes visual inferences. In such a case, the primary relationship is between two segments of text, not between two images. Chapter 7 explores image-texts in depth, but here I limit discussion to a single key inference: that the images relate not to each other directly but to their accompanying text and so do not trigger any of the above types of juxtapositional inferences.

In *Was She Pretty?*, Leanne Shapton includes text on each left-hand page and a drawing on each right-hand page. In most cases the text states a fact about a character's ex-lover, and the image appears to illustrate the statement. In Illustration 5.3, "Owen was Agnes's ex-boyfriend. He had introduced her as his 'friend' one too many times" appears opposite of a man drawn as if facing the reader (2016: 146–7). The next two-page spread features "Sarah was Michael's ex-girlfriend for ten years, but would eventually be his wife" and a drawing of a woman looking down in profile (2016: 148–9). The relationship between the two images, a man looking forward and a woman looking down, is primarily linguistic. Viewers know from the text that each is an ex-lover in a list of ex-lovers and need not relate the two images beyond the relationship established by the text. This would be so even if the text and image pairs appeared on the same pages or within traditional panel frames with both panels arranged on the same page. Stainbrook would describe each panel as containing "image-to-text cohesion" and their juxtaposition as "text-to-text cohesion" with no "image-to-image cohesion" (2016: 151). Without the text, the contiguously juxtaposed images might be experienced as non-sequiturs.

Linguistic inferences are prevalent in work that emphasize what McCloud terms a "word-specific" picture–word relationship, where images largely illustrate text (1993: 153). Lynda Barry's memoir *One! Hundred! Demons!* places text in the top half of each panel and images in the bottom half. Though a text-only reading of each sequence would be comprehensible, an image-only reading would not be. Cohn categorizes such a sequence under "Verb Dominance," "such as when text combines with purely illustrative image—as in newspapers, magazines, academic papers" (2003: 311).

10. Clarifying McCloud

McCloud's panel transition types may be understood as follows: moment-to-moment and action-to-action involve recurrent, spatial, and forward-moving temporal inferences. Aspect-to-aspect involves recurrent and spatial inferences, with possible ambiguity between simultaneous and forward-moving temporal inferences. Subject-to-subject involves spatial inferences, with possible ambiguity between simultaneous and forward-moving temporal inferences and probably no discursive inferences. Depending on the range of possible scene changes, scene-to-scene involves spatial and temporal inferences, possibly with no recurrence. And a non-sequitur, because it lacks all diegetic and discursive recurrence, produces no juxtapositional inferences—unless a viewer still experiences associative inferences and so partial recurrence.

As discussed above and as McCloud acknowledges, non-sequitur transitions are difficult to produce because juxtaposition encourages inferences. Looking back at Illustration 1.2, a reviewer who did not know that Vermeer's and Gentileschi's paintings are unrelated might draw a range of conclusions. Perhaps the content of the second image is described in the letter in the first image, making the second image the reading woman's mental experience of the written events. If so, the two images are temporally simultaneous, or, if the second image is understood as the actual event independent of the woman's imagining of it, the juxtaposition moves backward in time. Perhaps the letter instead is giving the woman instructions, and the second image is her imagining herself carrying them out, and so again is non-sensory, or is her actually carrying them after a significant forward leap in time. The woman would then be recurrent—an experience that may produce or be aided by a no-longer-coincidental discursive resemblance between Gentileschi's Judith and Vermeer's reading woman. Perhaps other viewers would draw other inferences, all of them due to juxtaposition.

Because so many combinational effects are possible, the categories offered here are not exhaustive. Future analysis or future artistic productions might reveal juxtapositional effects not accounted for here. Still, refining McCloud's closure as juxtapositional inferences and subdividing it into a range of types eliminates the term's ambiguity and provides a fuller lens for understanding sequenced images. I close the chapter by applying these inference types to close-viewings of four pages excerpted from works in the comics medium. Unlike McCloud's panel transitions which are limited to conceptually linear juxtapositions and Cohn's visual narrative grammar which is focused on conceptually linear sequences, the example pages involve multiple non-linear effects between directly and indirectly contiguously juxtaposed images. Since the analysis is of isolated pages, I refer minimally to content not directly represented and so will not refer to characters by name since no names appear on the pages themselves. These examples also preview the next chapter's discussion of image order, image viewing paths, and how image content produces the inferences that determine them.

Illustration 5.4, from Greg Rucka and J. H. Williams III's 2010 *Batwoman: Elegy*, demonstrates semi-continuous, non-sensory, spatial, continuous, temporal, and associative inferences.

The page divides into five sections. The black areas at the top and bottom function as caption boxes for writer and artist credits and so have no diegetic qualities, while the middle three sections combine to form the appearance of a figure's subdivided but otherwise continuous head as she speaks on a phone. That initial continuous effect turns semi-continuous when the seemingly continuous lines of hair from the eyes- and nose-framing panels align instead with the veil worn by an apparently different figure in the chin-framing panel. Viewers with prior subject knowledge would also recognize character-defining visual traits of two previously introduced characters and so understand that the red bangs and light skin tone in the eyes-framing panel contradict the literally white skin and lipstick pattern in the chin-framing panel.

The tone of the middle panel is ambiguous but is likely interpreted as a non-transparent use of color through non-sensory inferences. A viewer likely does not hypothesize that either woman's face has turned green or that there is any other diegetic explanation for the implied viewer's tinted perspective (since the phone is also green). Because there is no third implied character to ocularize the image, it could instead be understood as focalized through one of the two women's mental experience. Alternatively, the non-sensory color could be an aspect of image-narration alone, perhaps suggesting a transitional stage between the more distinctly character-defined panels above and below it. The non-sensory green might even suggest a merging of the two characters, creating an implied third entity that is neither but somehow both. If so,

Illustration 5.4 From Rucka and Williams's *Batwoman: Elegy.*

the role of non-sensory inference is crucial since the metaphorical effect violates a literal interpretation of the image.

Because the hair lines and curls are continuous with the eyes-framing panel, the content of the nose-framing panel appears to be aligned spatially with it. As a result, the initial continuous effect returns (or remains depending on the viewer) because the black zigzagging line produces no diegetic division. One of the two white oval speech containers appear within each panel, with a white linking strip and a pointer directed inside the center image, further suggesting the two panels are spatially unified despite their discursive color difference. Also, the first three black speech containers have no pointers and are scalloped, presumably to evoke the effect of a disembodied voice heard through a phone, but the fourth container is oval-shaped with a pointer directed at the lower figure's mouth, further suggesting only two diegetic spaces despite three discursively distinct areas on the page. Only the second black zigzagging line indicates a spatial leap to a different location. Though viewers know little or nothing about either setting, a spatial inference establishes that two distinct locations are involved, one for the eyes- and nose-framing panels, and a second for the chin-framing panel. Because the two characters are talking on a phone, the two locations are also presumably remote relative to each other.

In addition to continuous, the first zigzagging line produces a temporal inference, though the effect is primarily the result of the sequenced speech containers embedded in the panels. Without words implying the passages of time required to speak them within the diegesis, a viewer would likely understand the three sections of the semi-continuous face to represent a single moment, indicating two women holding the same pose in two different locations simultaneously. The speech containers instead produce a zigzagging but always downward-moving reading path that produces the same or similar temporal leaps between the subsections of the combined face.

While not necessarily involving juxtapositional inferences, the shapes are themselves significant, because viewers with prior subject knowledge may recognize the black zigzag as associated with the top figure. The black curling shapes protruding from the margins are similarly associated with the lower figure. Though, like the author credits and framing effects generally, the shapes do not exist literally within the diegesis, they do have representational qualities and so may a trigger associative inference if recognized. If all other representational content were eliminated, the page would still feature the interaction of these two character-linked design motifs, which by association could represent the interaction of the two characters diegetically.

A range of interpretations is open, but discursively the two sets of shapes are mostly distant, with the zigzags occupying the center of the page and the curls occupying the corners. The viewing path produced by the speech containers, including the last container apparently spoken by a third character from out of frame, ends in the bottom right corner where the curls are most prominent, including their extension into the non-diegetic area of the artist credit where the motif switches to red as though continuing from the red letters of the artist's name. If the curls are interpreted as having their own temporal sequence or are linked to the diegetic flow of time in the face subsections, then the curls are growing. Interpreted associatively, the relationship between the shape motifs parallels the diegetic struggle between the two pictured figures, suggesting the lower figure has gained an advantage—an interpretation that aligns with and so reinforces the content of the dialogue.

Illustration 5.5, from Dennis Hopeless and Javier Rodriguez's 2016 *Spider-Woman: Baby Talk*, demonstrates continuous, spatial, temporal, and semi-continuous inferences.

Though the page features a 3 × 3 grid, five of the panels produce a unified image through continuous inferences. Numbered by Z-path viewing, panels two, five, six, seven, and eight are a single discursive and diegetic unit. Because that unit is the dominant feature of the page, it likely encourages a viewer to apprehend the page as a whole first rather than beginning in the top left corner as the viewing norms of a 3 × 3 grid would prompt. The centered "KOOF" art in panel five also likely attracts a viewer's eye to the center of the page and so to the center of the continuous unit first. Switching to Z-path viewing requires some loosening of the continuous effect to apprehend each panel individually. Even though it contains only an ellipse and so indicates no spoken sound, the presence of a speech container in the top left panel encourages a Z-path by drawing a viewer's eye to its starting point. The sequence then follows the comic medium's spatiotemporal expectations.

In terms of spatial inferences, the setting is minimal and is represented only by an undifferentiated green background discernable in most panels. The green is likely perceived as transparently literal, even if its slight discursive variations are not. The discursively white background in the bottom left panel, however, is likely diegetically erased or, if noticed, understood non-transparently through non-sensory inference. Since the substitution of white for green probably suggests nothing diegetically, it likely does not trigger associative inferences. The white then is only for discursive effect.

Spatial inferencing also explains the differences between each pair of panels as the result of the differences in the position of the implied viewer in relation to the central and unmoving figure. The first juxtaposition involves a change in the implied viewer's proximity and angle. The second juxtaposition involves both, too, but while the proximity of the third image follows the trajectory of the first two images (the implied viewer is nearing the figure), the angle instead reverts back to the forward-facing view of the first panel. Because such movements do not correspond to the movements of an implied character, the spatial inference suggests no ocularization. But the final image could be ocularized by either of the two characters present in the backgrounds of panels six and seven. Even if non-ocularized, the implied viewer has rotated 180 degrees, explaining why the central figure is no longer facing forward. Alternatively, the figure has turned herself around as inferred through a causal inference. If so, she is now facing the two background characters, who, due to framing, do not appear in the image. I suspect most viewers would interpret the figure's ending posture as speaking over her shoulder to the characters behind her, and so no causal inferences would be involved. If the figure did turn around, a viewer would experience a different kind of temporal inference, one indicating a slightly greater period of time to account for the implied action.

Temporal inferencing is also necessary for parsing the five-panel continuous unit. The unit, because it appears more than once in the linear panel progression, represents more than one diegetic moment despite being discursively recurrent. Calling the

Illustration 5.5 From Hopeless and Rodriguez's *Spider-Woman: Baby Talk*.

combined continuous unit "A," the linear viewing sequence is: 1, A(2), 3, 4, A(5–6), A(7), A(8), 9.

First, note that temporal inference combines panels five and six into a two-panel continuous unit within the larger five-panel unit because the mid-air position of the flying fragments indicates the same moment. The space between panels five and six therefore divides neither spatially nor temporally. The space between panels seven and eight does divide temporally because the placement of a speech container within each segments time. Similarly, the space between four and five is temporal because of the action of the figure crushing the object (identified in the story as a phone). The change in the color of her glove from red to white is presumably the result of the electrical discharge from the crushed phone. The three changes (untightened to tightened fist, red to white glove, whole to shattered phone) all produce the temporal inference.

Temporal inferences also challenge the transparency of the apparent five-panel continuous image. Though panels A(2) and A(5–6) appear to represent a unified image and so a unified moment, panel four establishes that the phone is not yet broken during the moment of A(2), meaning the effect between A(2) and A(5–6) is not continuous but semi-continuous. It only appears to be a single continuous image, but the corresponding position of her fingers during the moment of A(2) could not match. In the first panel, which is temporally closer to A(1) than to A(5–6), the figure has not formed a fist yet since one of her fingers is higher on the phone. Temporal inferences produced by the speech containers also requires that A(7) and A(8) represent different moments from the rest of the apparent continuous unit, producing instead a semi-continuous unit of a single, stationary figure viewed from the same angle and proximity, but subdivided into four temporal units.

Illustration 5.6, from Matt Fraction and David Aja's 2012 *Hawkeye: My Life as a Weapon*, demonstrates continuous, spatial, temporal, causal, and associative inferences.

Uniform vertical and horizontal negative spaces divide the page into twelve rectangular but otherwise irregular images. The presence of words from a continuous statement ("Okay—this looks bad . . . Don't die.") placed inside caption boxes in the top left corner and the bottom right area encourage a general top left to bottom right viewing, but the norms of either Z-path rows or N-path columns are disrupted by the image arrangement and image content, producing no clear viewing order or even a method for naming images discursively. If viewers do begin with the first captioned word, they likely switch to apprehending the page as a whole, focusing first on the largest panel and the dominant content of the two figures diving underwater as bullets speed past them. Because the bullets' paths through the water follow the same lines as those in the top left corner, continuous inferences unite the panels a single unit, even though they share only corners and no borders. After closer inspection, the bottom left panel likely joins the same continuous unit.

The bullet trajectory lines in the top right corner also follow roughly the same pattern, so a viewer's eye may be drawn there next. Spatial inferencing establishes a more distant implied viewer since the bullet lines (which are through air rather than water and so literal only if understood as a kind of blur) and the figures are smaller. The contrast in distance blocks the continuous effect otherwise encouraged by the layout, since the top right panel content is also "above" the diegetic content of the larger panel

Illustration 5.6 From Fraction and Aja's *Hawkeye: My Life as a Weapon*.

below it discursively. Since the two are viewed from similar angles, it is only the difference of proximity that divides them diegetically. That almost continuous effect is further suggested by the near alignment of the pool edges in the top corner panels, which is itself heightened by the placement of a horizontal negative space between the middle panels in the same row, creating the discursive illusion of an intermediary step between the differing representations of the pool edge.

The second panel along the left margin also features a similar pattern of bullet trajectories, but spatial inferencing again divides the panel from the continuous unit, this time through an implied viewer placed in contrastingly close proximity to the bullets. Two other panels in the top left region stand apart discursively because of the accenting use of yellow. The two are also diegetically linked because they feature the guns firing the bullets. Diegetically, the second panel along the top margin belongs above and to the left of the first panel—a mental rearrangement that a viewer experiences through spatial inferences. The content of the second yellow-dominated panel is also diegetically "below" the discursively higher panel, but with the same change in proximity of the implied viewer as the panel abutting it, so that the bullets in the water and the bullet shells in the air are similar sizes. The two yellow panels also produce their own two-panel viewing path that cuts diagonally across the opposite diagonals of both the paths of the bullets and the reading path of the captions.

The seven panels described so far could occur simultaneously. The smallest remaining panel, the lone square positioned near the center of the page but grouped with the close-up panels, appears to represent a similarly close view of churning water and so is also likely understood to occur at the same moment. Four images remain. Two are ambiguous because their content is not overtly related, and the other two produce temporal inferences distinct from the rest of the page.

First, the figure in a bikini from the top right panel recurs in a lower left panel; instead of being struck by a bullet and falling from a standing position, the figure is floating face down in the water. The diegetic trajectory of the figure's previous falling posture aligns spatiotemporally with the body's later position in the pool, producing a causal inference. The juxtaposition also requires a new implied viewer position situated on the other side of the pool and so opposite the implied viewer of the other images. The apparent stillness of the figure and the water suggest a similar temporal leap to a later moment well after the action depicted in the surrounding images. The recurrent figure also creates a two-panel viewing path that echoes the path between the two yellow-dominant panels that appear discursively "before" them if a viewer is attempting a general top left to bottom right direction. The second pair of panels are more discursively distant to each other than the first pair, but in the same diagonal relationship, and so their placements also echo the widening trajectories of the bullets in the continuous unit.

The final image in the bottom right corner features the recurrent figure of the diver discursively above it, producing the spatiotemporal inference that he is no longer descending into the water from the force of his dive but has now slowed. Though his arms are framed out of the image, they appear to be at his sides. The temporal inference would divide the two images by roughly seconds. This means that the "last" discursive image on the page is not the "last" diegetic image because the previously described panel containing the floating corpse would follow it temporally.

Finally, two of the panels feature graphic designs surrounded by uniformly black areas that seem disconnected from the diegetic events, in part because they do not suggest the illusion of three-dimensionality. Viewers with prior subject knowledge will recognize the higher panel's spiral pattern as the symbol of the story's villain featured on his hat, producing an associative inference. Viewers without prior knowledge will be introduced to the symbol and character six pages later, applying the associative effect retroactively. The juxtaposition of the spiral icon beside the image of the firing guns may suggest that they are being fired either by the villain or, since there are multiple guns, on his behalf. A lower left panel contains another ambiguous icon, also later revealed to be associated with another villain employed by the first for similar foreshadowing.

Illustration 5.7, the first page of Ta-Nehisi Coates and Daniel Acuna's 2019 *Black Panther*, demonstrates embedded, non-sensory, spatial, temporal, and linguistic inferences.

The page is divided ambiguously. The central kneeling figure appears to occupy the foreground with three pillar-like images positioned as if diegetically behind him. This impression is challenged by the presence of a separate set of background details of rocks and vegetation that seem to exist spatially with the figure but not with the rectangular images. Those naturalistic background details also extend beyond the left and right edges of the rectangles, ending in unframed vertical edges and fading into an unframed bottom edge. The rectangular images instead have black frame lines separated by white negative spaces visible behind the figure.

Assuming a viewer rejects the impression of a spatiotemporally unified image, the pseudo-depth effects produce an embedded inference, dividing the foregrounded figure from the rectangularly shaped images that are only discursively "behind" him. The interpretation is aided by differences in color. The foregrounded figure and setting are brighter than the subdued colors in each of the three rectangular images. The subdued colors are likely understood metaphorically since the image content appears to be memories focalized by the kneeling figure. Non-sensory inferences explain the color differences as psychological and so non-literal.

Spatial inferencing establishes that each rectangular image is occurring in a unique setting, because, in addition to color differences, each has a distinct implied viewer positioned in a different proximity and angle to the centered subject. The four settings have no clear relationships between them and so produce no further spatial inferences.

A temporal inference likely identifies the unframed foregrounded image as occurring in the present moment, but the temporal order of the three remembered images is ambiguous. Though viewing norms prompt a discursive left-to-right movement through diegetic time, the arrangement may not encourage that assumption. If not, it may be due to the embedded effect superseding the background juxtapositions by encouraging an atypical reading path. If the centered foregrounded image is identified as A and the rectangular images as 1–3, the viewing path may be: A, 1, A, 2, A, 3. The effect of the three muted figures looking at and addressing the foregrounded figure reinforces this impression. Temporally then, the sequence moves back and forth from the present to moments in the past remembered by the figure in the present moment. Since the experience of memory is temporally ambiguous—recalling a

Illustration 5.7 From Coates and Acuna's *Black Panther*.

memory can be instantaneous and so unrelated to the period of time that passes within a remembered event—the foregrounded image may represent a single present moment as three memories flow through the figure simultaneously. Alternatively, the single image represents multiple moments, albeit fleetingly brief.

Assuming the images are memories, the implied viewer is the foregrounded character, making the images focalized in the foregrounded image's present moment and ocularized by the same character in the three past moments. If so, the figure is represented four times, once overtly and three times indirectly through spatial inference. Because the subjects in the remembered images appear to be looking at the foregrounded character, the three implied recurrences of the character occupy the same discursive area of the page, including through the illusion of three dimensions produced by the paradoxical combination of four contradictory diegetic spaces. Analyzed discursively, the three remembered subjects form a half circle around the foregrounded figure's rounded back. The foregrounded figure is literally and so metaphorically surrounded by his memories. Each remembered figure is also centered in relation to the vertical edges of its frame, creating a partial match effect.

The rectangular images are also linked through a linguistic inference, in which the content of the words rather than the content of the images is primarily related. Each image includes one white oval speech container directed toward its subject, and the statements relate as expressions of rejection and loss communicated by a speaker. The thematic connections are an aspect of focalization, and the four black caption boxes reinforce that impression by implying the internal speech of the kneeling figure who is also dressed in black. Because the black containers are all positioned above the white speech containers, viewers could read them as two rows or in an up-and-down pattern reinforced by the negative spaces between the rectangular images that enclose each set of words. That up-and-down pattern also mirrors the larger images' relationship to the foregrounded image below them: black–black, white; black, white; black, white.

Having addressed the qualities of single juxtapositions in Chapters 3, 4, and 5, I next move to the qualities of multiple juxtapositions in Chapter 6.

6

Sequences

The case studies at the end of the previous chapter involved multiple contiguous juxtapositions. This chapter extends that analysis by clarifying two kinds of image order (discursive and sequential), two kinds of multiple-image content (sequences and sets), two kinds of viewing paths for contiguously juxtaposed images (directed and variable), and how image content creates relationships (hinges) between juxtaposed images that produce those orders and paths. The chapter then explores the possible distinctions between sequence and narrative, before applying the above analysis of image relationships to determine a six-part typology of the comics form. The last section then applies narrative to explain and constrain McCloud's closure—specifically spatiotemporal juxtapostional inferences—by offering an event-defined analysis of inferred content.

1. Image Order

Though fourteen of the seventeen definitions of comics excerpted in the Introduction include the words "sequence," "sequential," or "series," plus one equivalent phrase, "a certain order," their precise meanings contain an ambiguity. According to the *OED*, a sequence requires only "the following of one thing after another in succession," but as a verb, to sequence means "to arrange in a definite sequence or order." Is a "definite order" (a phrase echoed in McCloud's definition) the same as Abel and Madden's "certain order," and if so, what does it mean for an order to be definite and certain, since by implication an order could instead be indefinite and uncertain?

When unmodified by adjectives, "order" seems synonymous with "succession." Successive things follow the order of their succession, but are all successive things in a definite order? In one sense they are because they are a series, what the *OED* defines as a "number of discrete things ... following one another in succession over time, or in order of appearance or presentation." Is "order of appearance" a "definite" order? If you shuffle a deck of cards and turn each over in succession, the cards' order is their order of appearance. If you shuffle the deck and turn them over again, the cards will still be in their order of appearance, though almost certainly not in the same order. Since order of appearance changes, it presumably is not "definite." The entries of a dictionary are in a definite order: alphabetical order. If the entries were printed on separate cards, they could be turned over either in order or out of order. That definite order makes a dictionary a sequence and not simply a series. If a comic is defined formally as a sequence, it must have a single correct order in which the images are to be viewed. That implies that there are also wrong orders—or at minimum orders that do not produce the aesthetic result that the preferred order produces. Defining the comics form as serial images would mean order doesn't matter. Images could but would not need to follow in a single conceptually linear succession.

Though Inge uses "series" in his definition, it seems unlikely that he is intending the above distinction since the comics he describes are all sequences. Groensteen also uses "series" in his comics definition, but since he also uses the word elsewhere to designate groups of braided images that appear within "narrative sequences," it is not clear whether comics are necessarily narrative sequences or if the series that define what he considers "the central element of comics" also define the form (2007: 146, 18). Hatfield's explanation is clearer: "the author's task is to evoke an imagined sequence by creating a visual series" and "the reader's task is to translate the given series into a narrative sequence" (2005: 41). Since Hatfield's series/sequence dichotomy reflects the discourse/diegesis division, the distinction is not related to order, which would be the same for both. Mag Uidhir acknowledges the two terms' "precise, mathematical senses … *sequence* as a linearly ordered collection of elements, *series* as the sum of the elements of a sequence," but finds those definitions "wholly inadequate" because "not only are the ordering relations on standard examples of so-called serial works of art structurally more varied than this would allow but also in many cases there are multiple distinct ordering relations—not all of which are linear" (2013: n.p.).

Because "sequences" and "series" are sometimes synonyms, *Creating Comics* divides comics into "sequences" and "sets," the first being ordered, and the second unordered (Gavaler and Beavers 2021: 95). Some sets of images are explicitly unordered while remaining literary and artistic. For its tenth anniversary the literary journal *The Diagram* released the 2019 anthology *10 of Diagrams* in the form of a deck of playing cards, with an image-text by a different author on each card. Beginning in 2012, the collective arts project *Playing Arts* has produced five similar decks. Since cards have actual rather than notional manipulability, viewers control not just the pace of viewing but the nature of juxtaposition by creating their own contiguously juxtaposed arrangements or temporally juxtaposed stacks.

Other sets have a permanent order of presentation due to publication formats. This may indicate what Lefèvre and Dierick mean by "fixed" when defining comics as "the juxtaposition of fixed (mostly drawn) pictures." The ten woodcut prints of Felix Vallotton's 1898 *Intimités* are a set that when published in a book must appear in some discursive order, but not order that is an aspect of the art. A viewer need not begin with the woodcut printed on the discursively first page and is free to flip backwards or forwards at any time without disturbing an aesthetic effect. Even two juxtaposed images such as William Hogarth's 1751 *Beer Street* and *Gin Alley* might be viewed in either order and so in either direction depending on the placement of the images in a publication or display. Hogarth preferred *Beer Street* to be viewed first, to heighten the shock of *Gin Alley*, but even when printed side by side with a left-to-right order implied by the norms of reading English, nothing prevents a viewer's attention from moving right to left, and viewers likely look back and forth multiple times, making the notion

EN DEHORS GARDE BINGO

Hitch a ride home from the feminist bookstore with woman in red pickup truck	Write poems instead of articles about your research	Keep a stash of tampons past menopause because a sister might need help	Suffer neurasthenia	Rises from the subconscious… carcass covered with bluebottles (your country)
Fall silent because you can't speak about theory unless you 100% understand it	Message allies on FB because you'd rather be spied on by Russians than your bosses	Count citations and make sure 51% come from women	Ask someone who promotes human rights abuse to leave your restaurant	Hide because everyone hates ambition in women, plus you need this job
Insist that grids perpetuate the patriarchy & redesign this board as a spiral	Skip the meeting but steal boxed lunches with a friend & discuss body dysmorphia	**EPIPHANY: THERE IS NO FREE SPACE**	Create a travel guide to a planet you've never visited	Call out panels/ publishing venues populated only by white men
Volunteer to throw department party/ bring baked goods then descend into rage	Reserve the word "genius" for POC and white people who identify as women	Teach books that scare you in a good way	Blizzard the attorney general with sanctimonious snowflakes	You've gestated for so long—give birth to yourself
Discuss sexual harassment in a gender-binarized restroom	Vote for candidates who defend social justice energetically	Tell the least self-confident brilliant students that they're brilliant, convincingly	Listen to everyone except people who don't think you have a right to speak	Refuse to play bingo unless everyone wins

Illustration 6.1 Wheeler's "En Dehors Garde Bingo."

of order moot. Sets even occur in publications that consist primarily of words. Lesley Wheeler's visual poem "En Dehors Garde Bingo" in Illustration 6.1 arranges its twenty-five, color-coded sentences into a 5 × 5 grid. They may be read in any order, which is a significant aspect of the poem's aesthetic qualities.

Unordered image juxtapositions (including image-text juxtapositions like Wheeler's) are not sequences and so are not comics according to the majority stated definitions listed in the Introduction—assuming "sequential" is used strictly. Cook's is a notable exception ("two or more visually distinct part … looked at separately") because it implicitly acknowledges the possibility of a comic that juxtaposes images without requiring a specific order. The concept is akin to the linguistic term "semantic field," which is essentially a list of thematically related but randomly organized words. The visual quality is common in fine art. The multi-image arrangements of Warhol's *Marilyn* silkscreen works are deliberate, but a viewer's eye need not begin, for example, in the top left corner and proceed to the right in a Z-pattern in order to best appreciate the recurrent portraits. If a viewer instead focused first on the center square and then scanned up and to the left or in any other direction, the aesthetic effect would not change. Order does not matter.

Describing sets as a type of comic is atypical because the overwhelming majority of works in the comics medium are sequences. I adopted sequenced images as a working definition of the comics form because "sequence" and "images" are the two most common terms in extant definitions. The absence of "sequence" in Inge, McCloud,

Cook, and Lefèvre and Dierick, however, may not distinguish them from other definitions if the other definers do not use "sequences" as distinct from "series." Only Abel and Madden appear to exclude sets by requiring comics images "to be read in a certain order," unless order means only physically fixed.

To clarify the two types of order, I refer to "sequential order" as the image order of sequences, following some principle beyond the needs of physical presentation, such as book design and the arrangement of frames on a gallery wall. Since sequence is a diegetic quality and a diegesis is a product of its discourse, sequential order and discursive order are identical for sequences. Since non-sequences must occur in some physical order, too, discursive order also describes the successive arrangement of a set, reflecting perhaps happenstance or convenience but no diegetic principle. (The order of diegetic parts might also be perceived independently from discursive order when the two are not synchronized, a variant discussed later in this chapter.)

Since both a set and a sequence may consist of only two units, a work such as Hogarth's paired *Beer Street* and *Gin Alley* can be viewed as either. If it is a two-image sequence, the two units are viewed in a prescribed order involving image content; if it is a two-image set, the units are viewed in either order, regardless of their discursive order when printed in a book or mounted on a wall. This presents a challenge to the comics form since juxtaposition alone may be sufficient to define sequence if "sequence" is used without distinction from "series." By identifying sequential order as a dominant convention in the comics medium, Forceville, Refaie, and Meesters also tacitly acknowledge that sequentiality is not a necessary quality: "In a mainstream comics' album, the reader/viewer is expected to access the panels in a specific order, although in exceptional cases there may be some freedom" (2012: 458). Gravett is more explicit: "By avoiding clear, aligned sequences of panels, some comics artists have deliberately sought to create an orderless page," citing examples by Jim Steranko, Osamu Tezuka, François Rivière and Andreas, and Luke Pearson (2013: 64–8). In her discussion of poetry comics, Bennett also notes that in "abstract, experimental and non-linear comics, segments are without enforced order" (2014: 115).

Since sequence is used ambiguously in the formal definitions excerpted in the Introduction, they do not necessarily exclude juxtapositions that follow only a discursive order. As a result, juxtaposition alone may be sufficient to define images in the comics form. However, because only three of the definitions include "juxtaposition" or "juxtaposed," I retain "sequenced" but acknowledge both its precise and imprecise meanings.

2. Image Path

Temporal juxtapositions must follow some discursive order when printed in book form because a bound spine requires it. If the images are sequenced, the discursive order and the sequential order are the same. But contiguously juxtaposed images may have no discursive order unless a viewer perceives a diegetic one. Viewing images in sequential order is commonly described as "linear," but the meaning is paradoxical since the discursive presentation for content requiring more than a page's width does not follow a line because the images must descend the page and, if requiring more than a page, continue to a next page in a sense that is conceptually but not physically linear.

Though neither contiguous nor temporal juxtaposition are synonymous with what is variously referred to as "linear," "sequential," or "panel-to-panel transitions," viewing sequenced images often requires both. Sequenced images within a row or column are directly contiguous, but the continuation of the sequence to a next row or column typically requires a visual leap to a non-adjacent image on the same page and so is an indirectly contiguous juxtaposition. If the sequence continues past a page turn, the transition requires a temporal juxtaposition before likely returning to direct and then indirect contiguous juxtapositions. Juxtaposition is also distinct from viewing paths. The first images in two abutting parallel rows are directly contiguous (the bottom of the higher image abuts the top of the lower image), but they are not sequenced if the rows are viewed in a Z-path. The same work may also be presented in more than one format. When published online at *Slate*, the square panels of Lynda Barry's *One! Hundred! Demons!* appeared in a single column (or the illusion of a column moving within the unchanging frame of a computer screen), but when published in book format, the same images are printed side by side, two to a wide page, producing a literally linear four-image path for each two-page spread, interrupted by each page turn.

Whether image order is discursive only or discursive and sequential both, viewing a divided visual field produces a viewing path. If the divided images are a sequence, the path is determined by image order. Viewing a set results in paths, too, but not ordered ones. "Words and images in a series," observes Bennett, "may be read in multiple directions, or as equal to one another rather than left to right or up and down" (2014: 113). This describes viewing Warhol discussed above.

A visual field consisting of discrete elements with no directed path may define collage, which according to the *OED* is: "An abstract form of art in which photographs, pieces of paper, newspaper cuttings, string, etc., are placed in juxtaposition and glued to the pictorial surface." The adjective "abstract" is unclear since photographs and newspaper excerpts are typically representational, so the abstract quality must be relational. Since "collage" in French means sticking or gluing, the connections between units define the form, suggesting the same experience as viewing an undivided visual field. Miodrag similarly observes how page composition can function "as a network, rather than a sequence: exploiting the possibilities specifically offered by the comics form, it gains its aesthetic impact by partially overriding sequential narrative progression" (2013: 165). The first, maze-like page layout of Jim Steranko's *Captain America* #111 (March 1969) is a notable example—though it is included in an otherwise specifically ordered comic book.

Smolderen's analysis of William Hogarth typifies unordered viewing. While the engravings are units in sequences, each engraving also individually depicts "swarming spaces" that are "rife with isolated incidents," "inviting the reader to a 'winding walk' from one detail, one clue, to another," creating "a slow read, one that invites the eye to lose itself in the details and to return to them in order to generate comparisons, inferences, and endless paraphrase" (2014: 5, 6, 8). Each engraving then is composed of smaller units that cannot be fully perceived simultaneously. Each "isolated incident" could instead be individually framed and sequenced—as Bryan Talbot demonstrates by reformatting details of *Beer Street* and *Gin Alley* in 3x3 grids (2007: 198, 201). Hogarth instead allows multiple and simultaneous viewing paths, even ones that defy chronological content order. Although continuous space implies that all incidents occur at a single moment, *A Harlot's Progress* plate 2 depicts pieces of a tea set slipping from the edge of an overturning table while on the ground other pieces already lie in motionless shards, a temporal contradiction apparent through unordered scanning. Because of the "variable, zigzagging circulation of the reader's gaze," each tableau is sequential only if understood as a unit within a larger sequence (2014: 5). Each engraving is a set only if viewers perceive the isolated incidents as isolated images. I suspect most viewers instead perceive each as discursively unified. If so, the individual engravings are not in the comics form.

Applying Smolderen's analysis to contiguously juxtaposed images, viewing is either variable, allowing a range of "winding walks," or directed, prescribing a single path. McCloud might tacitly acknowledge variable paths when describing his aspect-to-aspect transition as setting "a wandering eye on different aspects of a place, idea, or mood," unless the wandering is by the implied viewer within the diegetic space (1993: 72). Like image division, viewing paths are products of individual perception. As discussed in Chapter 3, there is no intrinsic criterion that distinguishes an image part from an image. Viewers may look at an image as a single unit or they may look at an image as multiple units. And just as image content can guide image division, it can also guide image order and so paths. As Groensteen explains, even a non-representational image "crisscrossed by orthogonal lines (Mondrian-style)" can "invite a linear decoding, this is to say a reading," where "contiguous images are perceived as consecutive" in "one-after-another apprehension" (2013: 13).

Groensteen does not analyze how such viewing is determined since some visually subdivided images do not produce it and some visually unified images do (recall Rios's *Pretty Deadly*). He notes only that it occurs if the page's "apparatus" (the "conventional configuration" of panels, frames, and gutters) "is recognized as being typical of comics" (2013: 13). What does it mean for a canvas to be "typical of comics"? Groensteen calls a layout of frames and gutters "the device upon which the language is founded" (2007: 28), and so his understanding of one-after-another apprehension is modeled on word-after-word apprehension. To view images in a specific order is to "read" them. This approach is pervasive in comics scholarship and accounts for why viewers are referred to as "readers" even when they are viewing wordless comics. Witek argues that "reading" is the defining quality of comics: "to be a comic text is to be *read* as a comic" with "an evolving set of reading protocols" (2009: 149). If those protocols necessarily produce directed paths, Witek would not consider a set of contiguously juxtaposed images to be a comic. "Reading" then is viewing images in a directed path. Since reading and viewing both require viewing, I adopt "viewing" as the umbrella term.

Reading text requires more than perceiving units in a sequential order. I do not know French, but I can look at a page of French text and perceive that it consists of words and that those units follow a specific order. This is not reading. This is recognizing the norms of typeset prose. Word-after-word apprehension does not necessarily follow the norms of prose typesetting in which the directed path (for English and French) moves left to right in a column of descending rows. As seen in Wheeler's "En Dehors Garde Bingo," reading paths can instead be variable. While each of Wheeler's boxed sentences still follows prose typesetting norms for directed word-to-word apprehension, poems by Susan Howe include sections termed "word squares," "word-grids," and "word-arrays" (Reed 2004), in which sets of words are spatially isolated, inviting the sort of slow, winding read Smolderen describes for viewing Hogarth. Apprehension of a Howe poem is still word-to-word, but it does not always follow any specific word-to-word order. Even if viewers do perceive a directed path, they do not have to follow it or to follow it exclusively. Readers of Eugen Gomringer's concrete poem "Silencio," which consists of the title word repeated fourteen times in an unframed 5x3 grid with the middle space empty, probably do not read left to right either. Groensteen describes an equivalent comics approach, "seriation," in which "the same image would be repeated in every panel of the multiframe, producing a kind of 'wallpaper' effect" (2013: 17), presumably like Warhol's *Marilyn Diptych* and so allowing variable viewing paths.

An arrangement of frames on an otherwise undrawn page is the equivalent of the lines in an unused notebook or the squares in a form that indicate where to write each letter of your name and address. Neither is the founding of a language. Independent of layout, Groensteen analyzes image order in linguistic terms, treating each image as a syntagma (a smallest linguistic unit) forming a "triad composed of the panel that is currently being read, the panel that preceded it, and the panel that immediately follows it" (2007: 111). Since an image is not a linguistic unit, Groensteen's application is metaphorical. Non-linguistic images combined into evolving triads have no linguistic qualities. Syntagmatic analysis also focuses on rules of syntax, how a language orders types of words and phrases, whether, for example, an adjective precedes or follows a noun, or how a verb should be conjugated if the subject is plural. For syntax to apply to images, images need to be sequential (because in syntax order matters), but they also need to fall into syntactic categories, such as parts of speech or types of phrases and clauses. Groensteen does not indicate such categories, so his analysis is not syntagmatic. He only identifies that image-to-image apprehension occurs. Groensteen does note that it "is common in comics that panels find themselves 'automatically' reinforced by the fact that they occupy one of the places on the page that enjoys a natural privilege, like the upper left hand corner, the geometric center or the lower right hand corner" (2007: 29), but such reinforcement is not language-related either because the privilege of the center is true of visual fields generally, and the privilege of first and last positions is true of discursive order generally.

Cohn also analyzes the comics medium in linguistic terms, clarifying that "comics *are written in* visual languages in the same way that novels or magazines *are written in* English" (2013: 2). He further clarifies that "the combination of images may be closer to the structure used between whole sentences" and so working "at a higher level than syntax" (2013: 65). Since grammar does not typically pertain to how complete sentences are combined to make larger units like paragraphs, stanzas, chapters, or acts, Cohn's "Visual Language Grammar" is not grammar in a standard sense (his initial but unpublished term was "macro-syntax," which better suggests the higher and lower level distinction). While Cohn equates "narrative structure" and "grammar," Todorov instead recognizes only "a profound analogy" between "the categories of language and those of narrative" (1969: 74).

Unlike Groensteen, Cohn does not imply that image arrangements have any syntactic qualities: "While layout and content likely interface in important ways, they are ultimately different structures" (2013: 92). He instead analyzes contiguously juxtaposed images primarily in terms of viewing paths, asking "How do people know how to navigate through page layouts?" (2013: 92). Groensteen also assumes that image position alone determines viewing paths: "it is from localization of the different pieces of the multiframe that the reader can deduce the pathway" (2007: 34). While image content and image paths can be analyzed separately, they are not independent if content can determine paths—as was already demonstrated in Illustrations 5.4–7. Layout alone can be indeterminate, and so additional qualities between images are necessary.

3. Image Relationship

Todorov describes narrative as an "organized succession of clauses" with "relations between the clauses" typically "causal" (1969:74). While images are not clauses, the relations between images create the order and so the organization of the succession of images in a sequence. Because Cohn's layout experiments use pages featuring frames surrounding negative spaces, they reveal how viewers navigate panels that contain identical content and so identical relationships between images. Since panels that differ in content are often navigated differently, image content is a factor in determining image order. When image content is not considered, Cohn identifies the path conventions of the comics medium according to frame spacing and alignment alone, deriving an eight-part flow chart for the learned preferences of contemporary viewers (2013: 97–8). Image content can disrupt any of these norms, creating different orders and paths.

Groensteen refers to "a laborious sequence of arrows" determining paths (2007: 34). Like numbers in numbered panels, discursive arrows are not part of the primary diegesis, but they are a kind of content that conveys information independently from image arrangement. Witek argues that both largely antiquated devices are "reminders that the delicate negotiation between sequentiality and simultaneity which we now call 'comics' came into being . . . in stages of new ways of perceiving the myriad relationships between word and image on a page" (2009: 150).

Other images convey order with only content. Illustration 6.2 demonstrates that adding black and gray squares creates image phrases (as discussed in Chapter 3) that alter Cohn's page-viewing norms by applying them to panels within each phrase and to the sequence of the phrases themselves. Rios's multiply embedded panel discussed in Chapter 3 disrupts all of Cohn's norms, requiring viewers to discover image order by processing image division without regard to paths. As discussed in Illustration 3.1, Maroh employs pseudo-depth to create the illusion of an unframed figure positioned as if on top of a page's conventional layout. Though the figure occupies the center of the page and so is two-dimensionally below the first row of panels, it will likely be experienced as three-dimensionally above them and so viewed first. As analyzed in the previous chapter, Dennis Hopeless and Javier Rodriguez's *Spider-Woman: Baby Talk*,

Illustration 6.2 Four 6×4 grids with varying visual phrases and viewing paths.

Ta-Nehisi Coates and Daniel Acuna's *Black Panther*, and Matt Fraction and David Aja's *Hawkeye: My Life as a Weapon* all present varied viewing paths.

Although also based on Z-path viewing, Matt Baker's layouts regularly violate Cohn's protocols. The "Sky Girl" excerpt from *Jumbo Comics* #83 (January 1946) in Illustration 6.3 requires a non-diagonal leap over an unread panel between panels three and four, a reversed right-to-left path between panels five and six, and a leap over a previously viewed panel between panels six and seven (Earle and Gavaler 2021). Baker also reveals a challenge to how the internal area of an image is viewed. Groensteen asserts that "the eye does not apprehend the panel … in the way that it takes in a painting" because "it always arrives … from another point situated within the" viewing path and an "exit is always indicated, pointing to another" panel (2007: 48–9). If true, viewing paths would paradigmatically run from the top left corner to the bottom right corner of each panel before leaping to the top left corner of the next panel. Pederson and Cohn instead explain the "relationship between panels by approximating the centrepoint of a panel in relation to the centrepoint of the narratively preceding panel" (2–16: 12). Neither approach explains Baker. Following Cohn's protocols for Baker's "Sky Girl" page would likely produce one of the following paths: 1, 4, 6, 2, 5, 3, 7 or 1, 2, 3, 4, 6, 5, 7, both of which contradict image content. Viewers may instead apprehend image order according only to salient content areas. While an order derived from bottom right corners is counterintuitive, Baker's content-driven path and a path based only on image entrance areas (typically the top left area for both Z-path and N-path layouts) are the same, meaning a viewer may orient by entrance areas only, disregarding image exit areas (typically the bottom right).

Even more fundamentally, viewers may not apply Cohn's path norms if they perceive image division without image order, making all paths ultimately dependent on the presence of perceived image order. According to Cohn's norms, Illustration 6.4 should be viewed in Z-path rows, and Illustration 6.5 should be viewed in N-path columns. If the images were identical, including if they consisted only of frames enclosing white space, Cohn's rules should be predictive, but the image content of the two Illustrations may instead produce no directed viewing paths. This is because both are image sets. Their representational content is related—6.4 features nine photo illustrations of Lesley Wheeler and 6.5 features nine adapted stills from the film *Lady Frankenstein*—but unordered.

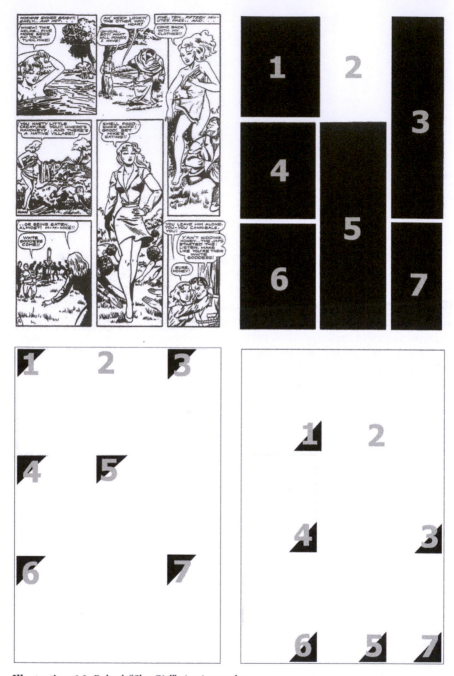

Illustration 6.3 Baker's "Sky Girl" viewing paths.

Illustration 6.4 "Snapshots, No. 1–9."

Illustration 6.5 *"Lady Frankenstein* (1971), No. 1–9."

Determining paths between images then involves determining the relationships between their content, including the inference types detailed in Chapter 5 and the fundamental quality of recurrence detailed in Chapter 4. Inferences produced by each contiguous juxtaposition can create image order and so a directed viewing path linking images. Since some juxtapositional inferences do not produce sequential order, an additional term for order-producing juxtapositions may be helpful. I suggest "hinge," since actual hinges physically link the actual panels of diptychs. *Creating Comics* introduced "hinges" to replace McCloud's "closure," but I offer it here only as a subset of juxtapositional inferencing that produce directed paths. When an inference determines the order of two images and therefore a path connecting them, the inference is a hinge. Non-order producing inferences (such as continuous inferences occurring simultaneously in multiple directions from each portion of an image subdivided into gutter-separated panels) involve no hinges.

Illustration 1.2 provides an example of both hinged and unhinged viewing. The images by Vermeer and Gentileschi have no relationship. Any juxtapositional inferences between them would be linguistic, and then only minimally so since the chapter discusses them separately and only as examples illustrating a larger point. Viewers likely experience no hinge in the negative space dividing them, and they attend to the left image first because the left image is discussed first in the chapter. If viewers attended only to the juxtaposed images and were unaware of each image's separate history, they might draw any of a range of inferences (as discussed in the previous chapter), all them diegetic and likely hinged. The content of the second image makes sense, or is made sense of, through its perceived relationship to the first.

A search for hinges is likely a continuous process that can be interrupted and restarted but begins with a brief global appreciation of the visual field and the resulting recognition of divided images. Eisner notes that a "viewer will often glance at the last panel first" (200: 42–3), and Bateman observes: "If there is a large colourful object on the right of an image, then the eyes will probably be drawn to it first; there may then be a much smaller, less prominent figure on the left of the image that will be attended to afterwards" (2014: 61). Chute describes how the "movement of the eye on the page instantly takes in the whole of grid of panels and its particular opening elements at once ... This duality—one's eye may see the whole page even when one decides to commence reading with the first box of the first tier—is a defining feature of comics" (2010: 8). The key verb is "decides," and the subject, "eye," suggests the decision is subconscious and nearly instantaneous. Since not all divided visual fields direct viewers to the top left corner, the perception of the "first box of the first tier" as "its opening elements" already indicates that the viewer has decided hinges are present—or at least has detected elements that suggest the hypothesis and is beginning to test it. Abbott describes a similar response to Roy Lichtenstein's 1962 *Eddie Diptych*:

> Upon first glancing at the work, the eye goes right to the girl's strongly delineated features ... After a brief moment for the girl's troubled expression to register a preliminary visual impact, the eye eagerly moves to the top left corner of the left panel for elucidation from the text.
>
> 1986: 161

Mikkonen and Lautenbacher support these assumptions:

> Global attention appeared essentially in the starting phase of the reading, regularly focusing on the center of the double-page spread, but also in the refocusing or checking for possibly meaningful elements during and at the end of reading.
>
> 2019: 23

Viewers choose "pathways due to an interrelation between the layout and the narrative content of the images," and so viewing paths are not "separate from meaning" (2019: 6).

Cohn may not detect the roles of global viewing and image content because of his experiments' materials and procedures. Participants were given "packets containing page layouts with empty panels" and "asked to number the panels in the order that they would read them if seen in an actual comic book" (Cohn and Campbell 2015: 4, 6). In an earlier experiment, Cohn describes the panels as "empty of content," and participants were "instructed to number the panels in the order that they would read them" (2013: 3, 5). The verb "read" assumes not only a Z-path, because the participants were English readers, but that the panels are already ordered and therefore hinged. Since the interior of each frame is identical, the only indicators of order and path are the spatial relationships of the frames themselves.

Actual reading can undermine Cohn's preference norms, too, because the positioning of text within image-texts is unrestricted. Abbott describes the non-Z-path movement of his attention when viewing Lichtenstein's comics-inspired *Eddie Diptych*, noting that "the text influences the perception of the panel image and exerts ... a limiting or guiding influence in deducing the picture's meaning," and therefore Abbott sees "the subordination of the pictorial to the literary in comics art" (1986: 159, 156). Instead of following the panel layout's Z-path, a viewer's eye may instead be guided from block of text to block of text, in a path that subordinates images and ignores panel and gutter composition entirely. Such a reading-focused viewer may still look at areas of the page that do not include words, but doing so may create atypical viewing paths.

Juxtaposed images are not necessarily hinged, even those with related content. Illustrations 6.4 and 6.5 have minimal discursive recurrence, and both produce partial diegetic recurrence. Though each image's abstract qualities may or may not result in the perception of each set's figures representing a single individual, each image represents a human face or figure, establishing at minimum thematic recurrence and making each canvas a representational set. Regarding "Charade II" in Illustration 4.6 again, the non-representational work divides into two braided phrases with four partially discursively recurrent images in each. Like those in 6.4 and 6.5, the images are unordered and so the viewing path is variable. Recurrence alone then, whether discursive or diegetic, is not sufficient to produce image order and directed paths.

Because two images can represent aspects of a shared setting without indicating order and direction, spatial inferences do not necessarily produce hinges either. This is especially clear with continuous inferences since the spatial unity creates the impression of a single image, which, if representational, likely also represents a single moment in time. Temporal inferencing is typically key. "Cape Cod, May 2019" in Illustration 3.7 creates temporal inferences through the causal inference that the three figures are further apart from each other because they have moved themselves during the implied time period between the depicted moments. The image order is therefore diegetically chronological, and any potential confusion in viewing paths is resolved by reference to that chronology. Illustration 6.6 is nearly diegetically identical. A viewer would likely attempt a Z-path, as indicated by Cohn's norms, but finding the resulting sequence diegetically confusing due to the non-chronological shifts would instead test for vertical hinges and, finding the results more diegetically satisfying, instead accept an N-path.

Illustration 6.6 "Cape Cod, August 2019, No. 2."

Linguistic inferences, or just the discursive directional flow of words in juxtaposed image-texts, is enough to produce hinges, too. Other inferences types (embedded, associative, non-sensory, match-cut, and semi-continuous) might not be sufficient in isolation, but if a path has already been established, the experience of any juxtapositional inference could suggest a hinge at a discursive crossroads. In Illustration 6.7, a page in Nick Sousanis's 2015 *Unflattening* directs a viewing path from right to left, something unaccounted for by Cohn's protocols. The hinge between panels three and four is produced by a continuous inference with the arrow-like extension of the teapot spout,

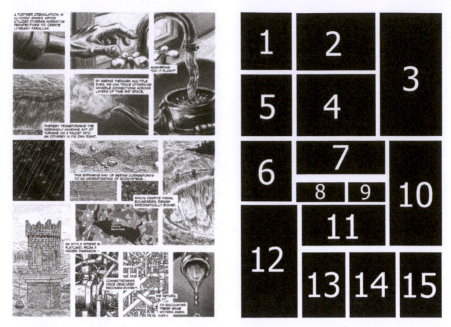

Illustration 6.7 From Sousanis's *Unflattening*.

which prepares a viewer for a similar directional hinge between panels ten and eleven, creating a boustrophedon (literally "to turn as oxen plow") pattern common in ancient Greek texts.

4. Narrative

Hinge inferences regarding image relationships determine image order and, for contiguously juxtaposed images, directed viewing paths. Hinges therefore create, or are created by, sequences. They may also have the same relationship to narratives—though it is ambiguous what precisely a narrative is and how it might differ from a sequence, if at all.

"Dubbing comics 'narratives,' Kukkonen asserts, "is hardly contested" (2013: 1). Thirteen of the eighteen complete definitions of comics excerpted in the Introduction include the word "narrative" or "story" or, for Duncan and Smith, "diegesis" used in the same sense. Cook instead asserts that a comic might be some "other meaningful agglomeration." Meskin similarly describes a "unifying link" between images (2007: 372), Pratt a "unifying device" (2009: 107), and Groensteen "causal links" (2013: 17), meaning the images are "correlated in some fashion" (2007: 19), all without stipulating that the causal or unifying or correlating or agglomerating quality is narrative. Lefèvre clarifies that

relations can be of quite different kinds, including purely formal aspects, such as graphic or abstract qualities pertaining to the form of the pictures, as well as content-related aspects, which can range from how objects are grouped into categories to all kinds of logical, rhetorical, and symbolic relations among the portrayed objects and events.

2011: 26

Meskin also lists character, theme, and form (specifically the arrangement and shape of panels) as possible non-narrative types of "significant connection," and Groensteen lists six "other principles according to which images may be related to each other": inventory, variation, inflection, decomposition, seriation, and fragmentation (2013: 17). Postema argues that an arrangement of panels is itself an organizing connection since "the comics form implies that a panel that follows another is somehow related to the previous one" (2013: 63).

Like the uses of "sequence" and "series," however, it is not clear what "narrative" or its absence in a definition necessarily indicates. Molotiu especially rejects narrative as a necessary element, establishing the subcategory of abstract comics which he defines not only by "the lack of represented objects in favor of an emphasis of form" but also "the lack of a narrative excuse to string panels together" (2009: n.p.). Though Molotiu does not define the stringing excuses that a work might employ instead of narrative, he does note that "even in the absence of a (verbal) story, [non-representational comics] can create a feeling of sequential drive, the sheer rhythm of narrative or the rise and fall of a story arc" (2009: n.p.). Lefèvre similarly concludes that even without an intended narrative, "interpreters will almost automatically look for some minimal coherence or narrative, especially if the various pictures are presented in the typical form of a comic" (2011: 26). Baetens also claims that such "narrative deciphering is almost unavoidable" (2011: 95), as does Davies, who argues that "readers 'naturally' seek out characters, actants and motivated action in what they see" and that this tendency "is not an additional interpretation imposed by a readership used to, expecting and insisting upon narrative content, but a basic way in which human beings perceive the world" (2013: 264).

It is unclear how narrative might differ from "minimal coherence" or from "a feeling of" narrative qualities, since a narrative presumably produces a feeling of those same qualities. Tabulo describes her experience of non-representational comics similarly:

in these non-narrative, wordless, sequential images there is an aesthetic energy or movement, which draws the viewer's sensors through the panel progressions by way of the graphic trace. However, I also found that there seems to be an innate desire to discover a narrative plot or theme, like any reader or viewer does who suspends disbelief when engaging with a fictional work or an abstract painting, and in the process surrenders to the possibilities of the work's sequentiality.

2014: 32

"Narrative" and "sequentiality" may reference the same quality, or narrative may be a viewer's experience of sequentiality. Without that interpretive experience, juxtaposed images have only discursive order.

Music suggests a parallel. A musical composition, even though (typically) non-representational, can be analyzed in narrative terms with character-like themes and plot-like linearity. Nattiez and Ellis emphasize that "the narrative, strictly speaking, is not in the music, but *in the plot imagined and constructed by the listeners* from functional objects" (1990: 249). They identify the two discursive features that enable an audience to experience narrative:

(1) a minimum of two objects, of whatever sort, must be provided for us, and
(2) these two objects must be placed in a linear and temporal dimension in order for us to be encouraged to establish a relationship between them.

1990: 246

These are the same conditions that define sequenced images. If "linear and temporal dimension" indicate diegetic order and a directed viewing path, then the parallel is only to the directed viewing paths of image sequences and not to the variable viewing paths of image sets. Sequential order and the directed paths determined by the image content of hinged juxtapositions may be sufficient to define narrative in the comics form. Alternatively, narrative is one possible causal or unifying or correlating or agglomerating quality of sequences, suggesting a larger category that could also include argument, description, and exposition—the four primary rhetorical modes codified by Newman in 1827, though other categorization systems may apply, too. Eisner similarly identifies two kinds of picture arrangements: those that "narrate a story or dramatize an idea" (2008: xi).

The most recent and comprehensive analysis of comics as narratives, Mikkonen's *The Narratology of Comic Art*, does not offer a definition of narrative but only identifies a tendency "to perceive certain features as constitutive," specifically "temporal sequencing" and "causal connection" (2017: 16). Bateman and Wildfeuer require two qualities to establish a "narrative relation" between two images: "(1) that there is a congruent temporal relationship across the two panels and (2) that they share a topic" (2014: 385)—which might be reduced to simply sequenced recurrence. Sometimes narrative is used synonymously with plot, which, since Aristotle's classical narrative structure, consists of a distinct beginning, middle, and end. Since the alphabetical entries of dictionaries and encyclopedia are not understood to be plotted, plot and narrative involve more than sequenced units. The *OED* dates the first use of narrative to 1539: "A part of a legal document which contains a statement of alleged or relevant facts closely connected with the matter or purpose of the document." Its non-legal meaning emerges later in the same century: "An account of a series of events, facts, etc., given in order and with the establishing of connections between them." Both meanings concern connected facts or events, as does the later literary critical meaning from 1843: "The part of a text, esp. a work of fiction, which represents the sequence of events, as distinguished from that dealing with dialogue, description, etc." The second two definitions both emphasize ordered "events," a ubiquitous but ultimately ambiguous term referring to "Anything that happens."

If images have no representational qualities, they cannot represent anything happening in a diegetic world. Non-representational images exclude the narrative qualities of settings (or environments), characters (or agents), actions (performed by agents), and events (which are the combination of agents, actions, and environments). Actions, when understood narratively, are causal and so are the most common connections that define and link what might otherwise be unrelated details. Without representational imagery, diegetic details cannot be linked into actions and actions into narratives because there is not "even a unified narrative space" in which events can occur. Without representation, images remain at the level of discourse.

The absence of a diegetic world peopled by characters performing actions in settings would seem to preclude narrative. Events are mental schema triggered by but not limited to their visual depictions, which might be understood as snapshot-like excerpts or approximations that frame larger swaths of diegetic time and space. Molotiu bars even "vaguely human shapes" or other character-representing abstractions such as "triangles and squares" because they "are not different in kind, but only in degree, from the cartoony simplification of, say, Carl Bark's ducks" (2009: n.p.). But two sets of non-representational marks can produce recurrence and so the inference that both sets represent a shared subject even if that subject is otherwise non-representational and exists in a non-mimetic world.

Can such non-representational characters have plots? Citing the previously discussed example of Baldi's *Petit trait* (or *Little Line*), Groensteen asserts: "the 'story' recounted is that of the transformations undergone by the line in question, through a kind of *physics*, whereby each new image is generated by the preceding one" (2013: 12). Drawing from film study, Postema argues that "transformations" alone define narrative action, an analysis especially suited to comics "since panels on a page show the various states together" (2013: 57). Baetens would seem to agree:

> The impact of our sequential reading habits is so strongly narrative that those habits help us make narrative sense of panels and drawings that seem to defy any direct figuration. From the very moment that material forms are changing from one panel to another, we seem to be able to read these transformations in a narrative sense.
>
> 2011: 100–1

Molotiu's anthology includes Ibn Al Rabin's "toads" in which two shifting abstract shapes appear to compete in dominance until dominated by a third. Though most of the works in *Abstract Comics* are less anthropomorphically plotted, their juxtaposed images are sequenced and can be read in terms of conflict, a highly common quality of narrative.

Conflict itself might be an anthropomorphic concept, but the ordered conflict of non-representational images remains at the level of discourse. The ordered conflict of board games suggests another parallel: while a game of chess is representational to the very limited extent that pieces are vaguely shaped after human agents, checker pieces are devoid of even that minimal visual likeness. The games' spatial apparatus of temporally sequenced competition resembles combat in only the most distant sense and so the narrative seems non-diegetic. Groensteen correctly asserts that the non-representational "visual content" includes:

colors, lines, form organized into motifs. These abstract "images" interact with each other. They establish relationships of position, contiguity, intensity, repetition, variation, or contrast, as well as dynamic relationships of interwovenness, etc.

2013: 12

Though Groensteen also argues that "[i]n principle, nothing in this list pertains to narration," the ability to "establish relationships" and to "interact with each other" are qualities of agents. This might be how their non-representational sequences create Molotiu's "feeling" of narrative.

Narrative structure is typically divided into progressive segments—such as obstacles and resolution or stages of balance and imbalance—segments that can be applied to non-representational imagery, provided some elements of the images are recurrent. Panels, according to Postema, "need a point of reference to create the cohesion between the separate images"; though this "cohesion tends to be provided by a character who appears across various panels," it might be provided by any recurring element (2013: 57). In the absence of sequenced conflict, recurrence alone may be enough to produce narrative if the recurrence is partial and so implies a transforming subject.

In traditionally representational sequences, recurrent elements are characters progressing in chronological time. In non-representational sequences, recurrent elements are repeated non-representational images juxtaposed in a specific order. Variations in the recurrences, as well as the absence of variations, may then be interpreted in terms of conflict and transformation and therefore be understood as narrative. Many non-narrative ordering principles offered to explain abstract sequences—variation, decomposition, etc.—may be the underlying discursive qualities of narrative generally. Shklovsky's literary analysis of plot is similar: "the introduction of interrupting digressions" produces the "story" (1970: 57).

Narrative typically combines sequenced recurrence with one extrinsic quality: theory of mind. The attribution of mental states, including intentions, motives, beliefs, and emotions, is a field of study in twenty-first-century cognitive science. Zunshine argues "that all narrative-oriented cultural representations, such as fiction, movies, plays, team sports broadcasts, as well as some forms of art, singing, and dance, reflect the workings of our theory of mind" (2011: 115). For example, "drained of all mindreading, tightrope walking is exactly as interesting as a wheel-o toy rolling back and forth on its magnetic axle," and "watching a basketball game without attributing intentions to the players is as enticing as watching falling snowflakes—both are random movements, interesting for about two minutes" (2011: 117). Zunshine notes that "our theory-of-mind adaptations do not distinguish between the mental states of real people and of fictional characters" (2011: 117), and that tendency appears to extend to non-representational imagery, too. A little line becomes Little Line through a reader's conscious or subconscious theorizing of mind. When a cluster of lines represents a face, the theory of mind is comparatively automatic. A cluster devoid of representational qualities can trigger theory of mind through sequenced recurrence, and that combination likely produces the "feeling" of narrative. Narratives, however, may not require that feeling. A sequence of discursive transformations, whether of representational or non-representation imagery, does not necessarily trigger theory of mind.

Despite the omnipresence of what might be termed "discursive narratives" within representational narratives, not all comics are narrative even in this expanded sense. In his list of panel transitions, McCloud includes "non-sequitur" in which there is "no logical relationship between panels whatsoever" (1993: 72). If this includes non-representational relationships, then the category precludes any linking principle, and so a series of juxtaposed images composed entirely of non-sequiturs, and so no hinges, would have no order, no sequence, no conflict or transformation, no "feeling" of narrative. Its use of the conventions of panels, frames, and gutters might, however, be sufficient to trigger the experience of a viewing path. If so, the external expectation conditioned by the viewing of previous works gives the otherwise unrelated images a discursive order. If the frame shapes themselves produce recurrence, the order may become diegetic and the images a narrative.

Some works consist of images that do have logical relationships but are still not ordered. As mentioned above, Meskin suggests character, theme, and form as possible organizing principles, ones that would not necessarily produce the sequenced conflicts of plot. Manju Shandler's 2003 *Gesture* combines theme, form, and certainly event, while avoiding viewing order. The work consists of 3,000 4" x 9" unframed paintings thumbtacked to exhibition walls. Where panels in the comics medium often possess notional manipulability, Shandler's units possess literal manipulability, with the background of a white wall creating the effect of gutters. Such formal uniformity is, according to Meskin, already a type of "significant connection," further heightened by each canvas shape evoking the World Trade Center towers and the number of canvasses referencing the number of victims. 9/11 is both unifying theme and diegetic event, elements that, despite the unsequenced order and variable viewing paths of the juxtaposed images, may be sufficient to classify the installation as a narrative—though, as mentioned above, perhaps another rhetorical mode (description, exposition, argument, idea) may apply also or instead, requiring a superordinate category that includes but is not limited to narrative. Regardless, *Gesture* is in the comics form if juxtaposition without hinges is sufficient to define the form.

Finally, Molotiu describes "comics that contain some representational elements" but "that do not cohere into a narrative" (2009: n.p.). Molotiu implies a spectrum, and Groensteen terms one pole "infranarrative comics" and analyzes three panels of Daniel Blancou's 2009 *Samuel Lipinksi* as an example. Blancou's first panel depicts tadpoles in a puddle; the second the face of a man looking down as though at a child as he says, "You're not going to bring that home?!"; and the third a gallery in which a woman is stepping out of frame as a perplexed man looks at a painting partially cropped out of frame. "It is not difficult to make a link between the first two panels," writes Groensteen, "even if the child that 'Dad' is addressing is not represented in either of them" (2013: 18). To explain the third panel, Groensteen posits that either the child grew up to be the artist who painted a partially obscured painting of a tadpole, or "the two situations bear no relationship to each other but the indecisive man has perhaps intimated that he is thinking about buying the picture, and his partner has replied 'You're not going to bring that home?!'" (2013: 18). The first interpretation is a traditional narrative told chronologically and unified by the undrawn but conceptually recurrent character of the child-artist. The second interpretation creates two diegetic events unified by the thematic repetition of the middle panel's speech. When Groensteen states that "the two situation bears no relationship," he means only no narrative relationship.

5. Typology

Combing the overlapping qualities of representation, image relationship, image order, and image viewing path produces six types of sequenced images. If the comics form is defined as sequenced images, a set of unsequenced images is not in the form. Because comics scholars do not typically differentiate between sets and sequences when referencing "sequences," sets are included in the typology.

1. Representational sequence: two or more related and sequentially ordered representational images. If the images are contiguously juxtaposed, hinges produce a viewing path. This describes the overwhelming majority of works in the comics medium and almost inevitably produces theory-of-mind processing and so the experience of narrative.

2. Non-representational sequence: two or more related and sequentially ordered non-representational images. Again, if the images are contiguously juxtaposed, hinges produce a viewing path. Molotiu cites Jackson Pollock's *Red Painting* 1–7 as an example of "a gradual transformation of form from image to image," which defines a discursive sequence devoid of a diegesis (2009: n.p.). Such sequences may still produce theory-of-mind processing applied to recurrent non-representational subjects and so an experience of narrative (and so perhaps a rudimentary diegesis). Since a representational sequence can be analyzed by its discursive qualities alone, so arguably all representational sequences also contain implicit discursive sequences or sets. Molotui draws a similar conclusion when arguing that "representational comics" are "not only narrative and mimetic" but also discursively dynamic in their use of iconostasis and "the life of the graphic trace, strewn across the trajectory of reading" (2012: 91). The division also allows the possibility that a work's representational sequence and non-representational sequence will not align.

3. Representational set: two or more related but unordered representational images. If contiguously juxtaposed, the images are not viewed in a directed path. Even if a set of juxtaposed images includes frames and gutters, those conventions do not trigger a specific path—if they did, the visual field would become a representational sequence. Derik Badman created *Flying Chief* by copying only representational setting elements from *Tarzan* comic strips, producing panels that include both representational details and inexplicable white space. The pages of Luke Ramsey's *Intelligent Sentient?*, a series of "two page environments" with versions of "an anti-character," are viewed discursively from left to right but without a clear sequential effect (2015). Andy Warhol's *Marilyn* silkscreens and Manju Shandler's *Gesture* are also representational sets. At the opposite aesthetic extreme, posters in the tourist-marketed series "The Doors of" are representational sets through thematic recurrence. Because the effect may vary according to viewer, the same representational work may fluctuate between sequence and set.

4. Non-representational set: two or more related but unordered non-representational images, which, if contiguously juxtaposed, are not viewed in a directed

path. Non-representational sets include a range of works by abstract expressionist artists, including Robert Motherwell's 1948–67 *Elegy to The Spanish Republic* and Barnett Newman's 1948–53 *Onement I–VI*. In each, images are clearly related, but their order is only discursive. Though the pages of Tom Phillips's 1966 *A Humument: A Treated Victorian Novel* are bound and numbered, the order is likely experienced non-diegetically and so the result is a set, too. The experience of narrative is less likely but possible.

5. Representational arrangement: two or more unrelated and unordered representational images with no contiguous hinges and so variable paths. The term "arrangement" recalls the sense used by William Wordsworth when he explained the organizational principles used to group his collected poems in 1815: "poems apparently miscellaneous, may with propriety be arranged" (1908: 520). Here "arrangement" denotes non-sequitur image relationships, and so their discursive order follows no organizing rule. Groensteen terms these "amalgams," and, when the amalgam consists of representational content, "infranarratives." Sets and arrangements are distinguished by image content, which appears unrelated even thematically. While it is possible that any subdivided representational content will trigger relationship inferences, Daniel Blancou's *Samuel Lipinski* gestures toward this extreme through his intention "to write, in three panels, strips whose meaning was not 'nailed down'" (quoted in Groensteen 2013: 17). Michael Dumontier and Neil Farber's 2011 *Constructive Abandonment* provides a fuller example, which Cino Zucchi in his afterword describes in terms of incongruous strangers meeting in hotel rooms: "Icons cannot speak, Texts cannot see. They just stay close, touch, feel. Sometimes they don't match, or don't even recognize each other; they know their relationship will have no future" (2011: n.p.). Max Ernst's 1934 *A Week of Kindness* offers an earlier, surrealist example: "A book of this sort, appealing equally to the emotions and the intellect, can be freely interpreted by each reader according to his own experiences, by the lights of his own mental baggage" (1976: vii–viii). The sections of Ernst' novel, however, include clear visual motifs, and so might instead be experienced as representational sets. The unbound sets of representational images that Henry A. Moore and Christiana D. Morgan included in their Thematic Appreciation Test provide an example from clinical psychology. Morgan based them on illustrations from magazines removed from their explanatory contexts to create extreme ambiguity.

6. Non-representational arrangement: two or more unrelated and unordered non-representational images with no contiguous hinges and so variable paths. The juxtaposition of images of any kind are likely to produce the perception of relationships, but non-representational ones with no or minimal recurrent elements are more likely to produce non-sequitur effects.

The four rows of Illustration 6.8 provide four-image examples of the types. Since representational sequences are ubiquitous, the Illustration begins with the second category.

The first row is a non-representational sequence—or rather it is if a viewer experiences each image as the same recurrent subject transforming through some sort of a four-part progression. I doubt the recurrence will produce theory-of-mind motivations or any other kind of character-like inferences to explain the transformations,

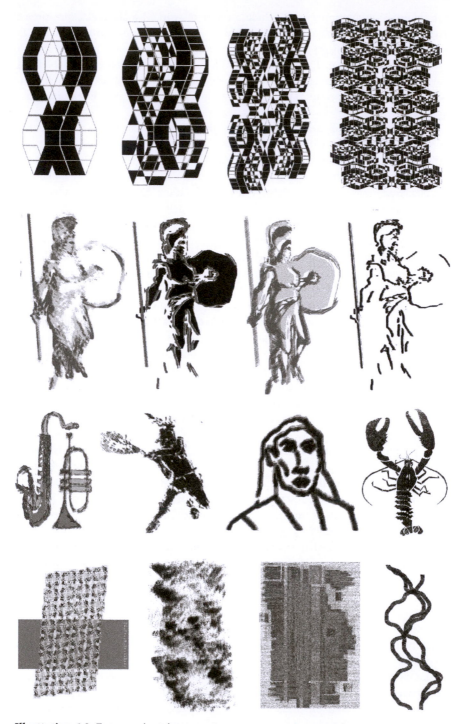

Illustration 6.8 Four comic strips.

but as long as it is a recurrent subject transforming, it can be analyzed as a narrative. Though hinged, the viewing path might be experienced in either direction, left to right or right to left, producing opposite "stories."

The second row is a representational set. Each image of the goddess Athena is partially discursively recurrent, but unless the differences are experienced as changes in a transforming diegesis, they would not produce a sense of order beyond the discursive one and so no sequence or narrative. They are four variant renderings of the same subject which is undergoing no spatiotemporal changes. The row is unhinged and so may be viewed variably, including with leaps over images.

For an example of the fourth category, non-representational sets, look back again at "Charade II" in Illustration 4.6. Unlike in the first row of Illustration 6.8, the images in the 2x4 grid are recurrent but their order is non-progressive because no hinges suggest a sequential progression through any of the variable viewing paths.

The third row of Illustration 6.8 is a representational arrangement. The images— musical instruments, tennis player, cropped figure, lobster—represent subject matter but without conveying relationships between them. Without relationships, their order is random, too. Arranging the four in different orders would not significantly alter the aesthetic effect, and whatever the discursive arrangement, viewers can move through it left to right or right to left or some combination beginning and ending at any point.

Finally, the fourth row is a non-representational arrangement. Not only are the images unrelated to diegetic subjects, they are unrelated to each other and to their discursive positions, producing no recurrence and therefore no transformation or sequence or story. Still, extended attention will likely lead to the perceptions of similarities. The second and fourth images share some elements of shape, and the first and fourth share elements of texture. If those similarities are experienced as recurrent, a narrative of transformation may follow, producing a non-representational sequence instead.

All six types require viewer interpretation and so no visual field intrinsically belongs to any category, and some visual fields may fluctuate according to viewers. Recall "Chess" in Illustration 3.3. If the incremental alterations in each chessboard produce causal hinges, then it is a representational sequence. Some viewers may disregard the title and the nominally representational quality of each chessboard and instead experience a non-representational sequence, especially since no actual boards could transform as depicted. Others may not experience causal hinges, allowing variable paths, including columns instead of rows. If so, it is either a representational or non-representational set, depending again on the perception of the image units as chessboards. It seems unlikely that it could be experienced as either kind of arrangement since the similarities between units relate them and the incremental changes create at least some degree of top-to-bottom transformation. Still, if a viewer does not experience individual images, then "Chess" falls into none of the six types because it is a single unified image.

The six categories contain at least one potential gap. Representation could be further divided between image content (as it currently designates) and the nature of sequential changes, creating a non-representational sequence featuring some representational content. Illustration 1.1 is an example. The three variations of the kissing figures are sequential because the images are recurrent and the changes are incrementally progressive. Though the representational qualities of the third image are obscured, they are still recognizable when viewed with the first two, and while the changes are non-diegetic (a viewer likely does not perceive the kissing figures undergoing any physical transformation), they produce a sequence. Rather than designating a seventh category (a non-representational sequence featuring partially representational content), I consider 1.1 to be a subcategory of representational sequences distinguished by its hybrid use of discursive juxtapositional inferences and non-representational changes to diegetically recurrent subjects to create hinges.

Combining the above typology of image relationships with the types of juxtaposition discussed in Chapter 3 produces further categories. Excluding distant juxtaposition (which may be juxtaposition in only a metaphorical sense), a work may be composed of images juxtaposed: A) contiguously only, B) temporally only, or C) both contiguously and temporally. The resulting eighteen-part typology is self-explanatory, and the majority of works in the comics medium fall into 1C: representational sequences contiguously and temporally juxtaposed.

Lastly, representational sets may also contain a significant subcategory, one that establishes one possible distinction between sequence and narrative. While I largely understand the two terms to be synonymous, narrative can also be understood as representational content in chronological order, and since sets have only discursive order (and so cannot be chronological) a set may contain or imply a kind of narrative if viewers recognize the diegetic position of each image independently of its discursive position. Imagine the contents of a family photo album randomly rearranged so that images taken years or decades apart follow each other discursively. Viewers, especially family members familiar with the documented events, would still experience an overall diegetic span of time through the randomly ordered fragments. Mikkonen analyzes Chris Ware in the same manner:

> the temporal open-endedness of *Building Stories* concerns primarily the *order of reading* the various printed works rather than the *sense of chronology* in the story. The story-time is not random even if the temporal relations between the different instalments are not clearly defined. How is this possible? First, the reader can make inferences about the order of the events on the basis of the image contents pertaining, for example, to signs of aging in the reoccurring characters, their changing relationships, homes, and milieu.
>
> 2017: 34

Narrative then has two kinds. As detailed above, a "discursive narrative" is defined by its sequential order and so is synonymous with sequence. The discourse/diegesis division then implies a seemingly redundant term: "diegetic narrative," which is instead defined by the perception of diegetic events unrelated to discursive order. When diegetic events follow discursive order, the distinction appears invisible. A discursive narrative of representational content could instead be termed "plot," since the *OED* notes that a narrative's "sequence of events" may be limited "to the story as it is supposed to have taken place," while "plot is used to refer to the way in which the story is revealed." Plot in this literary sense is sometimes used synonymously with discourse, and diegesis synonymously with chronological events, terms I have stipulated with different meanings for the purpose of visual rather than linguistic analysis.

The relationships between diegetic events and discursive presentation also provides a key for understanding one of the comics form's most significant effects: content that is undrawn yet somehow present.

6. Multi-Image Event Inferencing

McCloud gives *Understanding Comics* the subtitle *The Invisible Art* because, he argues, a "comics creator asks us to join in a silent dance of the seen and the unseen. The visible and the invisible . . . What happens between these panels is a kind of magic only comics can create" (1993: 92). Naming closure as the "grammar" that connects image fragments, he asserts that "comics *is* closure" (1993: 67). While other artforms are capable of triggering similar inferences, the connections perceived between images may be the comics form's most significant quality. However, Bateman and Wildfeuer identify a core challenge: "the operation of closure is unconstrained—just what connections may need to be drawn are left open" (2014: 383).

By referring to "the invisible" rather than to something that is absent, possible, hypothetical, or some other suggestive adjective, McCloud implies that sequenced images include content that is somehow present yet undrawn. The notion is not unique to images. Regarding prose-only novels, Wolterstorff describes a process of "extrapolation": "the activity of determining what is included in the projected world beyond what the author indicated" (1980: 116). Carrier observes the phenomenon in single images: "understanding the depicted scene does require imagining an earlier or later moment of the depicted action" (2000: 12); and he diagnoses the same challenge through an examination of an 1840 Daumier cartoon of a figure with a weight tied around his neck leaning over a river:

> In an instant, this poor man will be underwater dying . . . Logically speaking, many other alternatives are visually consistent with what we see. The man could detach the weight; what appears a weight could rather be a container filled with feathers; he could fall safely into a boat; an angel or a person with a flying suit like the one worn by Buck Rogers could rescue him. But . . . Daumier's success involves creating an unambiguous picture. . . . we are sure that this man is about to drown himself.
>
> 2000: 15

Carrier, however, does not explain how Daumier achieves that unambiguity. Grünewald similarly describes "autonomously narrative pictures" that are parts of "ideal sequences" because the single image prompts viewers to "create further images in our minds," making "non-material sequences" (2012: 176). The production and constraints of those "non-material" images remain open.

Carrier's and Grünewald's examples involve single images and so are not in the comics form (recall also the narrative qualities of Vermeer's *Woman in Blue Reading a*

Letter and Gentileschi's *Judith Beheading Holofernes* discussed in Chapter 1). Sullerot may be the first scholar to document the multi-image phenomenon in her study of Italian photocomics. Eco describes:

> She considers a sequence made of two frames: a firing squad in the process of shooting; the corpse of the condemned man lying on the ground. When they were asked about this sequence, the subjects of the tests tended to describe at some length an imaginary third frame showing the condemned man falling to the ground.
>
> 1965: 24–5

While the implied content is intuitive, the process behind such intuitions has not been explained. Since things that are undrawn are literally infinite, a complete theory of the comics form requires a means of constraining McCloud's closure (the subset of spatiotemporal juxtapostional inferences discussed in the previous two chapters) by differentiating between the merely possible and the undrawn content that can be identified as somehow actual.

As noted in Chapter 4, viewers are more likely to make temporal inferences that align with the qualities of the details that produce them. The time duration between moments depicted in two images of a character's shocked expression would typically be experienced in seconds or shorter, while the duration between moments depicted in identical images of a night sky might be minutes but not hours since the positions of the stars would be altered. While the assumption may seem intuitive, the temporal possibilities are far wider. The images could instead depict two consecutive nights, or they could be divided by weeks, months, years, or centuries. Even images of an identical facial expression could occur at distant moments without requiring the character to have maintained the expression during the interim. What then triggers and justifies the shorter temporal inferences?

Generally, viewers seem to infer as little as possible, suggesting that Occam's razor, the law of parsimony, applies to image juxtapositions: "Entities should not be multiplied without necessity." Determining what is minimally necessary requires a principle that applies across viewers since any individual may experience image juxtapositions differently. Acknowledging that perceptions will vary and that outliers exist, similarities in viewer perceptions produce similar diegeses that constrain inferences. As discussed in Chapter 5, most juxtapositional inferences are spatiotemporal, and as discussed in Chapter 4, a viewer's mental model of a diegetic world can effectively erase image details that contradict it. The same mental models may determine undrawn diegetic content.

If an image is akin to a photograph, depicting a single moment in time, and if a page includes three such images, that page visually represents only those three instances. But the diegetic time span of the page could be minutes, days, or decades, meaning the vast majority of the diegesis is not visually represented. Regarding illustrated prose novels, Mendelsund asks: "What do we *see* during the *unillustrated* part of the story?" (2014: 182). A reader may visualize, but, as Mendelsund points out, that visualization is hardly visual at all (2014: 192). For example, on the five-panel opening page of *Unterzahkn*

(2012), Leela Corman draws a young daughter following her mother through a market. In the second panel, the daughter is directly behind the mother, and in the third she is in front and to the side, selecting a roll of fabric from a vendor's stand as instructed. Does a reader therefore visualize the girl moving from her first location to her second? Almost certainly not. The diegetic event of her movement is, as Mendelsund says of prose-only reading, an "interaction of ideas—the intermingling of abstract relationships" (2014: 245). Viewers experience the abstract idea of the daughter's moving, not its visual enactment.

Viewers make inferences about a diegetic world based on image content in combination with independent knowledge and assumptions about the story world. Those assumptions are usually mimetic, applying, for example, laws of physics to objects and human psychology to characters. If an image includes a glass resting on a table, viewers assume that if the glass is knocked off the table, it will fall at the same rate as a glass falling from the same height in our world. Mimetic expectations are easily defied—Chuck Jones's cartoon Coyote exists to violate laws of physics—but the violations are violations only through contradictions of established expectations. If an image includes a figure with clenched fists, clenched jaw, and tensed brow, viewers will likely assume the features are the result of an internal experience such as pain or anger. Emotions and gravity are undrawn but implicit and so can be said to be part of the shared diegesis across multiple viewers' mental models. Similar qualities are accounted for in the experience of real-world events through a range of cognitive processes, including apparent motion, representational momentum, boundary extension, and the high-level features of goals and intentions; Radvansky and Zacks assert: "comics structure and schematize events. The constituents they use and their rules for combination inform us about the nature of the event representation they produce, and thus may tell us about event models constructed during normal perception" (2014: 93, 94, 98–101, 92).

Events are difficult to define. They are, according to Zacks and Tversky, "in the minds of the beholders," and each is "a segment of time at a given location that is conceived by an observer to have a beginning and an end" (2001: 3). An event therefore is a mental construct that requires at least two spatiotemporally ordered units. Those units, or event segments, "correspond to completions of goals and subgoals" (Tversky, Zacks, and Hard 20007: 449). In Jackendoff's event structure, those goals and subgoals are "Heads," and an event consists of a minimum of one unit, with two optional units: "a Head (the main action), with an optional Preparation (things that have to be done before the Head can be begun) and an optional Coda (things that are done to restore the status quo ante)" (2009: 201). He subdivides "making coffee" into twenty actions (2009: 202). Jackendoff also subdivides each action into the same Prep-Head-Coda construction, and so each alone consists of three units. The action "shaking hands" divides into three subactions: "grasp," "shake," and "withdraw" (2007: 117).

Newtson instead divides actions into "a series of cognitively discrete units" by identifying unit boundaries he terms "breakpoints," which are boundaries between larger multi-unit sections and are also units themselves (1977: 848). Breakpoints serve as "points of definition" for an overall action, where "each breakpoint is a point of reference, or comparison, from both the preceding and following breakpoints" creating an experience of "continuity ... between successive action units" (1977: 849). Newtson divides a video into still frames that he revealingly calls "an almost comic-strip summary of ongoing action sequences" (1977: 849). Jackendoff and Newtson might be harmonized since breakpoints seem to occur at the divisions of the Prep-Head-Coda structure. The resulting five-part structure is apparent in Jackendoff's complete "shaking hands" analysis, which includes five units: reach, grasp, shake, ungrasp, withdraw, with grasp and ungrasp paralleling Newtson's breakpoints (2007: 117).

These cognitive science approaches also parallel literary theories of plot and narrative. Freytag's pyramid analysis of dramatic composition, translated and published in English in 1900, is probably the most ubiquitous. Freytag divides drama into five parts, with three additional "crises," creating an eight-part formula:

1. "introduction";
2. "the exciting moment or force" (or "beginning of the stirring action");
3. "rise";
4. "climax";
5. "the tragic moment or force" (or "beginning of the counter-action");
6. "return or fall";
7. "the moment or force of the final suspense"; and
8. "catastrophe" (or "closing action"). (1900: 115, 137)

Freytag's pyramid is now counterintuitive because his "climax" refers to a turning point (such as Act III of *Macbeth*) rather than his "moment of the final suspense," which the word has evolved to mean. His three crises also parallel Newtson's breakpoints, and the two-sided pyramid consists of two Prep-Head-Codas: introduction-rise-climax and climax-fall-closing.

Referring to narrative and plot interchangeably, Todorov offers a similar structural analysis: "The minimal complete plot can be seen as the shift from one equilibrium to another ... The two moments of equilibrium, similar and different, are separated by a period of imbalance, which is composed of a process of degeneration and a process of improvement" (1969: 75). Dividing imbalance into two parts creates a four-part structure, which can be further punctuated by three breakpoints, producing a similar seven-part structure:

1. equilibrium;
2. disruption of equilibrium;
3. process of degeneration;
4. a turning point between degeneration and improvement;
5. process of improvement;
6. climax of process;
7. new equilibrium.

Freytag and Todorov can be harmonized by collapsing Freytag's steps 4 (his "climax") and 5 (beginning of the counter-action) into Todorov's step 4 (turning point).

The differences between the two dramatic structures and the two event structures are primarily of scale. Adding before and after equilibriums of hands at rest, the seven parts of Jackendoff's "shaking hands" is a complete plot with Newtson's breakpoints at Frytag's crises:

1. rest/equilibrium,
2. reach/disruption (breakpoint/crisis),
3. grasp/degeneration,
4. shake/turning point (breakpoint/crisis),
5. ungrasp/improvement,
6. withdraw/climax (breakpoint/crisis),
7. rest/equilibrium.

Analyzing comic strips, Cohn similarly identifies "arcs" defined by six types of narrative panels:

Orienter (O)—provides a superordinate information, such as setting
Establisher (E)—sets up an interaction without acting upon it
Initial (I)—initiates the tension of the narrative arc
Prolongation (L)—marks a medial state of extension, often the trajectory of a path
Peak (P)—marks the height of narrative tension and point of maximal event
  structure
Release (R)—releases the tension of the interaction (2013, 70)

Combining Cohn's first two narrative panel types into a single category parallel with Freytag's introduction and Todorov's equilibrium creates a five-part structure: Orienter/Establisher, Initial, Prolongation, Peak, Release. This parallels the five-part action structure introduced in *Creating Comics*, which harmonizes Freytag, Todorov, and Cohn, and Cohn's Initial-Peak-Release is partly based on and so aligns with Jackendoff's Prep-Head-Coda:

Balance   **Disruption**   **Imbalance**   **Climax**   **Balance**

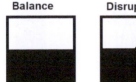

Illustration 6.9 Event Sequence.

"Action" is another problematic term because an action requires an actor and so connotatively a character performing motivated behavior. I will instead refer to events, which are commonly considered the units that comprise a narrative or plot. I also do not prioritize the *Creating Comics* approach over others.

Newtson further suggests why Cohn's Peaks, which are the defining element of his structure just as Heads are the defining element of Jackendoff's, are so significant because "action units are defined by a type of information uniquely available at breakpoints," and this is true primarily because breakpoints communicate "a meaningful change having occurred relative to the preceding breakpoint" (1977: 851). Hard, Recchia, and Tversky summarize this succinctly: "Breakpoints are bridges" (2011: 586). Breakpoints apply well to Todorov's three-part structure, because equilibrium, disequilibrium, and equilibrium are separated by a disruption and a restoration—or Cohn's Initial and Peak. Viewing them as breakpoints reveals how much less important other panel types are because they are one of many available "nonbreakpoints" within the equilibrium, disequilibrium, equilibrium spans. That accounts for why Cohn can divide the first phase into Orienter and Establisher, with multiple Prolongations in the middle phase, and (presumably) multiple Release panels in the third. Only Initials and Peaks then are unique and defining. The *Creating Comics* event structure visually literalizes the same two breakpoints, disruption and climax, by rendering them as actual breaks in the preceding line angles. For Newtson, the second breakpoint is the same as the first, since they are both disruptions (points of defining change) of a preceding status quo. However, since Newtson asserts that "Behavior is composed of coherent units with beginnings and endings" (1977: 848), first and second breakpoints are relative to each other and the differences in the two status quos, making each breakpoint distinct.

Breakpoints also apply to McCloud's original closure example for an action-to-action panel transition. In Illustration 6.10, the baseball batter's two poses are

Illustration 6.10 Action-to-action example from McCloud's *Understanding Comics.*

breakpoints between three segments: balance (holding the bat before swinging), imbalance (swinging the bat), and balance (holding the bat after swinging). The first image depicts either the last moment before the swing or the first moment of the swing, and the second image depicts either the last moment of the swing or the first moment of holding the bat after swinging. Both images are breakpoints.

Looking back at Illustration 4.8, McCloud's moment-to-moment images could be understood as depicting states of balance, the first establishing a status quo (eyes open), and the second establishing a new status quo (eyes closed). Though McCloud intends to illustrate what he ambiguously terms "moments," the contrast implies an action: she closed her eyes. Alternatively, the second image might be understood as a climax (if this is the moment her eyes fully close) and the first image as a disruption (if this is the moment they first began to close). If so, both are breakpoints, making the transition action-to-action. Understanding the two images instead as balances may reveal the difference McCloud intended: depicted breakpoints are linked to action-to-action transitions, and depicted nonbreakpoints are linked to moment-to-moment transitions. Both are aspects of event structure.

Though an infinite number of images can be drawn between breakpoints (assuming the Zeno effect), those possible images are still constrained by event structure. Revising McCloud's original claim, closure *is* event structure. The undrawn content viewers experience through the juxtaposition of two or more images is the minimal content required by a viewer's mental experience of a partially drawn but fully implied event. While anything could have occurred in the ambiguous lapse of time between any of the above pairings of depicted moments, viewers understand the images as parts of a discrete event. Any content that is not part of that discrete event is not implied and so did not happen—at least not through event inferencing. An author can always later assert that something previously unimplied did happen, retconning content that reveals an earlier omission.

Returning to Carrier's analysis of Daumier's image, though the man about to fall into the river "could fall safely into a boat" or "an angel or a person with a flying suit like the one worn by Buck Rogers could rescue him," nothing in the image implies those possibilities and so those events cannot be inferred. For them to be inferable, the image would presumably need to include a boat, angel, or a person in a flying suit, creating the possibilities of those rescues. Since Daumier draws only one image, the possibility would also create ambiguity about the outcome of the event, since viewers could no longer look at the first image and draw Carrier's conclusion: "we are sure that this man is about to drown himself" (2000: 15). Viewers would require at least one additional image to experience what event the first image initiated. If no additional image followed, event inferencing would remain blocked by a permanently indeterminate outcome.

Zacks and Tversky discuss event inferencing through schema theory:

> recognizing an event as an instance of a category consists of matching it to a schema stored in memory. Understanding what is going on consists of matching features of the perceptual world to variables in the schema. In ongoing perception, missing information is filled in by references to the patterns of intercorrelation

captured by the schema, leading to a fluid interplay of bottom-up and top-down processing.

2001: 13

Bottom-up indicates that cues in the discursive images motivate the processing, and top-down indicates that information already stored in the brain informs how cues are interpreted. Applied specifically to the comics form, event structure accounts for the undrawn but inferred content of an event represented through multiple images. Where event inferences can be applied generally to single or multiple images, the inference subcategory within the comics form applies only to multiple images. The juxtapositional inferences are constrained by the minimum required to satisfy undrawn event segments. Though it is possible that McCloud's two images of a baseball player could take place at unrelated moments and locations, the juxtaposition implies the unified event of a batter hitting a ball, and so that event and its minimally required details are part of the diegesis. Event inferencing therefore distinguishes between the merely possible and the diegetically actual.

Holbo makes a similar but flawed claim to suggest that closure applies to single images and therefore that single images are comics: "The not invariable but highly typical mechanism of the gag strip is to imply one unseen action or event: what happens next, or before," and since "Caravaggio's [*The Sacrifice of Isaac*] does not work differently, blood in the gutter-wise, than a gag strip … *any* image in which it can be seen what is happening is narrative art" and so a comic (2014: 9, 11). Since an unseen action or event is by definition not seen and so not a discursive image, Holbo either conflates discourse and diegesis or is speaking in a shorthand that obscures the distinction. Moreover, the relevant event inferencing is specific to sequenced images, but the "blood in the gutter-wise" inferences that Holbo refers to are the narrative effects of a single image and so are not "closure" even as defined by McCloud. "Narrative art" and the comics form are not equivalent, since some narrative artworks are not sequenced images, and some sequenced images are not narrative art.

Still, event inferencing of sequenced images and event inferencing triggered by a single image are deeply related. The first might be more fully termed "multi-image event inferencing," and the second "single-image event inferencing," both being subcategories of the larger category "image event inferencing." Since event inferencing may involve text or, when a work is prose-only, exclusively text, image event inferencing is a subset of event inferencing generally. When a work contains both images and text (as discussed in the next chapter), event inferencing may operate separately for each, or image and text may combine to co-produce the same inferences. Also, sequenced images need not imply any events, or they may imply multiple overlapping events, where one image or parts of one image represent different segments of different events simultaneously.

Because events can be experienced in a range of different ways, event inferences vary accordingly. Tversky, Zacks, and Hard note: "Events can be conceived of at many levels: a lifetime can be a single event, but so can eating a meal or folding a shirt" (2007: 459). A work representing "folding a shirt" through images and implied content might create an impression of nearly complete knowledge, but no sequence will create that impression for longer events. Consider Rudolph Zallinger's ubiquitous illustration "The March of Progress" in which silhouettes of walking figures progress from a small, hunched ape-like shape to a fully erect human. The event of human evolution is understood to occur over millions of years, but all of the details that take place in the time spans between each depicted moment are not inferable and so are not aspects of event inferencing. Event inferences then do not account for all content occurring between depicted moments. Note also that that transforming figure is paradoxically recurrent since each figure is also a separate individual, or a representative of an entire species of individuals, all of them beyond the constraints of event inferencing.

Events can also be extremely brief. Categorizing images by Cohn's panel types is often difficult when the primary represented action is a character speaking. Recalling Tversky's observation that event segments correspond to completions of goals, the image of a single talk balloon is an unsegmented event because it represents the complete goal-defined action of a speaker speaking. Talk balloons represent durations of time determined by the amount of time required for the speaker to speak the framed words. If the previous sentence were contained in a talk balloon, the balloon would represent a duration of roughly ten seconds. If that balloon were part of an image that included a representation of me speaking, the image would also appear to represent a static instant. That contradiction confuses event structure because any image that contains a word-filled talk balloon must somehow represent a duration of time, a single instance, and their ambiguous amalgam (a norm of image-texts discussed in the next chapter). Further, a single image that includes a speech balloon depicts a speaking event through single-image event inferencing, but if that image is also part of a sequence, it is also likely involved in multi-image event inferencing of additional events.

Though I have discussed several specific event and plot structures, event inferences are not dependent on any single paradigm, and any is potentially applicable—with the exception of Cohn's panels types. While event structure exists in a viewer's mind, Cohn's panels must exist in a physical visual field. There is no such thing as an invisible or undrawn Initial panel, even when there is a mental experience of a parallel disruption in a viewer's understanding of an implied event. Cohn's narrative panel types are event structure manifested discursively. Cohn acknowledges the role of implied content, distinguishing two sets of structures: "those related to the meaning of a visual sequence (spatial, referential, and event structures) and those related to its presentation (graphic and narrative structures)," noting that "each narrative category maps to prototypical event structures" (2019: 6, 8). However, studies in which participants "recognize which panels may have been deleted" from a sequence conflate discourse and diegesis by suggesting that the absence of a physical panel, rather than its parallel event structure content, is recognized (2019: 10). The deletion of a panel describes a step in the creative process of designing a test sequence, but the resulting sequence itself has no deleted panels. Participants' "longer viewing times" and "larger neural responses" linked to "reanalysis" are presumably the results of the sequences being unintuitive, but an artist need not draw and then delete an actual panel to produce such effects (2019: 12).

Finally, though event inferencing applies to representational images only, there are possible exceptions. The general rule follows from a lack of a mimetic world in which

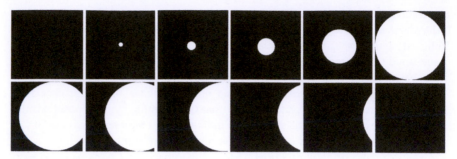

Illustration 6.11 Illustration 4.4 revised.

events can take place. Non-representational images produce no diegesis and so no diegetic world—except in the most limited sense. As previously discussed, two sets of discursively similar marks can be understood to represent a non-representational and yet recurrent subject. The first row of non-representational images in Illustration 6.8 is sequential and in some sense a narrative because it suggests an evolving subject. The progression is a kind of event. However, it is not clear whether undrawn content can be implied since there is no mimetic basis for comparison. The recurrent subject as it appears in each of the four images might be understood as the only stages in a four-part process, requiring and so implying no intermediate stages. Unlike McCloud's baseball player swinging a bat that must move through a range of physical points before reaching the point depicted in the second image, the nature of a non-mimetic object's transformation may be ambiguous.

Some images, however, can suggest a semi-mimetic setting that follows some form of physics, or if a progression displays a clearly incremental progression of changes, undrawn incremental steps can be implied as occurring between depictions. The ten-image non-representational sequence in Illustration 4.4 or the similar twelve-image sequence here in Illustration 6.11 could suggest undrawn content between images. Illustration 4.4 could also suggest the first and final black squares included in 6.11. The first black square is black because the circle is either too distant or too small to be seen, a fact that can be inferred in 4.4 by the images that establish the event of the circle's incremental changes. The last black square is black because the circle is no longer in the implied view's line of vision, an outcome of the inferred event of either the movement of the circle or an implied viewer's gaze. Either way, the non-representational images are actually semi-representational because they produce a diegesis that features a recurrent subject and setting that have at least rudimentary spatiotemporality. Event inferences then are still always diegetic and never exclusively discursive.

Having explored the qualities of images and sequences in the first six chapters, *The Comics Form* moves to a final chapter and a common subcategory: sequenced image-texts.

7

Sequenced Image-texts

Previous chapters have focused on images that do not include words (non-linguistic images). This final chapter explores the qualities of images with linguistic content (word-images), including word-images rendered as graphic art (word-image art), and images that combine linguistic and non-linguistic content (image-texts). Since sequenced images can but do not necessarily include image-texts, image-texts are not part of the comics form. Some scholars such as Rifkind, however, do consider text an essential feature, defining comics as "image-texts in sequence" (2019: 5). Image-texts then are at minimum a highly pervasive convention, and so a thorough understanding of how sequenced images work requires an understanding of the subset of sequenced image-texts.

The comics medium typically features both non-linguistic images and word-images, a fact observed as early as 1903 by Marble, who calls the "'picture section' of the Sunday newspapers" a "commingled art," an "alliance of picture and text" (2004: 8), and echoed by Greenberg's 1945 description of comics as the "mating of drawing with caption" (2004: 40). A half century later, Pratt similarly concludes that "it is a hybrid art form that employs narrative strategies closely connected to literature, on the one hand, and other pictorial media, on the other" (2009: 107). McCloud even argues against the perceived division: "But just how 'different' are they?" (1993: 47). Carrier agrees, describing comics as a "composite art" with a distinguishing "word/image unity" (2000: 4), but others, including Chute, argue that "words and images entwine, but never synthesize" (2010:5). Regardless of the nature of the various comingling, alliance, matting, hybridity, unity, or synthesizing, I set aside requirements such as Waugh's that works necessarily include "speech in the drawing" (1947: 14), though Inge and others are not wrong that works in the comics medium "often" do include "dialogue in balloons and narrative text" (1990: xi). If the image-texts are sequenced, the work is in the comics form.

The presence of words has also produced disagreement over their relative dominance. Abbott argues that comics art "must conform to an order of perception that is essentially literary" (1986: 156), Eisner asserts oppositely that images of "body posture and gesture occupy a position of primacy over text" (2000: 106), and Wartenberg articulates a middle position that it is typically "impossible to specify the story-world created by the comic without making reference to both the text and the image," and therefore "comics gives images and texts equal ontological priority" (2012: 101). Image-texts have no set relationship between words and images, allowing diverging claims to describe specific instances but not image-text sequences generally.

Though separable and variously related, words and images in the comics medium are often understood to create unified effects. In *The Avengers Annuals* #12 (November 1983), Rick Parker letters the speech of the Vision in word frames that penciller Butch Guice and inker Rick Magyar draw as corner-rounded rectangles to suggest the robotic quality of the android character's voice, an effect further heightened by colorist Carl Gafford's filling the interior areas in yellow. Scripter Bill Mantlo's dialogue coincides with the visual effect; when Wanda wakes from a nightmare, the Vision responds:

> "It was only a dream, my wife, made more real perhaps, because of your mutant
> sensibility to such unconscious states."
> Wanda: "Logic won't erase how awful it was."
> Vision: "No, but it should make you realize you have nothing to fear!"
>
> 1983: 21

Wanda's contrasting speech appears in white ovals, the standard talk balloon format. Because the words are attributed to the subjects as drawn by Guice and Magyar, they are also linked to the same moment that is depicted in the image, creating a unified impression. But the words and image also disrupt each other. The amount of diegetic time required for the characters to speak the framed words exceeds the apparent instantaneity of the image, producing a contradictory spatiotemporality that is a norm in the comics medium.

Image-texts can also be fundamentally disruptive. Hopkins presents six claims for pictorial representation:

1. "It is possible to refer to a particular thing using a word . . . without saying anything about it . . . In contrast, a picture must depict more"
2. "all depiction is from a point of view"
3. "only what can be seen can be depicted"
4. "there is only so much room for misrepresentation"
5. "one needs to know what the thing depicted looks like"
6. "I do not need much more than knowledge of appearance to understand pictures"

> 2005: 145–6

An image-text can depict the unseeable by labeling an image with identifying language. The abstract noun "Love" may be affixed to a scribble of lines, communicating that the scribble represents love even though the emotion cannot be seen. Similarly, any level of misrepresentation is acceptable if the accompanying language communicates the meaning. If the scribble of lines, which bears no resemblance to Chris Gavaler, is labeled "Chris Gavaler," the scribble is understood to represent me—and may do so later without the accompanying label. One need not even know what I look like to understand the labeled scribble. A labeled scribble also does not necessarily suggest a point of view and may communicate little if anything beyond its identifying label.

For similar reasons, sequenced image-texts are prone to metafictional effects, since the two communication forms interrupt each other and prevent unreflective immersion.

The dual nature of word-images also allows them to function as objects within a diegesis interacting with other diegetic content as part of an otherwise non-linguistic image—Eisner's *The Spirit* splash pages provide numerous examples—while still communicating their linguistic content. Since the presence of the letterforms violates the illusion of the diegetic reality (unless the letterforms are understood to exist literally in the way that the letterforms of a Robert Indiana *Love* sculpture exist three-dimensionally), viewers must understand them as non-literal while simultaneously understanding other non-linguistic elements in the same image-text literally. When the two kinds of images are interacting—as when Eisner draws characters climbing on letterforms—the paradoxical and metafictional effect is intensified.

Whether word and image combinations create unified, ununified, or paradoxical effects, analysis of sequenced image-text requires an understanding of the separate and interactive qualities of linguistic and non-linguistic content. Groensteen provides groundwork for such an approach, adapting Gaudreault's "monstration," the act of showing, to coin "monstrator," the agency of "putting into drawing" (2010: 4), and adapting "recitative" into "recitant," "the authority responsible for [verbal] enunciation" (2010: 6–7). Their coordination "is dependent on the authority of a higher narrative focus," which Groensteen terms simply the "narrator," through whom the monstrator and recitant "exercise, through delegation, some of its prerogatives" (2010: 14).

While pioneeringly useful, these terms and definitions present limitations, requiring further examination of each narration kind, text and image, individually, and the complexities of their combination into a third kind. I offer text-narrator, image-narrator, and image-text narrator and analyze their relationships as necessary qualities of any image sequence that includes text. Before discussing narrators, the chapter first explores the qualities of word-images and their juxtapositions.

1. Word-images

Though words are not necessary to the comics form, word-images are a kind of image, and sequenced images often include them. Describing some that do, Carrier observes:

> Comics are personlike in their unity of words and images [...] Philosophical theories of the mind–body problem aim to explain that unity or to dissolve it. Comics merely illustrate that dualism, without taking any stand on philosophical questions about the nature of the mind–body relationship.
>
> 2000: 73

Words and images involve independent parallel processes that combine to produce interconnected meanings, but a mind–body relationship instead suggests a hierarchy. Even if regarded as immaterial, a mind is in some sense a product of a body's brain, and so on a biological understanding a body can exist without a mind, but a mind does not exist without a brain.

Carrier's "personlike" simile does apply to word-images. The word "word" has at least two definitions. In alphabet-based writing, a word is a combination of letterforms, and it is also a set of meanings including connotations linked to that combination of letterforms and experienced in a reader's mind. Neither refers to a specific instance of a word's appearance as an image, which may be termed a "word-image." Miodrag observes similarly: "language participates in comics *through* its material configuration on the page" (2010: 324). Every word-image is a specific instance or token of a general category or type, and in prose-only contexts, its material configuration is typically ignored. This is why Goodman can correctly assert that "differences between [editions] in style and size of script or type, in color of ink, in kind of paper, in number and layout of pages, in condition, etc., do not matter" (1976: 115).

Like non-linguistic images, word-images have both discursive and diegetic qualities. They are physical marks on physical surfaces, but unless the words are pictographic and so have at least some minimal resemblance to their subjects, their discursive shapes are non-representational. As Walton explains, a "reader does not imagine his viewing of the words of the text to be the viewing of" the subject matter that the words prompt her to imagine, while for a viewer of a picture the "seeing" of the picture and the "imagining" of the subject matter "are inseparably bound together" (1990: 294–5). Since word-images trigger linguistic content, which is a kind of representational content, word-images are also an indirect kind of representational image.

Like other representational images, word-images can fail to represent content fully. A viewer can recognize the subject of an untitled portrait only if the portrait sufficiently resembles the subject—though a viewer might still recognize the intended portrait as an image of some unidentifiable person. Similarly, an illegible word is illegible because a viewer understands the cluster of marks as intending but failing to resemble letterforms that convey linguistic content. The failed resemblance for non-linguistic images is of the representational content itself. If a letterform cluster is called a scribble, it is distinct from other scribbles which are not understood to intend linguistic meaning. The failed portrait would be called a scribble for the same reason. It might be more accurate to say both "look like scribbles" if scribbles are non-representational marks distinct from failed representational ones.

Legible word-images may barely register as marks if a viewer's attention shifts primarily to their linguistic content seemingly bypassing their discursive presence. "What we are looking at when we read," explains Mendelsund, "*are* words, made up letterforms, but we are trained to see past them—to look at what the words and letterforms point toward. Words are like arrows—they *are* something, and they point *toward* something" (2014: 322). "To read," continues Mendelsund, "is: to look *through* [...] There is very little looking at" (2014: 334–5). Words-images in prose-only texts are most often typeset in a single font and color and with little variation. That uniformity communicates the graphic equality of the word-images' discursive features. If all words are rendered identically, word rendering communicates no meaning. Bendis describes the same convention in the comics medium: "Lettering should be invisible. You shouldn't notice it, unless it is a determined piece of storytelling in graphic design" (2014: 43).

Bendis correctly implies that some word-images are designed to disrupt readers' looking-through tendency. Bateman describes an example from Eisner: "The visual instantiation of the text plays just as strong a role in the expressive force of the panel as the facial expression and gestures of the depicted character" (2014: 27). The effect is also common outside the comics medium. William Faulkner proposed to print *The Sound and Fury* in colored inks to signify time shifts: "If I could only get it printed the way it ought to be with different color types for the different times in Benjy's section recording the flow of events for him, it would make it simpler" (quoted in Flood 2012). Aside from a 2012 Folio Society edition of 1,480 colored copies, the novel remains in its original uniformly rendered format, its black ink signifying nothing. Words rendered to be looked at are more common in fine art. Glenn Ligon's 1994 *Untitled: Four Etchings* repeats two sentences, "I do not always feel colored" and "I feel most colored when I am thrown against a sharp white background," on juxtaposed canvases. Henri Matisse treated the graphic qualities of his own handwriting as non-representational paint strokes. His 1947 *Jazz* begins:

> I'd like to introduce my color prints under the most favorable conditions. For this reason I must separate them with intervals of a different character. I decided handwriting was best suited for this purpose. The exceptional size of the writing seems necessary to me in order to be in a decorative relationship with the character of the color prints. These pages, therefore, will serve only to accompany my colors, just as asters help in the composition of a bouquet of more important flowers. *Thus, their role is purely visual.*
>
> 1985: xv

The word-images' non-linguistic qualities don't add meaning to their linguistic content; they replace it. Matisse likens the content to the unread court decisions he filled with fables as a law clerk because the importance of a trial was marked by the volume of paper it produced. For Matisse, the letterforms are shapes only.

Word-images in the comics medium are not purely visual, but, like Matisse's lettering, they are visually expressive and compositional. A reader reads them in the linguistic sense while also being influenced by their renderings, so the meaning of a word-image may be both linguistic and non-linguistic. Even "Spacing and typography," observes Miodrag, "mold the reception of text" (2013: 78). Words in the comics medium typically appear to be hand-lettered, consist entirely of capitals, employ bolding for word emphasis, and may change size, line-thickness, stylistic shape, and color to denote a range of meanings. John Costanza's lettering in the caption boxes of *Wonder Woman* #20 (September 1988) is set in a font similar to courier news, because the narrator is a character within the story who is drawn seated at a typewriter in an opening panel (Pérez 1988: 152). Words in speech frames still appear in standard hand-lettered style, differentiated from the character's first-person narration as he types his memoir which consists of the same words that appear in the captions. The captioned words, however, are not a direct representation of his sheets of typewriter paper because the caption boxes are too small and the line breaks too numerous. The rendered words hover between text and pictorial representation.

Hatfield refers to such word-images as "visually inflected," explaining that "visible language has the potential to be quite elaborate in appearance, forcing recognition of pictorial and material qualities that can be freight with meaning" (2005: 36–7).

Schwarcz, in his overview of visual communication in children's literature, devotes two chapters to such visual effects, "The Letter and the Written Word as Visual Element" and "Visual Sound," and identifies a dozen subcategories (1982). Eisner also describes how, when treated "'graphically,'" lettering "functions as an extension of the imagery," and so the lettering style of dialogue "tells the reader how the author wishes it to sound" and "evokes a specific emotion" (2008: 3–4). What Eisner calls the "visual treatment of words as graphic art" also complicates Walton's assumption that the "seeing" of a word and the "imagining" of the word's subject matter are separate, since the imagining is not simply the result of triggering a viewer's set of meanings associated with the word but is also influenced by the discursive qualities of the specific word-image that does the triggering. The discursive and linguistic qualities may synthesize.

2. Word-image Juxtapositions

Word-images pose a challenge to the comics form as defined as sequenced images, since, if any discursive word is a word-image and therefore an image, any two juxtaposed word-images would be in the comics form. However, the rendered two-word phrase "sequenced images" is not in the comics form for several reasons.

First, juxtaposed word-images typically form and are defined by larger units. The same is true of non-linguistic images. Isolating a set of marks—say, the ones that form my left eye in "Four Mode Self-Portrait" in Illustration 2.3—does not indicate that it is a separate image. Viewers most likely perceive my eye as only a part of an image. If it is part of the self-portrait as a whole, there is no juxtaposition. If the self-portrait is instead perceived as four juxtaposed images (as suggested by the 2x2 grid and the contrasting styles within each section), then "Four Mode Self-Portrait" is in the comics form. Similarly, the words inside each gridded square of Wheeler's visual poem "En Dehors Garde Bingo" in Illustration 6.1 are likely perceived as a single unit and not as multiple juxtaposed units.

Word combinations, however, do not address the core challenge, since any two larger word units (this and the previous sentence, for example) would be in the comics form when juxtaposed. Kay Rosen's 1998 six-canvas *The Ed Paintings* excerpted in

Illustration 7.1 *Surprise, Technical Difficulties, Part I of "Blanks," and Part II of "Blanks"* from Kay Rosen's *The Ed Paintings*.

Illustration 7.1 deepens the challenge since the words on each canvas are distinct, sequential, and together create a diegetic event and sound-based puns. What distinguishes *The Ed Paintings* from this page of text? One answer reverts to the publishing and social context criteria discussed in the Introduction, defaulting either to authorial intention or viewer reception. That approach does not preclude (and likely implies) the presence of formal features that influence such determinations. By graphically arranging words on this mass-producible page, a typesetter focuses attention on their linguistic qualities only. By graphically arranging words on a canvas, an artist focuses attention on either their discursive qualities or their discursive and linguistic qualities both. Arguably all word-images are visually inflected since a word-image cannot be non-visual or non-graphic, but if there is a spectrum, *The Ed Paintings* and this page of text are on opposite halves.

McCloud places "reality" and "language" at opposite ends of a horizontal "iconic abstraction scale," adding the vertical dimension of a "picture plane" to create an abstraction pyramid (1993: 46, 51). The language-picture dimension marks the degree to which an image, whether linguistic or non-linguistic, has symbolic meaning (its diegesis) or "simply 'means' what it is," (its discourse) "ink on paper" (1993: 50). Standard typeset prose falls at the bottom of the language–picture continuum, communicating only its linguistic meaning. McCloud draws the sound effect "SPLASH!" in large rounded unaligned letters with two water drops as an example of a word rendered one tier higher than a typically typeset word on his picture continuum. The majority of words in the comics medium would likely fall between McCloud's two tiers, with some appearing at or a tier above if the rendering of the word is emphasized over its linguistic meaning.

Critiquing McCloud, Holbo observes: "Typography *is* graphic design. Novels, being typed are *graphic* novels," and since "Letterforms *are* images," prose-only novels would appear to be in the comics form (2014: 15). McCloud addresses this concern by distinguishing between "pictorial" images and "other images," acknowledging that "juxtaposed static images" include words (1993: 8–9). Pictorial images and the implied category of non-pictorial images, however, do not clarify Hatfield's "visually inflected" category because visually inflected word-images are neither exclusively pictorial nor non-pictorial. Also, McCloud's "word/picture combination" list includes "montage," for "words and pictures combined pictorially" (2006: 130). The term is unfortunate since "montage" already refers to the juxtaposition of moving images (a meaning unrelated to McCloud's closure despite its parallel to panel transitions). McCloud also does not clarify the adverb "pictorially," since his category includes words that exist within the diegesis (he draws the example of a stop sign), sound effects (which exist within the diegesis non-visually), titles incorporated metafictionally into the diegesis (while remaining outside characters' experience), and words in word frames "with a strong pictorial sensibility" (2006: 139).

Distinguishing instead between "non-linguistic images" and "word-images" avoids McCloud's ambiguities. Eisner, Bendis, and Holbo use the modifier "graphic" to further distinguish between Hatfield's "visually inflected" word-images and word-images generally, but "graphic" is synonymous with discursive, and so all word-images are necessarily graphic, making the subcategory either unclear or contradictory. Calling "visually inflected" word-images "word-image art" offers a clearer distinction, while leaving the point on the implied spectrum to individual perception. Only a word-image that is rendered and experienced as graphic art is word-image art.

Sequenced word-images are in the comics form to the degree that a viewer experiences them non-linguistically and so as word-image art (which is also separated into distinct images and not a multi-word unit). Because word-image art incorporates word-images, a viewer presumably also experiences them linguistically. A work of word-image art may include a single word—Hannah K. Lee's two-page "Millennial" consists entirely of black letterforms, some nested, and two rendered to resemble dripping ink (2017: n.p.)—or a set of words, such as the graphic arrangement of words on each canvas in *The Ed Paintings*. The comics form then is sequenced non-linguistic images and/or word-image art, but not word-images only.

Since a non-linguistic image and a word-image may be perceived as a single unit, the relationship of word-images to the comics form requires further clarification.

3. Image-texts

An image-text is a visual field that includes both non-linguistic images and word-images or word-image art.

In the comics medium, hand-lettered or typeset words appear in frames termed "caption boxes" and in "balloons" or "bubbles" distinguished by the linguistic content of speech or thought, with "tails" or "pointers" directed at rendered subjects. The framed words typically divide into lines according to the discursive requirements of the frame and so with little or no linguistic consideration, but word frames can also produce units and rhythmic effects similar to lines or stanzas of poetry. The backgrounds of framed areas are sometimes different from the surrounding image, often with the same negative space as margins and gutters. Since these frames, like drawn frames generally, are not actual frames but representations, words in word frames are image-texts, with the non-linguistic elements communicating meaning. Pratt, for example, observes that "word balloons may also, through their style or even color, give pictorial cues to the reader as to the mental states and attitudes of their utterers" (2009: 110).

If frames and word-images are sufficient to make an image-text, then many PowerPoint presentations are in the comics form, including the story "Great Rock and Roll Pauses" in Jennifer Egan's 2010 *A Visit from the Goon Squad*, which is a PowerPoint both discursively and diegetically since it is created by a character within the story. The contiguously juxtaposed units of Wheeler's "En Dehors Garde Bingo" from Illustration 6.1 are also image-texts (the original version includes multiple shades of green, blue, and black ink, the visual arrangement is central to the poem's meaning, and the framing grid is itself a non-linguistic image), and so the visual poem would also be in the comics form. Many charts, graphs, and diagrams are image-texts, too, and so would combine in the comics form. Alternatively, such examples might be excluded from the comics form if non-linguistic images must display some minimal level of graphic-art quality to produce image-texts in combination with word-images. Such a spectrum would be subject to individual perception.

More often word-images are integrated elements of a larger image-text that includes non-linguistic images that are unambiguously art, creating a combined experience that vacillates between reading words and viewing images. The combination in isolation does not produce sequenced images. René Magritte's 1929 *The Treachery of Images* and Barbara Kruger's 1989 *Untitled (Your body is a battleground)* are each not in the comics form, but if printed side by side, they could be. Each alone would be in the comics form

II. Mourning Science

Behind the torn veil of her face, the dead bride of her inventor wrenches the gears into thought, steers the wheelhouse of her head up to blink at nothingness. Her eyes mirror the oil-black sky. Nobody home. Her God-husband grieved life into cogs, valves, pistons, and hope that things are only things, no fraud of a spirit to spark their ignition. He died. His wet machine disassembled its own parts, left her no memory to keep remaking her mistaken self, no hold on her ghostly code. She will never leap that divide. Not dead, not not dead. All wives are manmade, haunting their invented lives.

II. Mourning Science

Behind the torn veil of her face, the dead bride of her inventor wrenches the gears into thought, steers the wheelhouse of her head up to blink at nothingness. Her eyes mirror the oil-black sky. Nobody home. Her God-husband grieved life into cogs, valves, pistons, and hope that things are only things, no fraud of a spirit to spark their ignition. He died. His wet machine disassembled its own parts, left her no memory to keep remaking her mistaken self, no hold on her ghostly code. She will never leap that divide. Not dead, not not dead. All wives are manmade, haunting their invented lives.

Illustration 7.2 "Mourning Science."

only if a viewer experiences their words as discrete images and not as integrated elements of a single image-text. While this could vary by individual perception, I suspect most viewers experience most image-texts as single images.

Illustration 7.2 features "Mourning Science," the second page in the four-page sequence *Metropolis II*. The page divides into six units, each composed entirely of word-images. Those in the top right and middle left stanzas are legible and combine to produce the same sonnet. In terms of shape, the letterforms are Bauhaus, an art deco font evocative of the 1920s. The interiors of the letterforms are digital cut-outs of film stills that combine for gestalt effects, though neither image is legible until the letterforms are layered into overlapping units. The middle right stanzas combine the word-images to reveal a human face, the bottom left combines them to reveal a robot face, and the bottom right and top left stanzas combine both sets to produce amalgam faces. The layered words are not legible and so arguably are not word-images but the equivalent of paint strokes that produce the non-linguistic content. Like Matisse's *Jazz* text, their role is visual. When they are legible, their typography is thematically relevant, but likely not to the degree to categorize them as word-image art. Instead of word-image art, the page consists of images composed of word-images that are only minimally graphic art when not layered to produce non-linguistic content. Because the page juxtaposes multiple non-linguistic images, it is in the comics form, and because it includes word-images, it is also sequenced image-texts contiguously juxtaposed.

William Blake's 1789 *Songs of Innocence and Experience*, because it consists of sequenced image-texts (each page integrates an illustration and Blake's hand-rendered text) temporally juxtaposed, is in the comics form. Children's pictures books typically are, too. This book also includes image-texts on pages with illustrations, but the word-images of the typeset text on the majority of pages are not word-image art, and so their sequencing with the illustrations do not produce sequenced images. *The Comics Form* is not in the comics form.

4. Narrators

As discussed in Chapter 1, narrators are a convenient conceit for analyzing content, whether linguistic or non-linguistic. A prose-only work can have only one narrator, or only one kind of narrator. If a prose work includes multiple narrators, they are all text-narrators, because in prose a discourse of words alone produces the diegesis. Keen clarifies that narrator applies equally to "the many visual or hybrid narrative forms," too (2003: 34, 32). An image-text sequence has two kinds of narrators, a text-narrator and an image-narrator, as well as a third, an image-text narrator, that produces effects through the combination of the first two.

I set aside Groensteen's earlier terms for several reasons. Words and images can both be understood to "show," making the designation monstrator exclusive to images inappropriate. Secondly and more significantly, image-narrator has a broader application than the drawing-specific meaning that Groensteen stipulates for monstrator, since images need not be drawn. Groensteen asserts that the drawn image, as a manufactured creation, inevitably produces a signature of its creator. Drawing per se is an encoding and stylization of reality, it is produced by a reading of the world. As such, drawing cannot be separated from the hand of a specific enunciator.

2010: 4

While possibly true, such hand-specific images do not define images generally, and so while all monstrators are image-narrators, not all image-narrators are monstrators. Photo-based work, such as Joey Comeau and Emily Horne's 2016 *Anatomy of Melancholy*, image-narrate with no monstrator. Also, some image-narrators do not create but instead select from pre-existing images. In her memoir *Belonging*, Nora Krug includes pages comprised of historical photos (2018: n.p.). Since Krug is not the photographer, there is no monstrator even in an expanded sense. However, while no monstrator draws the content of Krug's photographic images, an image-narrator can be understood to select and position them, thereby giving them their context-specific meanings within the memoir.

Krug's approach further contradicts Groensteen's categories in which his overarching "narrator" is responsible for "cutting" and "page lay-out" (2010: 15), actions better attributed to the image-narrator. Groensteen appears to treat an image's diegetic content as separable from such discursive qualities as image size, framing, and page position, even though a page may also be understood as a single image sequenced into parts. Those parts, however, are not discrete and their relationships are image-to-image and so understandable through image-narration alone, making an addition of a second agency, Groensteen's "narrator," unnecessary. An image-only work employs only an image-narrator, just as a prose-only novel employs only a text-narrator.

Finally, the hand-specificity that Groensteen attributes to monstrators alone can apply instead to recitants. Most of the pages of *Belonging* include hand-written text, sometimes interwoven with photography, and so Krug's images do not suit the definition of a monstrator, and yet her text does. Grant even implies that all drawing might belong to a recitant since: "Cartooning can be seen as a performative mode of handwriting" (2019: n.p.). By recitant Groensteen might mean something that could be more precisely termed a language-narrator: a narrator that produces word meanings independent of word rendering. If so, the physical letterforms that trigger those meanings are not the product of a recitant but paradoxically of an image-narrator— and even a monstrator in Groensteen's stricter sense since letters are drawn, often by the same hand with the same pen that draws the accompanying images. Alternatively, Groensteen's recitant might be a text-narrator, a narrator that produces both words in the linguistic sense and their physical letterforms. This is perhaps closer to Groensteen's intention since his recitant does not merely conceive words but "enunciates" them, which in a visual medium would presumably indicate rendering.

This is a problematic division though, since the word-image art discussed above may serve a more visual-based than language-based function. While the text inside word frames is often rendered by a lettering artist different from the penciller and inker, sound effects are typically drawn by the primary artist in a style that emphasizes the expressive quality of the rendering over the meaning of the onomatopoeic word.

The same may be true of words intended as speech when rendering suggests volume or emotion. Alison Bechdel further problematizes any division between image and text when her image-narrator in *Fun Home* visually renders journal and book pages that include legible words, requiring viewers to read images that represent physical objects in the diegesis.

Despite these challenges, text-narrator may be the most practical term. A language-narrator cannot enunciate but through an image-narrator, but the hybrid text-narrator may be understood also to render its language into minimally graphic text (meaning not word-image art). While again no precise division along the spectrum is likely, when the expressive lines of rendered words overwhelm their language-based meanings, the image-narrator dominates and perhaps replaces the text-narrator. In Bechdel's case, when the linguistic content of drawn letterforms overwhelms their image-based meanings, the text-narrator dominates. Regardless, both linguistic and non-linguistic analysis is applicable and essential to interpreting hybrid cases.

Groensteen also conflates monstrators and actual artists when he asserts that a "drawing cannot be separated from the hand of a specific enunciator" (2010: 4). If a monstrator has an actual hand, it is the actual artist and so not a narrator. The two may merge in a graphic memoir, but in a work of fiction, a monstrator might be said to have a hand only if it is understood to be a character within the diegesis. Even then, such a character does not use her hand in the sense implied unless she is also understood to be an artist drawing the images within the represented world. Otherwise the images are a product of her filtered consciousness and so drawn only in a metaphorical sense. Either way, the hand Groensteen references belongs to the actual artist drawing the images that comprise the discourse.

By referencing a singular hand, Groensteen also assumes a single artist. Any given work, however, may involve the hands of multiple artists, including penciller, inker, and colorist, and multiple artists may perform each of those roles. When Marvel employed more than two inkers on a single issue, credit was sometimes attributed to "D. Hands," an abbreviation for "diverse hands" (Shooter 1978). Pencillers are often considered primary artists, but other collaborative relationships are less hierarchal. Niv Bavarsky and Michael Olivo describe themselves working "completely in tandem" when creating *Old Growth* (2020: n.p.), producing a single image-narrator. In contrast, for *Havok and Wolverine: Meltdown,* Jon Muth and Kent Williams's artwork each focuses on one of the two primary characters, creating two character-focalizing image-narrators often on the same page (1998).

Regardless of kind, narrators may be understood as aspects of a diegesis. This is explicitly true for first-person narrators of prose-only novels. As discussed in Chapter 1, the narrator of Margaret Atwood's *The Handmaid's Tale* is called Offred by other characters and exists only within the world of the diegesis. A narrator's relationship to discourse is circular: a narrator appears to create the discourse that when interpreted creates that narrator. The distinction between a narrator's language and a discourse's text is less relevant in prose-only works because the language-narrator is not understood to produce the typography of the discourse but to exist apart from it. The actual lines of ink that appear on the pages of *The Handmaid's Tale* are not understood to be Offred's, and so font, size, spacing, etc. are not linked to an authorial act. The distinction addresses Holbo's objection that, despite "a restrained and more or less self-effacing graphic design formula," a prose-only novel is still "a graphic product"; though true, such graphic design is not the author's, justifying why "writing a novel, of the traditional sort, is not traditionally conceived of as an exercise in graphic design" (2014: 15, 14). It is only a linguistic exercise.

Word-image art is the product of the image-narrator—though, again, the edges dividing image-narration and text-narration may be ambiguous and overlapping. In one extreme, images are literally shaped by letterforms. In Matt Faction and David Aja's *Hawkeye*, Aja draws a figure firing a gun within the letterforms of the onomatopoeia sound effect "BLAM" (2015: n.p.), and similarly in Kieron Gillen and Jamie Mckelvie's *Phonogram: The Singles Club*, Mckelvie draws a sex scene within the letterforms of song lyrics playing in the background (2013: n.p.). In both cases, gestalt inferences combine the drawn content into the impression of a single image viewed through a word-shaped window. In the reverse extreme, a non-linguistic image can be comprised of letterforms. H. N. Werkman's 1920s *Typeprint* series treats letters as pointillistic brushstrokes, effectively eliminating their linguistic qualities, but concrete poetry such as John Hollander's 1969 "Swan and Shadow" arranges words into shapes that reflect their linguistic content. When linguistic and non-linguistic content are so merged, the role of the image-text narrator may be primary.

Regardless of narrator divisions, according to Eisner, artwork that emphasizes its physical and so discursive presence "connects the reader with the artist" (2008a: 149), meaning an actual artist, not Groensteen's monstrator. If the reader is aware of a human hand that shaped the lines of ink (whether those lines form word-images or non-linguistic images), the discourse appears to make an actual author present in a manner that a prose-only text does not. The act of image-making is partially preserved in the images because they are artifacts (or facsimiles) of that creative process. In prose-only works, a single author may create a single narrator, but a single author of an image-text sequences must create both a text-narrator and an image-narrator. In graphic memoirs such as Bechdel's *Fun Home* and Julie Doucet's *My New York Diary*, the text-narrator, image-narrator, and implied author are all understood to be the actual author. If a work has multiple authors, including a scripter and one or more artists, the implied author cannot be mistaken for an actual person, a fact often ignored through an experience of unified intentionality (Goldberg and Gavaler 2019: 189).

The author–narrator relationships of a semi-autobiographical work such as Jonathan Ames and Dean Haspiel's 2008 graphic novel *The Alcoholic* is more complex. The presence of two authors strains the illusion of a single implied author, but the strain is greater because the semi-autobiographical experiences are understood to be exclusively Ames's. While the language can be understood as Ames's, the images are a visual interpretation of Ames's possible experiences as drawn by Haspiel. Even if Ames wrote a script with meticulously detailed visual descriptions of intended image content which Haspiel precisely executed, the drawn lines are Haspiel's and their physicality highlight Haspiel's contribution. Instead of a single author creating two narrators, two authors create two narrators who collaborate within the image-texts. In contrast, a multi-author prose-only novel may still produce a unified language-narrator whose discourse cannot be easily divided according to its actual authors' individual contributions.

The creative divisions of *The Alcoholic* are a norm of graphic memoirs, with a memoirist scripting and an artist illustrating. Li Kunwu and P. Ôtié's 2012 *A Chinese Life* reverses the norm, since the autobiographical content is the artist's. Whatever the authorial roles, the majority of works in the comics medium are multi-authored, and image-narrators and text-narrators often operate as if independently and so require the inference of an image-text narrator to produce a coherent whole.

5. Parallel Narration

Bateman defines the parameters of an image-text:

> the text and image need to have been *presented together* as joint contributions to a single, perhaps complex, "message." The crucial restriction drawn is then: *intended* co-presence of concrete text-material with concrete image material.
>
> 2014: 25

Bateman's definition also describes the role of an image-text narrator—though "message" is not an ideal term for analyzing works of art that may not be so reducible. Also, as discussed in Chapter 1, authorial intention is typically and perhaps necessarily unknowable. An image-text narrator is a viewer's perception of intentionality in the combination of word-images and non-linguistic images and the effects those combinations produce. Rather than describing them in terms of addition, Bateman labels the results "meaning multiplication," a metaphor he prefers over the verbs "blend" and "synthesize" (2014: 7). Regardless, words and images within an image-text have independent roles, as Varnum and Gibbons's critique of McCloud's description of words and images as dance partners implies: "His very metaphor suggests that although the partners move together, each retains its individual character" (2001: xiv).

McCloud describes seven word/picture combinations: word-specific, picture-specific, duo-specific, intersecting, interdependent, parallel, and montage. In the second to last, words and pictures follow "seemingly different paths without intersecting" (2006: 130), but even in the case of a "duo-specific" combination, in which both "words and pictures [are] sending roughly the same message" (2006: 130), the two narrators do not fully coincide. Early superhero comics often create duo-specificity by including captions that verbally duplicate images. In Batman's first 1939 adventure, Bill Finger scripts a row of three panels that includes one caption box each:

> "The 'Bat-Man' lashes out with a terrific right . . .
> ". . . he grabs his second adversary in a deadly headlock . . . and with a mighty heave . . .
> "sends the burly criminal flying through space . . ."
>
> Kane 2005: 6

The visual content of Bob Kane's three drawings is the same—or nearly the same. Eisner might consider this an "illustration," an image that "reinforces (or decorates) a descriptive passage. It simply repeats the text," as opposed to a "visual," a "sequence of images that replace a descriptive passage told only in words" (2008: 132). Instead of categorizing the image-texts as duo-specific, McCloud might prefer word-specific, where words provide "all you need to know, while the pictures illustrated aspects of the scene being shown" (1993: 130). If so, duo-specificity may be intrinsically impossible. As Hopkins explains: "It is possible to refer to a particular thing using a word [...] without saying anything about it. [...] In contrast, a picture must depict more" (2005: 145). Schwarcz observes the same: "There is never complete redundancy because the picture is more concrete than the word" and so "elaborates the texts" (1982: 14). Baetens and Frey apply that difference to narrative: "In verbal storytelling, these two modes are generally presented as mutually exclusive: either one narrates or one describes," but in visual storytelling "both aspects coincide: it is not possible to narrate without describing, and conversely all descriptions will be deciphered immediately in relationship with their contribution to the story" (2015: 180).

Finger's text-narrator does not mention that Batman's adversaries are wearing hats, or that one hat is green and the other yellow, or that the first adversary drops a gun when struck, or that a streetlamp is glowing in the distant background. The text-narrator never even identifies the location of the scene on a rooftop, or that the second adversary falls to his apparent death—as suggested only by the inclusion of his prone body on the sidewalk in a subsequent panel. Because none of the visual information contradicts the verbal information, the text might be deleted without losing diegetic content. If the images were deleted, a great deal of diegetic information would vanish with them. This reverses the creative process in which Finger's words prompted Kane's drawings, resulting in the inevitable creation of additional details through image-narration. Kane's drawings originated as illustrations of Finger's script, but they replace that script in the final product, and where the script's visual descriptions remain in the form of captions, those less informative captions, not the more informative drawings, become the redundant element. Because the text-narration seems unaware of its own redundancy, the effect is of two narrators working not in collaboration but along parallel paths, each seemingly blind to the other.

McCloud's duo-specificity is sometimes analyzed in terms of illustration in which images are understood to be dependent on words. Based on his reading of the 1941 collaborative photo essay *Let Us Now Praise Famous Men* by James Agee and Walker Evans, Mitchell identifies three requirements for images to be more than mere illustrations: equality, independence, and collaboration. The last two "are values that may work at cross-purposes, and a 'co-equality' ... is easier to stipulate than it is to achieve or even to imagine" (1994: 290). Images in the comics medium, however, often demonstrate all three. While Finger's and Kane's collaboration is unequal because Kane's contribution is dependent on Finger's, their narrators function independently.

Similar collaborations imply greater independence through contradictions. *The Defenders* #16 (October 1974) concludes after the villain Magneto and his allies have been transformed into infants by a god-like entity. Scripter Len Wein gives Doctor Strange the final words: "A godling passed among us today and, in passing, left behind a most precious gift! After all, how many lost souls are there who receive a second chance at life?" (1974). Penciller Sal Buscema, however, draws not just any children, but temperamental ones, their frowning tear-dripping faces repeating the geometry of the adult Magneto's shouting mouth from earlier panels. Because the images imply that the supervillains were always toddler-like in their immaturity, the babies appear innately bad, their inner characters unchanged by their outer transformations. The image-narration then contradicts the text-narration of Doctor Strange's hopeful conclusion.

Groensteen might identify *The Defenders* example as braiding (because of the visual repetition of the faces) that produces dramatic irony: "comics, because they are, unlike prose literature, a polysemiotic medium, have greater resources at their disposal and so can create dramatic irony by introducing all sorts of gaps, of dissonance, between a specific verbal assertion and a specific image that present different facts" (2010: 20). Dramatic irony, however, involves the recognition that one fact is correct and the other false or at least incomplete without the corrective addition of the first. In the above case, the differences create ambiguity: which is correct, the text or the image? The question is possible only because of the relative co-equality and independence of the two collaborating narrators.

Other image- and text-narrators contradict more overtly and with no ironic effect. For *Captain America* #111 (March 1969), Jim Steranko drew a sequence designed to be read clockwise, but editor Stan Lee "felt it would confuse readers, and rewrote the bottom tier to be read conventionally, which creates confusion regarding the victim's hands being free, then bound for no reason" (Lee, Kirby, and Steranko 2014: 280). Lee's so-called Marvel Method, in which he added text after an artist visually composed an issue, sometimes produced contradictory image and text narration. For the 1962 premiere of Spider-Man, Steve Ditko drew Peter Parker superhumanly leaping from the path of a car, an action that would presumably attract attention, but Lee's text-narrator states in the caption box that the action is "unnoticed by the riders" (Lee and Ditko 2009: 3). In the 1961 premiere of the Fantastic Four, Jack Kirby drew a forest fire accidently lit by the Human Torch. The flames stretch well above the heads of the four characters, yet Lee's text-narrator states: "Silently they watched the small fire he had started in the underbrush burn itself out!!" (Lee and Kirby 2008: #1, p. 13). According to O'Neil, text-narration commonly corrects image-narration. When "a penciller neglects to draw parts that may be quiet, but have to be present if the story is to make sense," the scripter will add "captions that explain the motives of the characters or describe events that aren't in the story" (2001: 28). Though not co-equal, such contradictions and corrections occur only if the two narrators are independent.

Even in the case of single-author works, text and image narrations diverge. In Bechdel's *Fun Home*, a caption box frames the text: "Maybe he didn't notice the truck coming because he was preoccupied with the divorce. People often have accidents when they're distraught" (2006: 28). The image beneath the caption depicts Bechdel's father crossing a road while carrying branch cuttings on his shoulder. Not only do his blank expression and relaxed posture not communicate "distraught," the cuttings are blocking his view of the oncoming truck and so they, not his preoccupation with his divorce, are the visually implied reason for his not noticing the truck. Bechdel's text-narrator states earlier that her father "didn't kill himself until I was nearly twenty" (2006: 23), the first reference to the memoir's core event, and yet one undermined by the image-narrator five pages later. If viewers believe the text-narrator, they must discount information implied by the image-narrator as incorrect and so construct an implied author who does not intend the image to contradict the text. If so, the differences are accidental and so imply nothing (discussed in Chapter 4 as diegetic erasure). If viewers instead believe the image-narrator, they must understand the text-narrator—who is typically understood as a direct verbal representation of Bechdel herself—as misguided in her assumption that her father committed suicide. This produces a different implied author, one represented more completely by the image-text narrator, who uses images to contradict text and so present her verbal persona as a faulty narrator: we and the image-narrator know things that "Bechdel" the text-narrator does not.

6. Pronoun-defined Narration

Groensteen would likely label the text-narrator of *Fun Home* a "delegated narrator," indicating "first person narration, namely by a character involved in the story ... who monopolises the use of recitatives, within which he or she says 'I'"; the delegated narrator is "the focus of explicit discourse" through "the fundamental narrator's delegation" (2010: 15). Groensteen, however, could not as easily clarify if the image-narrator is also a delegated narrator since it cannot say "I" in the discourse of the images.

Such complexities of image-narrator identification are a product of differences between text and non-linguistic images. First-, second-, and third-person text-narrators are easily defined and distinguished through their uses of "I," "you," and "she." Image-narrators have no parallel quality. Unless the image includes content that identifies its perspective with a character, "I," "you," or "she" could each equally occupy the point of view—as demonstrated by differences and overlaps of ocularization and focalization discussed in Chapter 2. It is possible that all image-narrators imply second-person, but it is also possible that any application of person-defined narration onto image-narration is flawed. Even when "I" refers to a first-person character text-narrating in caption boxes, it is not necessarily clear whether that character is also the image-narrator of the accompanying images.

Works of fiction highlight the ambiguity, since actual authors are unlikely to be taken for narrating characters. As seen in Illustration 7.3, the first time Peter Parker summarizes his origin story in *Amazing Spider-Man*, Steve Ditko draws the panels with the scalloped edges of a thought balloon, implying that both the drawn images and the accompanying text are the character's first-person narration (Lee and Ditko 2009: 15). Similarly a page later, Ditko draws Peter sitting at a table surrounded by thought balloons, one of which contains not words but an image of himself unmasked in jail as his aunt cries in a duo-specific image of his first-person text-narration: "if I were ever arrested and imprisoned it would break Aunt May's heart!" (2009: 16). Peter appears to be both the first-person text-narrator and the first-person image-narrator.

Anya Ulinich creates a similar effect in her *Lena Finkle's Magic Barrel* by drawing the first-person narrator's thought images in a different visual style. Lena, who appears comparatively naturalistic in most panels, is rendered in the simplified and exaggerated

Illustration 7.3 From Ditko's *Amazing Spider-Man* and Ulinich's *Lena Finkle's Magic Barrel.*

style of a cartoon during a sequence of childhood memories, an effect heightened by the lines and spiral edges of a notebook implying that the character Lena has literally drawn the images herself (2014: 21–30).

In both cases, Ulinich and Ditko seem to indicate that the first-person text-narrator is also the first-person image-narrator during these sequences, but how is a reader to understand the works' other images? In Illustration 7.3, Ulinich renders Lena's memories in a different style than current action. The visual change could indicate a change in image-narration, possibly from Lena's first-person to the image-narration equivalent of third-person omniscience. Lena's first-person text-narration, however, remains consistent. Because her text is the work's only text and because it accompanies all images, the different visual styles appear to be produced by Lena, too.

Amazing Spider-Man, however, does change text-narrators. The issue begins with the captioned words of a third-person omniscient narrator: "Our scene is the bedroom of Peter Parker, the teen-age student whom many consider to be a shy bookworm … But, oh, if they only knew!"; in the next panel, Peter addresses the reader directly, narrating at first in talk balloons, then in quoted text inside caption boxes, and finally in thought balloons (Lee and Ditko 2009: 15). Ditko renders Peter's first-person images in the same style as images that Peter's words do not co-narrate. If the lack of change indicates no change in image-narrators, then either Peter's first-person image-narrator narrates through all images or an omniscient image-narrator separate from Peter narrates all images including even those explicitly inside Peter's thoughts.

The focalization effect is common in prose where third-person narration is limited to a single character, allowing the selectively omniscient narrator access to that character's consciousness. Though still third-person, such a narrator will often adopt the idiosyncratic language of the focalized character, creating effects similar to first-person. Since an image-narrator can never say "I," most apparently first-person image-narrators may be better understood instead as focalized image-narrators. An exception would be characters who are artists within the depicted world creating the images and so merging discourse and diegesis.

Works of fiction or memoirs drawn by collaborating non-memoirists can create a default effect of omniscient image-narration because the image-narrator cannot also be identified within the primary diegesis as a text-narrator. In one sense, the image-narrator looks down on the world as she renders it on the page, a creative act encoded in the images in a manner alien to text-narration. The fictional character Peter does not appear to image-narrate his own thoughts, but the fictional character Lena does appear to image-narrate hers. Distinguishing the equivalent of first-person image-narration from the equivalent of third-person focalized image-narration may require a reference to the narrating character literally or at least figuratively creating images, something present in *Lena Finkle's Magic Barrel* but absent from *Amazing Spider-Man*.

The difference may also be linked to the contrasting levels of perceived fictionality. Although Ditko gives Peter qualities of his own, a reader cannot mistake Peter for Ditko. Lena, however, so closely resembles her creator that *Lena Finkle's Magic Barrel* is sometimes referred to as a graphic memoir. A *New York Times* reviewer observes: "Lena Finkle, as readers will quickly realize, strongly resembles the author, and the two also share numerous biographical similarities" (Waldman 2014). But how would a reader realize this, let alone quickly? The novel includes no similarities-revealing introduction, foreword, afterword, or acknowledgments, and Ulinich's backcover bio lists her professional accomplishments with a single sentence referencing her daughters and Brooklyn home. Yet a *Los Angeles Times* reviewer refers to Ulinich and Lena interchangeably:

> [the graphic novel] draws us into Lena's experience with the force of memory. Ulinich highlights this with her drawing . . . she uses the device of a notebook . . . to bring the process of her storytelling to life. The effect is that of seeing her working drafts — a useful strategy because so much of the book deals with her efforts to find a through line, to make sense of the disparate pieces of her life.
>
> Ulin 2014

Although "her drawing" are Ulinich's, "her efforts" and "her life" are presumably Lena's, but "her working drafts" might be either. Lena the image-narrator and Ulinich the actual artist merge in the creation of "her working drafts" because those images are both diegetically fictional and discursively real. The conflation is not limited to Ulinich. Hodgman responds similarly when reviewing Jessica Abel's *La Perdida*:

> I had presumed it to be a kind of dull expat memoir. Like her main character, the author is an American who lived for some time in Mexico City. And even when it becomes clear that Carla, [sic] is her own person, it takes some time before you shake the suspision [sic] that she's just a stand-in for Abel.
>
> 2006

Carla text-narrates in first-person, but it is unclear whether the stand-in effect also applies to the graphic novel's image-narration, which repeatedly views Carla from a perspective other than her own and so parallels third- or perhaps second-person. Since representational images typically create an implied viewer positioned in diegetic relationship to image content, second-person may be the default mode of image-narration.

7. Style, Tense, and Referents

In addition to person-defined narrator perspective, other differences between words and images further separate the parameters of text- and image-narrators. While a text-narrator may express attitudes toward its subject directly, an image-narrator expresses information that is not an element of the represented content sometimes through the style of the depiction.

As discussed in Chapter 2, Eisner calls style a visual "voice," one that not only "sets ambience" but has "language value" and "emotional charge" (2008a: 149, 153). If the rendering approach is consistent throughout a work, then style signifies a consistent attitude regardless of changing subject matter. It reflects on the diegetic world as a whole. Though Kane's Batman art, like superhero art in general, uses elements of naturalism, it depicts violence in a paradoxically violence-sanitizing style that evokes excitement rather than repulsion. The image-narrator therefore may be said to advocate the hero's violent actions. In *My New York Diary*, Julie Doucet draws herself and other characters in a stark cartoon style that can be read as her own critique of her former teenage self and circumstances. If Doucet had instead rendered her first sexual experience with a semi-predatory middle-aged man in a naturalistic style, the same subject matter would communicate different connotations.

If an image-narrator changes styles within a work, those changes can be linked to specific subject matter. Because Ulinich draws Lena in varying degrees of cartoon and naturalism, the image-narrator's implied tone varies accordingly. When Lena appears cartoonish, the image-narrator appears to be critiquing her for behaviors that are literally and thematically exaggerated and simplistic. When Lena and her surroundings appear naturalistic, she seems comparatively mature and her situation realistic, suggesting the image-narrator's more sympathetic tone. Bechdel also varies style with contrasting tonal effects. *Fun Home* is drawn primarily in a simplified style that lacks the satirical quality implied by exaggerated proportions. Each of the seven chapters, however, begins with a naturalistic rendering of a photograph. The privileged opening position places what follows in relation, emphasizing not only the reality that the images are based on, but that the images are inevitably interpretations multiply removed—simplifications of drawings of photographs of past events. Bechdel also renders photographs in a comparatively realistic style on four pages that are otherwise drawn in her simplified style, a visual contradiction made most stark when she draws her own hands holding a photograph in the novel's only two-page spread (2006: 100–1). Bechdel's fingers are little more than outlines, while the copied photograph—a semi-nude of a young man taken by her father—is meticulously detailed with multiple angles of cross-hatching. Taken literally, the people in the past are physically fuller, are composed of a greater number of lines, than people living in the present. The figurative possibilities are extensive—is Bechdel's life made comparatively flat and immaterial by the dense fragments of her father's past?—but all are produced by the image-narrator's tonal effect.

Groensteen differentiates consistent and varying artistic styles as "neutral" and "involved monstrators" (2010: 12), terms that complicate rather than clarify the distinction since, as noted above with Kane and Doucet, so-called "neutral" image-narrators can express a range of tones or opinions, none of them less "involved" than image-narrators that vary style. Text-narrators of course can vary styles, too, but those variations need not be linked to the narrator's relative level of neutrality.

Text-narrators also describe sensory imagery, but, as Baetens and Frey allude above also, the greater their descriptive detail the slower their narrative pace—a dilemma absent from image-narration since a viewer controls viewing pace and so may move quickly over a highly detailed image or pause to study details. A verbally detailed description is detailed because it involves more words which slow narrative pace by requiring a longer period of time to read them. Text-narrators can also directly and so more efficiently express non-spatiotemporal content—abstractions, summary, generalization, disembodied facts, opinions, etc. The two disparate systems obey different rules, and so their cross-sections achieve effects impossible by either in isolation. Emily Hyde, as discussed in Chapter 2, argues that Chinua Achebe's *Things Fall Apart*, when illustrated in the heavily shaded style of Dennis Carabine, is a realist novel, but, when illustrated in the sparser, surface-emphasizing style of Uche Okeke, it is a modernist one (2016: 20). *Fun Home* might be a realist memoir for similar reasons, and *My New York Diary* a modernist one.

Also unlike linguistic representations, visual representations do not have verb tenses—or only one: present. If image content appears to be historical, then the image occurs in the historical present. If the image content appears to take place in the future, the depiction is still in the equivalent of the present tense. Accompanying text might identify an image as occurring at some time other than the present, but the image itself cannot. In *My New York Diary*, Julie Doucet draws attention to this inability of images to change verb tense by vacillating colloquially between past and historic present in her text-narration across multiple captions and panels: "So here I am, moving in with Mario. It was in September, two weeks after school had started [...] Mario is 22. He's studying Philosophy ... He's very clever [...] I learned a lot from him" (2013: 13).

An image within a sequence may through contrast mark itself in a way that suggests a difference in time with other images in the same sequence, but an isolated image cannot. All representational images occur during a "now" linked to the actual present moment of the viewer. If the image incorporates qualities understood to signify the equivalent of past or future tense, such as a wavy border or a sepia color filter, it still achieves that effect through contrast with other images. To visually depict more than one moment requires more than one image, but even if the juxtaposition communicates two moments, each image as it is viewed represents only its own present.

In *Action Comics* #5 (October 1938), Jerry Siegel's text caption states "The Valleyho dam is cracking under the strain of a huge downpour!" beside Joe Shuster's image of a cracking dam; in the next panel, a flood of water sweeps away a house beneath the caption: "Should it give way, a mountain of water will sweep down the valley, killing thousands and destroying the fertile land!" (Siegel and Shuster 2006: 60). The two captions differ in verb tense—the first is present, the second is future conditional—and so a reader understands that the dam has not yet and may not ever break. The image-narration communicates the opposite: a dam is cracking and then the escaping water is destroying a house, producing the causal inference of the dam breaking between the two depicted moments. Not only does the image-narrator not indicate that the second event occurs in the future relative to the text-narration, it does not indicate that the event may never occur.

Groensteen claims that images have a "temporal imprecision" that artists manipulate through conventions (2010: 5). Manga images would be in the present tense due to the use of motion lines, fragmentation, insets, and onomatopoeia, but western comics images would be in the past, which he understands as the default tense of a page because it includes multiple images: "at the very instant when my attention is focused on one of them, I can already perceive the following frames—I can see the future is *already there*" (2010: 6). Yet viewers can also see previous frames that are in the past relative to the ever-changing current image, instead implying present tense. Moreover, a reader of a page of prose also necessarily focuses on one word or phrase at a time while also perceiving that more words follow. This does not reveal anything about the content of those yet-to-be-read words, including their tense because tense is a diegetic quality. Groensteen conflates diegesis and discourse. The division is most overt when a page ends in a flashback, requiring the diegetic content of an "*already there*" image to be understood as taking place prior to the diegetic content of a discursively earlier image.

It seems only text-narrators can make direct propositions regarding time. "She walked home," "She is walking home," and "She will walk home" are instantly distinguishable statements, all implicitly referencing two moments in time: the moment of the event and the moment of the telling of the event. If depicted visually, the three statements would be indistinguishable because an image typically does not (and perhaps cannot) divide an event from its telling, because the act of viewing a subject is incorporated in the image of the subject through the angle and proximity of the implied viewer's perspective. While the present-tense caption "The 'Bat-Man' lashes out with a terrific right" contains little information not expressed by its accompanying image, the caption "She walked home" accompanying an image of a woman walking would: the event occurred in the past relative to the present moment of the image-text narration.

A reader might also assume that "She" refers to the woman, but even that assumption can only be tentative. Stainbrook explains that: "Two disparate sign systems work together in visual narratives, according to common connective principles, to create a shared representation of conceptual schemas" (2016: 153). While typically true, image-narrators and text-narrators might instead work separately to create cross-representations of different schemas. The separate text- and image-narrations may produce a double image-text referent, in which a word has one meaning according to its linguistic context and a different meaning according to its visual context. Alan Moore and Dave Gibbons typify this approach in *Watchmen*. In Illustration 7.4, the first panel of issue #2 depicts a statue of an angel in a cemetery, under the caption: "Aw, willya look at her? Pretty as a picture an' still keepin' her figure! So, honey, what brings you to the city of the dead?" (1988: n.p.). The "her" and the "city of the dead" of the text-narrator's ambiguously quoted speech reference the statue and cemetery when read in the context of the image, but in the next panel, they are revealed to have referenced a daughter visiting her mother in a retirement home. Similarly, the first panel of *Watchmen* #3 depicts the black triangle and yellow background of a fallout shelter sign, under the caption: "Delirious, I saw that Hell-bound ship's black sail against the yellow Indies sky, and knew again the stench of powder, and men's brains and war" (1988: n.p.). In its image context, the text "black sail against the yellow" seems to reference the sign, but subsequent panels reveal the words' meaning in the context of a pirate comic book being read by a character seated in the foreground.

McCloud partially notes this effect, clarifying his descriptions of parallel combinations: "words and pictures don't connect at all—though their paths may bend toward each other in later panels" (2006: 138). Seth's 1996 *It's a Good Life, If You Don't*

Weaken extends those paths to atypical lengths. The caption box in the second panel of page one begins: "Cartoons have always been a big part of my life," while the panel image depicts a snowplow on a city street and an unidentified figure walking on the sidewalk. The third panel centers the same figure, implying a link between the character and the narrating "I." But it is intentionally ambiguous whether the narration is the equivalent of thought balloons, linking the production of the words to the moment depicted in the image. The text-narration extends for sixteen panels, without an overt reference to the settings and actions of the panels, instead describing "an old Charlie Brown strip" with no relationship to the actual panels enclosing those words. Instead of Charlie Brown, the images depict the figure walking, pausing at a used bookstore window, entering, browsing, selecting a book, purchasing it, and leaving. It is only with the thirteenth panel that the text retroactively explains its relationship to the preceding images: "it was on this day that I happened upon a little book that opened up a whole new world of cartooning for me." That event occurs visually on the previous page in panels that include caption boxes enclosing diverging text, as seen in Illustration 7.4.

Even referents seemingly shared by text- and image-narrators divide. A viewer of a Superman comic might expect the word "Superman" to be matched to the visual representation of the character in his iconic costume and the words "Clark Kent" to be linked to any of a range of non-superheroic-looking appearances. But Jerry Siegel and Joe Shuster's early works do not establish those norms. In *Action Comics* #2 (July 1938), when the character infiltrates a foreign army, Shuster draws him in a brown military uniform, eliminating the visual markers of both alter egos, Superman's costume and Clark Kent's glasses. Siegel's caption, however, identifies the visually indeterminate image as Clark Kent: "Kent, in his disguise as a soldier, overhears an astounding bit of information" (2006: 26). Similarly in #3, Siegel writes: "Kent, disguised as a miner, approaches the pit. Pretending to slip, Clark tumbles into the lift-shaft!" (2006: 32). Shuster's visual representation remains consistent in the following panel, but the next caption reverses attribution: "Down plunges Superman in a fall which would have meant death for any ordinary man!" (33), and three pages later: "Superman, clad in a miner's garb, drops out of the sky" (2006: 36). The first two references to Kent suggest that Kent is the character and Superman is the name of his disguise, but the two references to Superman suggest the opposite. Visually, neither Kent nor Superman are linked to a specific drawn appearance. Alternatively, the character is Kent when behaving humanly and Superman when behaving superhumanly, a kind of dual-identity based on changing descriptions rather than on stable references. Since the interpretation is not definitive, the nature of the character remains indeterminate, and the text and image referents ambiguous.

Double referents and ambiguous referents are possible because image and text referents are never simply identical—their juxtaposition only creates that impression. As with Finger and Kane's blindly duo-specific Batman sequence, Moore and Gibbons's and Seth's image- and text-narrators seem unaware of each other, too, requiring an image-text narrator that coordinates both to produce effects possible only through their combination.

Illustration 7.4 From Moore and Gibbons's *Watchmen* and Seth's *It's a Good Life, If You Don't Weaken.*

8. Embedded Narration

Zunshine provides a tool for understanding the relationships between the three overlapping narrators. She defines "socialcognitive complexity"

as the depiction of a mental state embedded within another mental state. "I am sad" is less sociocognitively complex than "He knew she was sad," which in turn is less complex than "Surprisingly, he knew that she was sad," because "surprisingly" implies someone else's mind—perhaps the narrator's?—contemplating a mental state of one character who is aware of the mental state of another character . . .

2011: 119

Zunshine's example describes text-narration, but image-narration communicates similar socialcognitive complexity. "He knew she was sad" might be depicted through the image of a woman with a sad expression being observed by a man with a thoughtful expression. Image-narration, however, is incapable of expressing the surprise of a narrator that exists outside of the scene. An image-narrator cannot express its own internal experience directly. An image-narrator is typically a disembodied eye seemingly selecting subject matter, which can only imply an attitude, as with the Kane and Doucet examples discussed above. The image-narrator is also incapable of directly depicting the internal experience of other characters. A character's thoughts and emotions are present to the extent that the character outwardly demonstrates them or that the image-narrator represents them associatively through style or visual metaphors. When Lena and a former boyfriend sleep together and then immediately separate afterwards, Ulinich draws a heart in a freezer bag at Lena's feet (2014: 45). Non-visual senses are present only through visually depicted behaviors that signify an internal experience of those senses or through non-literal representations such as emanata, such as the wavy lines Ditko draws around Spider-Man's head when he feels his spider-sense "tingling."

Zunshine establishes a norm for text-narration: "third-level complexity—a mind within a mind within a mind, as in the above case of 'Surprisingly, he knew . . .'—is the baseline for fiction" (2011: 119). Third level might be a baseline for prose-only works, but image-texts may be prototypically more complicated. While "the third level of embedment is this 'sweet spot' for engaging readers in literature," and written texts that exceed fifth-level complexity "tend to be incomprehensible," the effects of embedment "achieved primarily by means of body language and unconscious inference as opposed to explicitly articulated propositions . . . is less clear" (Whalen, Zunshine, and Holquist 2012). Body language and verbal language overlap to produce combinational effects similar to image-text narrators' coordination of image-narrators and text-narrators.

The text-narrator of *Amazing Spider-Man* depicts the mental state of those who consider Peter Parker "to be a shy bookworm," while also depicting its own mental state in response to their ignorance, "But, oh, if they only knew!" (2009). The image-narrator simultaneously depicts the mental state of Peter, drawing him with an angry expression as he throws his costume. Those three mental states—angry Peter's, those who consider him a bookworm, and the amused text-narrator's—are embedded within the image-text narrator.

Embedded narrators are a norm in nonfiction works, too. The image-text narrator of *Fun Home* embeds the text-narrator's depiction of the father's suicidal state and his unawareness of the oncoming truck due to his preoccupation with his divorce—as well as people who in general have accidents when distraught. The image-text narrator also embeds the image-narrator's depiction of the father crossing the street while carrying branches. It therefore holds three different fathers defined by three distinct mental states: one who committed suicide by intentionally stepping into the path of a truck, one who was unaware of the truck due to his distraught preoccupation, and one who was unaware of the truck due to the branches on his shoulder. The image-text narrator further embeds the mental state of the text-narrator who expresses separate beliefs about the existence of the first two fathers—the suicidal and the preoccupied—but not the unaware father depicted only by the image-narrator. Since the image can be understood as an expression of image-narrator's belief that the father's death was merely the result of carelessness, the image-text narrator embeds five mental states—or six if "people" are included. The viewer also experiences the image-text narrator as an intentionality and so an additional mental state. Which of the three fathers does the image-text narrator believe is accurate and therefore which of the opinions of the subordinate narrators does the implied author endorse? Even if a viewer concludes that the image-text narrator is unable to draw a conclusion, that still describes a mental state.

The image-narrators and text-narrators, however, do not embed each other, because, as Stainbrook observes above, they are "two disparate sign systems." If both are minds in a shared socialcogntive complex, each remains unaware of the other. Shuster's panel of a flood sweeping away a house depicts that event, but with no visual element that identifies the depiction as occurring in a possible future. Doucet's panels depict a sequence of moments unfolding in New York, with no visual element that identifies those moments as having already occurred in the author's remembered past. Gibbons's panels depict a statue and a fallout sign, with no awareness of the double-referents created by the accompanying texts, just as the texts contains no verbal element that identifies any inherent relationship to the images. Image-narrators and text-narrators embed multiple mental states, including sometimes the same mental states of the same characters, but the embedding occurs separately even when simultaneous and aligned. Understood as mental states themselves, the two narrators remain ignorant of the other's presence. Text and images can be juxtaposed, but even when the juxtaposition is within the level of letterform artistry, the two modes are processed separately by reader-viewers. While image-narrators and text-narrators are separated by formally exclusive qualities, image-text narrators combine them for paradoxically unified effects that form the complexly embedded narratives of image-text sequences.

9. Embedded Relationships

Finally, embedded narrators produce combinational meanings not previously accounted for. Miodrag observes: "Critics often seize upon particular ways of combining image and text as being definitive of the form, though these definitions tend to account for a limited range of possible conjunctions" (2013: 83). Specifically, they tend to account only for interactions between the linguistic content of word-images and the subject matter of representational images. This is what McCloud means by word/pictures relationships, and this is the primary way image-texts in the comics medium have been analyzed. Interactions, however, also occur at both images' representational and stylistic levels. For word-images, style can be described in typographic terms, and for other representational images style can be described in terms and degrees of stylistic abstraction. This produces two levels of interaction within images and within word-images separately:

1. between a word-image's linguistic features and typographic features
2. between an image's representational features and stylistic features

And four broad categories of representational image-text combinations:

3. between a word-image's linguistic features and an image's representational features
4. between a word-image's linguistic features and an image's stylistic features
5. between a word-image's typographic features and an image's representational features
6. between a word-image's typographic features and an image's stylistic features

Although Bateman does not give "systematic attention" to "the deliberate use of the visual form of texts as graphical units in their own right," he does distinguish between "internal" relationships, "where the text 'is' the image," and "external" relationships, "where the text . . . relates to other images" (2014: 27). The first relationship category is internal in Bateman's sense, and, though he doesn't identify it, so is the second. The remaining four are external. The first relationship is also the domain of a text-narrator, the second is the domain of an image-narrator, and the remaining four are of an image-text narrator.

The four kinds of interactions introduced in *Creating Comics* can be applied to each of the categories (Gavaler and Beavers 2021: 147):

Duplicate: the two sets primarily overlap each other, neither contributing uniquely to the whole.
Complement: the two sets primarily correspond, one or both providing additional but congruent qualities to the whole.
Contrast: the two sets primarily contradict, each providing incongruent qualities to the whole.
Diverge: the two sets appear primarily unrelated, neither contributing to a whole.

These divisions simplify, clarify, and expand McCloud's word/picture combinations: word-specific, picture-specific, and duo-specific combinations duplicate; additive (or intersecting) and inter-dependent either complement or contrast; parallel diverge; and montage can duplicate, complement, contrast, or diverge. Varnum and Gibbons's critique of McCloud's combinations highlight similar points. Noting that pictures that "are said 'merely' to illustrate a text, they always add a layer of meaning," Varnum and Gibbons describe features that complement; by noting that words and pictures can "stand in ironic juxtaposition" and that pictures "can belie words," they identify features that contrast (2001: xiv).

Eco introduced one of the first analyses of image-text relationships, identifying related categories. The first, "a close inter-relationship between word and picture: at a simple level they serve to complement each other's deficiencies. Thus the words can convey an attitude which the picture is unable to convey in all its implications," overtly complements; the second, "Or else the spoken part is deliberately pleonastic, and continually intrudes to explain what the pictures have already made explicit ...," duplicates; the third, "Or again, we meet a kind of ironic independence between the picture and the text," contrasts; and the fourth, "Finally, there are cases where the visual detail is carefully fitted with matching remarks by the characters, so that the overall effect suggests a good film sequence," is another example of complementing, leaving divergent relationships unaccounted for because the 1947 comic strip Eco analyzed, Milton Caniff's *Steven Canyon*, provided no examples (1965: 24).

The four kinds of interactions proposed above also harmonize approaches originating outside of the comics medium. Expanding Barthes's initial semiotic analysis, Kloepfer divides image and texts relationships into two central kinds: divergent relationships contrast or diverge, and convergent relationships duplicate or complement, including when their additive features modify or amplify each other (quoted in Bateman 2014: 72). Schwarcz identifies two primary relationships between texts and images: congruency (including elaborating, amplifying, extending, and alternating) complements, and deviation (including veering away, opposing, negating, and counterpointing) contrasts (1982: 14–18). Nikolajeva and Scott's symmetrical picture books duplicate; complementary and expanding or enhancing picture books complement; counterpointing picture books contrast; and sylleptic picture books diverge (2016: 12). "As usual," Bateman observes of McCloud's combinations, "there are some patterns which continue to recur" (2014: 99), echoing his observation of Schwarcz: "It is in fact striking just how often similar lists are suggested in different areas without, apparently, very much interaction between the distinct inquiries" (2014: 73). The recurring patterns reflect an underlying logic, which can be represented conceptually by three Venn diagrams:

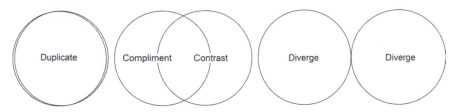

Illustration 7.5

Duplicating features mostly overlap; both complementing and contrasting features partially overlap (and are distinguishable in relation to their shared duplicating features); and diverging features do not overlap (and so suggest no basis for comparison or contrast).

The above six-part list of relationship levels also reveals that previous approaches are external only and so do not account for internal relationships. Beginning with the first relationship category, Bob Wiacek and Todd McFarlane's *The Incredible Hulk* #340 (February 1988) title design is a word-image with linguistic and typographic features that complement. The linguistic meaning of "HULK" and the stylistic rendering of the letterforms as blocks of stone communicate similar impressions. René Magritte's 1950 painting *The Art of Conversation* employs a similar typographic approach, rendering the French word for dream, "RÈVE," in blocks of stone for a contrasting effect. Examples described earlier in this chapter also apply to the first category's internal relationship. The word-images from *Wonder Woman* #20, the multi-color edition of *The Sound and Fury*, and the drawn diary entries in *Fun Home* all display complementary linguistic and typographic features. John Hollander's "Swan and Shadow," a concrete poem with words arranged in the shape of a swan and its shadow, displays linguistic and typographic (meaning word-style) features that duplicate, but Werkman's letterform-based images have no linguistic content and so no internal word–image relationship.

Other earlier examples display external relationships. *Detective Comics* describes word-image linguistic features and image representational features that duplicate or complement, and *Fun Home* and *The Defenders* describe word-image linguistic features and image representational features that contrast. The large, hand-written word-images in Matisse's *Jazz*, because they are "in a decorative relationship with the character of the color prints," display typographic features that compliment with the image's stylistic features. Since letter-shaped framing is both a stylistic feature of the image of a villain firing a gun and a typographic feature of the onomatopoeic word "BLAM," and since each echoes the word's linguistic and the image's representational content, Aja's example from *Hawkeye: Rio Bravo* combines all four external relationships with duplicating or complementing features (see Illustration 7.6).

Because image-texts contain many additional combinational possibilities, an account of image-texts sequences requires attention to the embedded relationships of each combination. The range would require twenty-four examples, so the three remaining examples included in Illustration 7.6 focus primarily on style combinations because style, including word-image typography, is an under-analyzed aspect of image-texts, one that Bateman intentionally excludes (2014: 27).

In Dave McKean's *Black Dog: The Dreams of Paul Nash*, McKean juxtaposes non-representational green paint strokes with representational image-texts of World War I trenches. When viewed with the words, "But there is green—little dabs of grass and clover / push through the earth" (2016: n.p.), the non-representational images seem to refer either overtly or metaphorically to the vegetation, even though the images would not suggest that content in isolation. Were the words absent, the non-representational and representational images would instead diverge. Since the image consists entirely of stylistic qualities (merging the two meanings of abstract), the image–text relationships demonstrate word-images' linguistic features and the images' stylistic features that complement.

In Will Eisner's June 7, 1942 *The Spirit*, Eisner renders the title in a distinctive but thematically ambiguous font. In combination with the visual tropes of a woman's longing expression and her apparent focus on the atypically bare-chested title hero, the font and image evoke romance instead of the work's expected genre of adventure. The linguistic reference of the title remains the same, but the image clarifies the connotative meaning of the word rendering, an example of a word-image's typographic and an image's representational features duplicating or complementing.

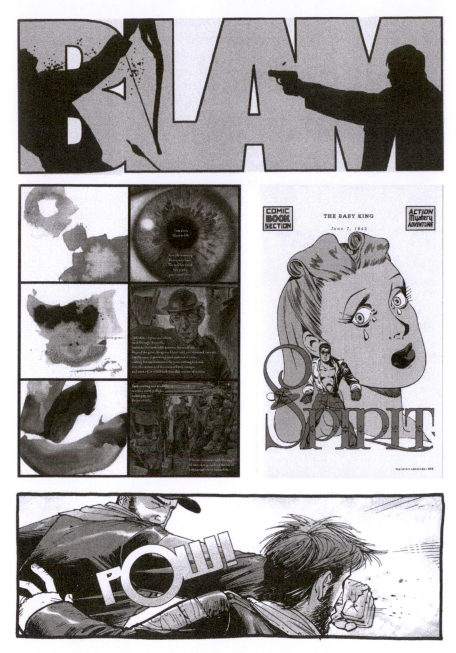

Illustration 7.6 From Fraction and Aja's *Hawkeye: Rio Bravo*, McKean's *Black Dog*, Eisner's *The Spirit*, and Kirkman and Moore's *The Walking Dead*.

In Robert Kirkman and Tony Moore's *The Walking Dead: Days Gone Bye*, Moore draws sound-effect words in a typographic style distinct from both the lettering of spoken words, and with an expressive line quality distinct from the line quality of accompanying images (2010). Because the sound effects are integrated into the images, the overlapping styles suggests the synesthesia effect of visually rendered sounds since the lines of the letters would not be visible to characters who are drawn in a different style. The result is an example of a word-image's typographic features and an image's stylistic features contrasting. Note, however, that "POW" is a word convention that strains a literal understanding of sound effects, since the actual sound of a fist striking a face bears little if any resemblance to the pronounceable word.

The roles of words and images in sequenced images are complex but not chaotic. Though words are not a necessary aspect of the comics forms, this chapters offers a framework for analysis when they do. The next and final section concludes *The Comics Form* with a summary of its main observations.

Conclusion

A poem consisting of fourteen blank-verse lines following an ABABCDCDEFEFGG rhyme scheme is a Shakespearean sonnet because it is in the Shakespearean sonnet form. A work in the comics form is formally a comic for similar reasons. Unlike Shakespearean sonnets, however, a comic may be defined by other than form. A work may be a comic contextually, stylistically, conventionally, or by other criteria independent of or non-exclusive to form. Though it may be a comic according to multiple sets of defining criteria, if the work satisfies one set but not another set, it is both a comic and not a comic. The apparent paradox is due to each set using the same term, even though each usage is distinct. A "comic" is not a "comic" is not a "comic."

The Comics Form defines the comics form by extracting the two most common physical features from a range of comics definitions and combining them as sequenced images. Sequenced images may or may not define comics generally, but if a work consists of sequenced images, the work is in the comics form and so can be analyzed formally as a comic. Although that may be sufficient for the work to be considered a comic, others might understand that a work must be, for example, a mass-produced replica or be created, produced, and purchased with the understanding that it is a comic. I refer to such media-defined works as the comics medium. A single-image cartoon in a newspaper comics section is in the comics medium, but because it is not in the comics form, it is outside the scope of this study.

The terms "discourse" and "diegesis" differentiate images' physical qualities and representational qualities. All images have discourses, and many also have diegeses. Since I derive "image" from extant comics definitions, I also infer its discursive constraints: an image in the comics form is a visual, static, flat image juxtaposed with another. If it is also a representational image, it represents some subject matter: the diegesis experienced in the mind of a viewer interpreting its discourse. Like "discourse," "diegesis" has other usages, but I adopt an expansive meaning: all representational content, either overtly depicted or implied, including the larger context of a world. Diegeses vary between viewers but also presumably overlap significantly. Non-representational images have no diegeses, only discourses—which must still be mentally experienced, but without the construction of a mental model with diegetic qualities understood to be separate from the discourse.

Analyzing representational images involves a range of approaches for relating their discursive qualities to the diegetic qualities they produce. Rather than focusing on unknowable authorial intentions or the illusion of intentions in characters, I focus on viewers' experiences of intentionality in author-constructed narrators, focusing first on image-narrators, which communicate diegetic content through an image's discursive qualities. An image's style is in one sense discursive: an arrangement of marks on a surface. In another sense, style is diegetic: subjects depicted in a certain manner. Style may then be understood as semi-representational: discursive qualities that represent subjects non-literally and indirectly. Style may follow certain norms or modes, including cartooning and naturalism, as well as other combinations of exaggeration and simplification. Those norms are understood to represent subject matter through overspecified or underspecified details that are not aspects of the diegesis, except indirectly through connotations. Viewpoint and framing effects are similarly semi-representational.

To be in the comics form, a work must include more than one visual, static, flat image. Distinguishing multiple images from a single image with multiple units poses a challenge. Common terms "panels," "frames," and "gutters" are metaphors to describe drawn qualities that are not determining. Unless images are physically divided—two framed paintings hanging on the same wall, for example, or two facing pages—image division is determined by viewer perception. A physically unified page or canvas of visual subunits consists of multiple images only if a viewer perceives it to be multiple images. Like style, a layout of gutter-divided panels straddles discourse and diegesis. The division of images is neither a discursive quality nor a diegetic quality in the same sense as the images' subject matter, because the divisions are not part of that diegetic world. Where style seems diegetically transparent (subjects are drawn as if accurately reflecting their literal appearance in their world), image divisions seems discursive (images are drawn as if separated physically in the discourse). Distinguishing the two effects, style is semi-representational and layout is pseudo-formal. Because pseudo-formal qualities are not physical qualities like page dimensions and divisions, pseudo-form is a kind of diegesis, but one separate from the primary diegesis of the representational content, and so a secondary diegesis.

For images to be sequenced, and so to be in the comics form, they must be juxtaposed in one of three possible ways: 1) contiguous: images appear simultaneously within a single visual field; 2) temporal: an image appears immediately after a previous image in the same visual field; or 3) distant: a non-contiguous image that does not immediately follow a previous image is mentally recalled while observing a current image. Contiguous juxtaposition describes the pages of most works in the comics medium in which viewers understand panels to be separate images. Temporal juxtaposition is the norm of films but occurs in static images when, for instance, a viewer turns a page. Distant juxtaposition is dependent on memory and so may be juxtaposition in only a metaphorical sense. A viewer of a sequence may at any time recall a previous image and relate it to a current image, discursively, diegetically, or both. Contiguous juxtaposition also includes braiding effects (with and without repetition) in which the discursive relationship of visual elements influences a viewer's understanding of their corresponding diegetic qualities.

Juxtaposed images trigger inferences. The most fundamental inference is recurrence: marks in separate images are understood to be representations of the same subject. Recurrence is reinforced by a parallel phenomenon, diegetic erasure, in which discursive qualities that would produce diegetic contradictions are ignored. Juxtaposition produces ten additional types of inferences: 1) spatial: images share a diegetic space; 2) temporal: images share a diegetic timeline; 3) causal: undepicted action occurs between depicted moments; 4) embedded: one image is perceived as multiple images; 5) non-sensory: differences between representational images do not represent sensory reality; 6) associative: dissimilar images represent a shared subject; 7) semi-continuous: discursively continuous but representationally non-continuous images are perceived as a single image; 8) continuous: images are perceived as a single image; 9) match: otherwise dissimilar images share matching similarities; and 10) linguistic: images relate primarily through accompanying text. These first seven are diegetic only; the second two can occur both discursively and diegetically, or discursively only; and the last is not primarily a result of image juxtaposition and so arguably is not a type of juxtapositional inference. While the subtypes of diegetic inferences are only discernible through analysis of the story world, discursive inferences must be analyzed at the level of the page. Purely discursive inferences involve only discursive marks understood in terms such as shapes and values without reference to representational content.

For images to be sequenced, they must be juxtaposed, but the relationship between sequence and juxtaposition is ambiguous. The juxtaposed images of a sequence follow a specific order. The juxtaposed images of a non-sequence, or set, follow no specific order. Since a set can be juxtaposed contiguously, when, for example, organized into a book or gallery, order has two kinds: 1) discursive order: the successive but non-diegetic arrangement of images, reflecting only happenstance, convenience, and/or the needs of physical presentation; and 2) sequential order: the successive arrangement of the images, reflecting some diegetic quality of the representational content. Sequential order and discursive order are identical for sequences.

When images, whether sets or sequences, are contiguously juxtaposed in a visual field, viewing them produces a viewing path that is either: 1) directed: determined by the image order of the sequence; or 2) variable: indeterminate and so open to multiple discursive orders. Since image orders and image viewing paths are apprehended simultaneously, both are an additional type of juxtapositional inference in which a viewer determines relationships between contiguous images. If other inferences (recurrence, spatial, temporal, etc.) suggest a sequential order organized in a directed viewing path, the images are hinged. Unhinged viewing describes variable viewing paths of a set arranged discursively but non-sequentially.

The image qualities of content, relationship, order, paths, and hinges suggest a six-part typology: 1) representational sequence: two or more related and ordered representational images, with, if contiguously juxtaposed, hinges that produce a directed viewing path; 2) non-representational sequence: two or more related and ordered non-representational images, with, if contiguously juxtaposed, hinges that produce a directed viewing path; 3) representational set: two or more related but unordered representational images, that, if contiguously juxtaposed, are viewed in variable paths; 4) non-representational set: two or more related but unordered non-representational images, that, if contiguously juxtaposed, are viewed in variable paths; 5) representational arrangement: two or more unrelated and unordered representational images with no contiguous hinges; and 6) non-representational arrangement: two or more unrelated and unordered non-representational images with no contiguous hinges.

Representational sequences also provide a means to explain and constrict McCloud's closure. Viewers make inferences about a diegetic world based on image content in combination with independent knowledge and assumptions about the depicted world. Those assumptions are usually mimetic, applying, for example, laws of physics to objects and human psychology to characters. The undrawn content that viewers experience through the juxtaposition of two or more representational images is the minimal content required by a viewer's mental construction of a partially drawn but fully implied event, consisting of definable subunits. While anything could occur in the ambiguous lapse of time implied by paired images of discreet moments, viewers understand the images as parts of a unified event. According to event inferencing, any content that is not part of that event is not implied.

Though text is not a necessary quality of the comics form, many sequenced images contain text. An image-text is an image that combines linguistic and non-linguistic content, and sequenced image-texts are in the comics form. Since all text is necessarily images, there are two types: 1) word-image: an image with linguistic content; and 2) word-image art: a word-image rendered as graphic art. Since word-images and non-linguistic images function as though on parallel and independent paths, image-texts involve three kinds of narrators: 1) image-narration of non-linguistic content; 2) text-narration of linguistic content; and 3) image-text narration of combinational effects of linguistic and non-linguistic content, which produces embedded relationships including double referents.

These are the qualities of sequenced images, which together explain the comics form.

Works Cited

Abbott, Lawrence L. (1986), "Comic Art: Characteristics and Potentialities of a Narrative Medium," *Journal of Popular Culture*, Vol. 19, No. 4, pp. 155–76.

Abel, Jessica (2006), *La Perdida*, New York: Pantheon.

Abel, Jessica, and Matt Madden (2008), *Drawing Worlds and Writing Pictures*, New York: First Second.

Abouet, Marguerite, and Clément Oubrerie (2015), *Aya: Life in Yop City*, Montreal: Drawn & Quarterly.

Adams, Neal, and Roy Thomas (1969), *X-Men* #58 (July), New York: Marvel Comics.

Adams, Sam, Noel Murray, Keith Phipps, and Leonard Pierce (2009), "Reinventing the pencil: 21 artists who changed mainstream comics (for better or worse)," avclub.com, 20 July. Available online: http://www. avclub.com/article/reinventing-the-pencil-21-artists-who-changed-main-30528.

Amash, Jim, and Eric Nolen-Weathington (eds.) (2012), *Matt Baker: The Art of Glamour*, Raleigh: TwoMorrows.

Ames, Jonathan, and Dean Haspiel (2008), *The Alcoholic*, New York: Vertigo DC.

Arr, Don Christensen (1982), *How-To-Draw Tips from the Top Cartoonists*, Woodland Hills, CA: Donnar Publications.

Ault, Donald (2004), "Imagetextuality: 'Cutting Up' Again, pt. III," *ImageTexT: Interdisciplinary Comics Studies*, Vol. 1, No.1. Available online: http://www.english.ufl. edu/imagetext/archives/v1_1/ault/>.

Auster, Paul, Paul Karasik, and David Mazzucchelli (2004), *City of Glass*, New York: Picador.

Avermaete, Roger (1976), *Frans Masereel*, New York: Fonds Mercator and Rizzoli.

B., David (2005), *Epileptic*, New York: Pantheon.

Baetens, Jan (2001), "Revealing Traces: A New Theory of Graphic Enunciation," Robin Varnum and Christina T. Gibbons (eds.), *The Language of Comics: Word and Image*, Jackson: University Press of Mississippi, pp. 145–55.

Baetens, Jan (2011), "Abstraction in Comics," *SubStance*, Vol. 40, No. 1, #124, pp. 94–113.

Baetens, Jan, and Hugo Frey (2015), *The Graphic Novel: An Introduction*, Cambridge: Cambridge University Press.

Baetens, Jan, and Hugo Frey (2017), "'Layouting' for the plot: Charles Burns and the clear line revisited," *Journal of Graphic Novels & Comics*, Vol. 8, No. 2, pp. 193–202.

Balaban, Halely, Keisuke Fukuda, and Roy Luria (2019), "What can half a million change detection trials tell us about visual working memory?" *Cognition*, Vol. 191.

Barker, Martin (1989), *Comics: Ideology, Power and the Critics*, Manchester: Manchester University Press.

Barry, Lynda (2017), *One! Hundred! Demons!*, Montreal: Drawn & Quarterly.

Barthes, Roland (1977), *Image-Music-Text*, trans. Stephen Heath, New York: Hill and Wang.

Bateman, John (2014), *Text and Image: A Critical Introduction to the Visual/Verbal Divide*, New York: Routledge.

Bateman, John (2017), "Triangulating transmediality: A multimodal semiotic framework relating media, modes and genres," *Discourse, Context & Media*, Vol. 20, pp. 160–74.

Bateman, John (2019), "On the track of visual style: a diachronic study of page composition in comics and its functional motivation," *Visual Communication*, Vol. 20, No. 1, pp. 1–39.

Bateman, John, and Janina Wildfleuer (2014), "Defining units of analysis for the systematic analysis of comics: A discourse-based approach," *Studies in Comics*, Vol. 5, No. 2, pp. 373–403.

Bavarsky, Niv, and Michael Olivo (2020), *Old Growth*, Seattle: Fantagraphics.

Bearden-White, Roy (2009), "Closing the Gap: Examining the Invisible Sign in Graphic Narratives," *International Journal of Comic Art*, Vol. 11, No. 1, pp. 347–62.

Beaty, Bart (2012), *Comics versus Art*, Toronto: University of Toronto Press.

Bechdel, Allison (2006), *Fun Home*, Boston: Mariner.

Beineke, Colin (2017), "On Comicity," *Inks: The Journal of the Comics Studies Society*, Vol. 1, No. 2, pp. 226–53.

Bell, Roanne, and Mark Sinclair (2002), *Pictures & Words: New Comic Art and Narrative Illustration*, New Haven: Yale University Press.

Bendis, Brain Michael, and David Finch (2005), *Avengers Disassembled*, New York: Marvel.

Bendis, Brian Michael (2014), *Words for Pictures: The Art and Business of Writing Comics and Graphic Novels*, Berkeley: Watson-Guptill.

Benefiel, Rebecca R., and Holly M. Sypniewski (2015), "Images and Text on the Walls of Herculaneum: Designing the Ancient Graffiti Project," A. E. Felle and A. Rocco (eds.), *Off the Beaten Track: Epigraphy at the Border, Proceeding of the VI Eagle International Meeting*, Oxford: Archaeopress, pp. 29–48.

Bennet, Tamryn (2014), "Comics Poetry: Beyond 'Sequential Art,'" *Image and Narrative*, Vol. 15, No. 2, pp. 106–23.

Berger, John (1971), *Ways of Seeing*, London: BBC and Penguin.

Berger, Itamar, Ariel Shamir, Moshe Mahler, Elizabeth Carter, and Jessica Hodgins (2013), "Style and Abstraction in Portrait Sketching," *ACM Transactions on Graphics*, Vol. 32, No. 4, pp. 55.1–55.12.

Beronä, David A. (2012), "Wordless Comics: The Imaginative Appeal of Peter Kuper's *The System*," Matthew J. Smith and Randy Duncan (eds.), *Critical Approaches to Comics*, New York: Routledge.

Blackbeard, Bill, and Dale Crain, (1995), *The Comic Strip Century: Celebrating 100 Years of an American Art Form*, Englewood Cliffs, NJ: Kitchen Sink Press.

Brosgol, Vera (2011), *Anya's Ghost*, New York: Square Fish.

Brown, Eliot (1985), cover art, *Amazing Spider-Man,* #262, New York: Marvel.

Brunetti, Ivan (2011), *Cartooning: Philosophy and Practice*, New Haven: Yale University Press.

Burns, Charles (2005), *Black Hole*, New York: Pantheon.

Buscema, Sal, and Len Wein (1974), *The Defenders*, #16, New York: Marvel.

Carney, James, Robin Dunbar, Anna Machin, Tamás Dávid-Barrett, and Mauro Silva Júnior (2014), "Social Psychology and the Comic-book Superhero: A Darwinian Approach," *Philosophy and Literature*, Vol. 38, No. 1A, pp. A195–A215.

Carrier, David (2000), *The Aesthetics of Comics*, University Park: Pennsylvania State University Press.

Carroll, Emily (2014), *Through the Woods*, New York: Margaret K. McElderry Books.

Chabon, Michael (2008), "Secret Skin: An essay in unitard theory," *The New Yorker*, 10 March, pp. 64–9.

Christiansen, Hans-Christian (2000), "Comics and Film: A Narrative Perspective," A. Magnussen and H.-C. Christiansen (eds.), *Comics and Culture: Analytical and Theoretical Approaches to Comics*, Copenhagen: Museum of Tusculanum Press, pp. 107–21.

Chute, Hillary (2010), *Graphic Women: Life Narrative and Contemporary Comics*, New York: Columbia University Press.

Chute, Hillary (2011), "Materializing Memory: Lynda Barry's *One Hundred Demons*," Michael A. Chaney (ed.), *Graphic Subjects: Critical Essays on Autobiography and Graphic Novels*, Madison: University of Wisconsin Press, pp. 282–309.

Chute, Hillary (2016), *Disaster Drawn: Visual Witness, Comics and Documentary Form*, Cambridge, MA: Harvard University Press.

Coates, Ta-Nehisi, and Daniel Acuna (2016), *Black Panther: A Nation Under Our Feet*, New York: Marvel.

Cohn, Jesse (2006), "Translator's Comments on Benoît Peeters, 'Four Conceptions of the Page,'" *ImageTexT: Interdisciplinary Comics Studies*, Vol. 3, No. 3. Available online: http://imagetext.english.ufl.edu/archives/v3_3/cohn/.

Cohn, Neil (2003), *Early Writings on Visual Language*, Carlsbad, CA: Emaki Productions.

Cohn, Neil (2005), "Un-Defining 'Comics,'" *International Journal of Comic Art*, Vol. 7. No. 2, pp. 1–11.

Cohn, Neil (2007), "A Visual Lexicon," *The Public Journal of Semiotics*, Vol. 1. No. 1, pp. 35–56.

Cohn, Neil (2010), "The Limits of Time and Transitions: Challenges to Theories of Sequential Image Comprehension," *Studies in Comics*, Vol. 1, No. 1, pp. 127–47.

Cohn, Neil (2013), *The Visual Language of Comics*, London: Bloomsbury.

Cohn, Neil (2016), "A Multimodal Parallel Architecture: A Cognitive Framework for Multimodal Interactions," *Cognition*, Vol. 146, pp. 304–23.

Cohn, Neil (2019), "Your Brain on Comics: A Cognitive Model of Visual Narrative Comprehension," *Topics in Cognitive Science*, Vol., 12, No. 1, pp. 1–35.

Cohn, Neil (2021), *Who Understands Comics? Questioning the Universality of Visual Language Comprehension*, London: Bloomsbury.

Cohn, Neil, and Stephen Maher (1915), "The notion of the motion: The neurocognition of motion lines in visual narratives," *Brain Research*, Vol. 1601, pp. 73–84.

Cohn, Neil, and Hannah Campbell (2015), "Navigating comics II: Constraints on the reading order of page layouts," *Applied Cognitive Psychology*, Vol. 29, pp. 193–9.

Cohn, Neil, and Kent Worcester (2015), "Visual Language: Neil Cohn and Kent Worcester in Conversation," *International Journal of Comic Art*, Vol. 17, No. 1, pp. 1–23.

Cook, Roy T. (2011), "'Do Comics Require Pictures? Or Why *Batman* #663 Is a Comic," *Journal of Aesthetics and Art Criticism*, Vol. 69, No. 3, pp. 285–96.

Cook, Roy T. (2012), "Drawings of Photographs in Comics," *The Journal of Aesthetics and Art Criticism*, Vol. 70, No. 1, pp. 129–40.

Cook, Roy T. (2015), "Judging a comic book by its cover: Marvel Comics, Photo-covers, and the objectivity of photography," *Image & Narrative,* Vol. 16. No. 2, pp. 14–27.

Cook, Roy T. (2015a), "My Definition of Comics," *Hooded Utilitarian*, March 29. Available online: http://www.hoodedutilitarian.com/2015/03/my-definition-of-comics.

Corman, Leela (2012), *Unterzahkn*, New York: Schocken.

Cruse, Howard (1995), *Stuck Rubber Baby*, New York: DC.

D'Salete, Marcelo (2019), *Angola Janga*, Seattle: Fantagraphics.

DeConnick, Kelly Sue, and Emma Rios (2014), *Pretty Deadly*, Vol. 1, Berkeley: Image.

Daniels, Les (1998), *Superman: The Complete History, The Life and Times of the Man of Steel*, San Francisco: Chronicle.

Davies, Paul Fisher (2013), "'Animating' the narrative in abstract comics," *Studies in Comics*, Vol. 4, No. 2, pp. 251–76.

Dean, M. (2000), *The Ninth Art: Traversing the Cultural Space of the American Comic Book*, Dissertation, Milwaukee: University of Wisconsin-Milwaukee.

Delporte, Julie (2019), *This Woman's Work*, Montreal: Drawn & Quarterly.

del Rey Cabero, Enrique, Michael Goodrum, and Josean Morlesín Mellado (2021), *How to Study Comics & Graphic Novels: A Graphic Introduction to Comics Studies*, Oxford: Oxford Comics Network.

Dolezel, Lubomir (1998), *Heterocosmica: Fiction and Possible Worlds*, Baltimore: Johns Hopkins University Press.

Doucet, Julie (2013), *My New York Diary*, Montreal: Drawn & Quarterly.

Drimmer, Sonja (2017), "The Manuscript as an Ambigraphic Medium: Hoccleve's Scribes, Illuminators, and Their Problems," *Exemplaria*, Vol. 29, No. 3, pp. 175–94.

Dubose, Mike S. (2007), "Holding Out for a Hero: Reaganism, Comic Book Vigilantes, and Captain America," *The Journal of Popular Culture*, Vol. 40, No. 6, pp. 915–35.

Duncan, Randy (2012), "Images Functions: Shape and Color as Hermeneutic Images in *Asterios Polyp*," Matthew J. Smith and Randy Duncan (eds.), *Critical Approaches to Comics*, New York: Routledge.

Duncan, Randy, and Matthew J. Smith (2015), *The Power of Comics: History, Form, and Culture*, London: Bloomsbury.

Earle, Harriet E. H. (2021), *Comics: An Introduction*, New York: Routledge.

Earle, Monalesia (2019), *Writing Queer Women of Color: Representation and Misdirection in Contemporary Fiction and Graphic Narratives*, Jefferson, NC: McFarland.

Earle, Monalesia, and Chris Gavaler (2021), "Misdirections in Matt Baker's *Phantom Lady* Viewing Paths," Qiana Whitted (ed.), *Desegregating Comics: Debating Blackness in Early American Comics, 1900–1960*, New Brunswick: Rutgers University Press.

Eco, Umberto (1965), "A Reading of Steve Canyon," *Comic Iconclasm*, London: ICA, pp. 20–5.

Egan, Jennifer (2011), *A Visit from the Goon Squad*, New York: Knopf.

Eisner, Will (1995), *Signal from Space*, New York: Norton.

Eisner, Will (2001), *Will Eisner's The Spirit Archives*, Vol. 4, New York: DC.

Eisner, Will (2008), *Comics and Sequential Art: Principles and Practices from the Legendary Artist*, New York: Norton.

Eisner, Will (2008a), *Graphic Storytelling and Visual Narrative*, New York: Norton.

Ernst, Max (1976), *Une Semaine De Bonte: A Surrealistic Novel in Collage*, Mineola, NY: Dover Publications.

Evens, Brecht (2016), *Panther*, Montreal: Drawn & Quarterly.

Evnine, Simon J. (2015), "'But Is It Science Fiction?': Science Fiction and a Theory of Genre," *Midwest Studies in Philosophy*, Vol. 39, No. 1, pp. 1–28.

Finck, Liana (2019), "How to Make Comics & Cartoons: A Very Particular Guide," *New York Times Book Review*, Sketchbook, October 13, p. 27.

Flood, Allison (2012), "William Faulkner's *The Sound and the Fury* to be published in colored ink," *The Guardian*, July 4. Available online: http://www.theguardian.com/books/2012/jul/04/william-faulkner-sound-fury-coloured-ink.

Forceville, Charles (2002), "The identification of target and source in pictorial metaphors," *Journal of Pragmatics*, Vol. 34, pp. 1–14.

Forceville, Charles, Elisabeth El Refaie, and Gert Meesters (2012), "Stylistics and comics," Michael Burke (ed.), *Routledge Handbook of Stylistics*, New York: Routledge.

Fortress, Karl E. (1963), "The Comics as Non-Art," David Manning White and Robert H. Abel (eds.), *The Funnies: An American Idiom*, New York: The Free Press.

Foster-Dimino, Sophia (2017), *Sex Fantasy*, Toronto: Koyama Press.

Fraction, Matt, and David Aja (2015), *Hawkeye: My Life as a Weapon*, New York: Marvel.

Fraction, Matt, and David Aja (2015), *Hawkeye: Rio Bravo*, New York: Marvel.

Freytag, Gustave (1900), *Technique of the Drama: An Exposition of Dramatic Composition and Art*, Chicago: Scott, Foresman and Company, Internet Archive. Available online: https://archive.org/details/freytagstechniqu00freyuoft/page/114.

García, Santiago (2010), *On the Graphic*, trans. Bruce Campbell, Jackson: University Press of Mississippi.

Gavaler, Chris (2018), *Superhero Comics*, London: Bloomsbury.

Gavaler, Chris, and Leigh Ann Beavers (2021), *Creating Comics: A Writer's and Artist's Guide and Anthology*, London: Bloomsbury.

Gavaler, Chris, and Nathaniel Goldberg (2019), *Superhero Thought Experiments: Comic Book Philosophy*, Iowa City: University of Iowa Press.

Gertler, Nat (ed.) (2002), *Panel One: Comic Book Scripts by Top Writers*, Thousand Oaks, CA: About Comics.

gg (2017), *I'm Not Here*, Toronto: Koyama Press.

Gillen, Kieron, and Jamie McKelvie (2013), *Phonograph: The Singles Club,* Berkeley: Image.

Gillen, Kieron, and Jamie McKelvie (2014), *The Wicked + The Divine: The Faust Act*. Berkeley: Image.

Gloeckner, Phoebe (2001), *A Child's Life and Other Stories*, Berkeley: Frog Books.

Goldberg, Nathaniel, and Chris Gavaler (2020), *Revising Fiction, Fact, and Faith: A Philosophical Account*, New York: Routledge.

Goldstein, Sophie (2015), *The Oven*, Richmond, VA: AdHouse Books.

Gombrich, E. H. (1960), *Art and Illusion: A Study in the Psychology of Pictorial Representation*, Princeton: Princeton University Press.

Goodman, Nelson (1976), *Languages of Art: An Approach to a Theory of Symbols*, Indianapolis: Hackett.

Gordon, Ian (1998), *Comic Strips and Consumer Culture: 1890–1945*, Washington: Smithsonian Institution Press.

Grant, Pat (2019), "The Board and the Body: Material Constraints and Style in Graphic Narrative," *The Comics Grid: Journal of Comics Scholarship*, Vol. 9, No. 1, p. 4. Available online: https://www.comicsgrid.com/articles/10.16995/cg.145/.

Gravett, Paul (2013), *Comics Art*, New Haven: Yale University Press.

Greenberg, Clement (2004), "Steig's Cartoons: Review of *All Embarrassed* by Willilam Steig," Jeet Heer and Kent Worcester (eds.), *Arguing Comics: Literary Masters on a Popular Medium*, Jackson: University of Mississippi Press, pp. 7–8.

Grennan, Simon (2017), *A Theory of Narrative Drawing*, New York: Palgrave Macmillan.

Groensteen, Thierry (2007), *The System of Comics*, trans. Bart Beaty and Nick Nguyen, Jackson: University Press of Mississippi.

Groensteen, Thierry (2010), "The Monstrator, the Recitant and the Shadow of the Narrator," *European Comic Art*, Vol. 3, No. 1, pp. 1–21.

Groensteen, Thierry (2013), *Comics and Narration*, trans. Ann Miller, Jackson: University Press of Mississippi.

Groensteen, Thierry (2016), "The Art of Braiding: A Clarification," *European Comic Art*, Vol. 9, No. 1, pp. 88–98.

Grünewald, Dietrich (2012), "The Picture Story Principle," *International Journal of Comic Art*, Vol. 14, No. 1, pp. 171–97.

Hague, Ian (2014), *Comics and the senses: A multisensory approach to comics and graphic novels*, New York: Routledge.

Hamm, Jack (1967), *Cartooning the Head and Figure*, New York: Perigee.

Hard, Bridgette Martin, Gabriel Recchia, and Barbara Tversky (2011), "The Shape of Action," *Journal of Experimental Psychology*, Vol. 140, No. 4, pp. 586–604.

Harvey, Robert C. (1979), "The Aesthetics of the Comic Strip," *Journal of Popular Culture*, Vol. 12, No. 4, pp. 640–52.

Harvey, Robert C. (2005), "Describing, Discarding 'Comics,'" Jeff McLaughlin (ed.), *Comics as Philosophy*, Jackson: University Press of Mississippi, pp.14–26.

Haskett, Maggie Shapiro (2019), "Animating Questions: An Introduction to Miriam Libicki's *Glasnost Kids*," *Shenandoah*, Vol. 68, No. 2.

Hatfield, Charles (2005), *Alternative Comics: An Emerging Literature*, Jackson: University Press of Mississippi.

Hatfield, Charles (2017), "Introduction: Comics Studies, the Anti-Discipline," Matthew J. Smith and Randy Duncan (eds.), *The Secret Origins of Comics Studies*, New York: Routledge.

Hayashi, Seiiche (2018), *Red Colored Elegy*, Montreal: Drawn & Quarterly.

Hayman, Greg, and John Henry Pratt (2005), "What Are Comics?", David Goldblatt and Lee B. Brown (eds.), *Aesthetics: A Reader in Philosophy of Arts*, Upper Saddle River, NJ: Prentice Hall.

Hayward, Susan (2000), *Cinema Studies: The Key Concepts*, New York: Routledge.

Herriman, George (2010), *Krazy & Ignatz: 1916–1918*, Bill Blackbeard (ed.), Seattle: Fantagraphics.

Hick, Darren Hudson (2014), "The Language of Comics," Aaron Meskin and Roy T. Cook (eds.), *The Art of Comics: A Philosophical Approach*, Oxford: Wiley-Blackwell, pp. 125–46.

Hoffman, Alex (2017), "Review: I'm Not Here by GG," *Sequential State*, October 9. Available online: https://sequentialstate.com/?s#eqi#pc27m#plnot#plhere.

Hodgman, John (2006), Review: *Comics Chronicle, The New York Times*, June 4. Available online: http://www.nytimes.com/2006/06/04/books/review/04hodgman.htm l.

Holbo, John (2014), "Redefining Comics," Aaron Meskin and Roy T. Cook (eds.), *The Art of Comics: A Philosophical Approach*, Chichester: Wiley-Blackwell, pp. 3–30.

Hong, Yeon-sik (2020), *Umma's Table*, Montreal: Drawn & Quarterly.

Hopeless, Dennis, and Javier Rodriguez (2016), *Spider-Woman: Baby Talk*, New York: Marvel.

Hopkins, Robert (2005), "The Speaking Image: Visual Communication of the Nature of Depiction," Mathew Kieran (ed.), *Contemporary Debates in Aesthetics and the Philosophy of Art*, Oxford: Blackwell, pp.145–59.

Horrocks, Dylan (2001), "Inventing Comics: Scott McCloud's Definition of Comics," *The Comics Journal* #234, June, pp. 29–38.

Hyde, Emily (2016), "Flat Style: *Things Fall Apart* and Its Illustrations," *Publications of the Modern Language Association of America*, Vol. 131, No. 1, pp. 20–37.

Inge, M. Thomas (1990), *Comics as Culture*, Jackson: University Press of Mississippi.

Jackendoff, Ray (2007), *Language, consciousness, culture: Essays on mental structure* (Jean Nicod lectures), Cambridge, MA: MIT Press.

Jackendoff, Ray (2009), "Parallels and Nonparallels Between Language and Music," *Music Perception*, Vol. 26, No. 3, pp. 195–204.

Jacob, Mira (2015), "37 Difficult Questions From My Mixed-Race Son," *Buzzfeed*, June 8. Available online: https://www.buzzfeednews.com/article/mirajacob/questions-from-my-mixed-race-son.

Johnson, Rikuo (2005), *Night Fisher*, Seattle: Fantagraphics.

Jousselin, Pascal (2018), *Mister Invincible: Local Hero*, Magnetic Press.

Kane, Bob, and Bill Finger (2005), *The Batman Chronicles,* Vol. 1, New York: DC.

Karasik, Paul, and Mark Newgarden (2017), *How to Read Nancy: The Elements of Comics in Three Easy Panels*, Seattle: Fantagraphics.

Keen, Suzanne (2003), *Narrative Form*, New York: Palgrave Macmillan.

Khordoc, Katherine (2001), "The Comic Book's Soundtrack: Visual Sound Effects in *Asterix*," Robin Varnum and Christina T. Gibbons (eds.), *The Language of Comics: Word and Image*, Jackson: University Press of Mississippi, pp. 156–73.

Kintsch, Walter (1998), *Comprehension: A Paradigm for Cognition*, Cambridge: Cambridge University Press.

Kirby, Jack, and Stan Lee (2008), *Essential Fantastic Four*, Vol. 1, New York: Marvel.

Kirkus Review (2019), Review: *Good Talk*: A Memoir in Conversations, Available online: https://www.kirkusreviews.com/book-reviews/mira-jacob/good-talk/.

Kirkman, Robert, and Tony Moore (2010), *The Walking Dead, Volume I: Days Gone Bye*, Berkeley: Image.

Klein, Cheryl (2019), "Brown, Black and White in America: PW Talks with Mira Jacob," *Publishers Weekly*, March 5. Available online: https://www.publishersweekly.com/pw/by-topic/authors/interviews/article/79433-brown-black-and-white-in-america-pw-talks-with-mira-jacob.html.

Kornberg, Dianne, and Celia Bland (2014), *Madonna Comix*, Portland, OR: Media F8.

Kress, Gunther, and Theo van Leeuwen (1996), *Reading Images: The Grammar of Visual Design*, New York: Routledge.

Krug, Nora (2018), *Belonging: A German Reckons with History and Home*, New York: Scribner.

Kukkonen, Karin (2013), *Contemporary Comics Storytelling*, Lincoln, NE: University of Nebraska Press.

Kwa, Shiamin (2020), *Regarding Frames: Thinking with Comics in the Twenty-First Century*, Rochester: RIT Press.

LaValles, Victor, and Dietrich Smith (2018), *Destroyer*, Los Angeles: Boom! Studios.

Lee, Hannah K. (2017), *Language Barrier*, Toronto: Koyama Press.

Lee, Stan, and Jack Kirby (2008), *Essential Fantastic Four*, Vol. 1, New York: Marvel.

Lee, Stan, Jack Kirby, and Jim Steranko (2014), *Marvel Masterworks: Captain America*, Vol. 3, New York: Marvel.

Lee, Stan, and Steve Ditko (2009), *Marvel Masterworks: The Amazing Spider-Man*, Vol. 1, New York: Marvel.

Lefèvre, Pascal (2000), "The Importance of Being Published," Anne Magnussen and Hans-Christian Christiansen (eds.), *Comics and Culture: Analytical and Theoretical Approaches to Comics*, Copenhagen: Museum Tusculanum Press, pp. 91–107.

Lefèvre, Pascal (2009), "The Construction of Space in Comics," Jeet Heer and Kent Worcester (eds.), *A Comics Studies Reader*, Jackson: University of Mississippi Press.

Lefèvre, Pascal (2011), "Some Medium-Specific Qualities of Graphic Sequences," *SubStance* Vol. 40, No. 1, #124, pp. 14–33.

Lefèvre, Pascal (2012), "Mise en scène and Framing: Visual Storytelling in Lone Wolf and Club," Matthew J. Smith and Randy Duncan (eds.), *Critical Approaches to Comics*, New York: Routledge.

Lefèvre, Pascal (2016), "No Content without Form: Graphic Style as the Primary Entrance to a Story," Neil Cohn (ed.), *The Visual Narrative Reader*, London: Bloomsbury, pp. 67–87.

Libicki, Miriam (2016), *Toward a Hot Jew: Graphic Essays*, Seattle: Fantagraphics.

Libicki, Miriam (2019), "Laying Down One Line After Another," *Shenandoah*, Februay 7. Available online: https://shenandoahliterary.org/thepeak/laying-down-one-line-after-another/.

Lucie-Smith, Edward (1981), *The Art of Caricature*, Ithaca: Cornell University Press.

Lynch, John Gilbert Bohun (1927), *A History of Caricature*, Boston, MA: Little, Brown, and Company.

McCloud, Scott (1993), *Understanding Comics: The Invisible Art*, New York: Kitchen Sink Press.

McCloud, Scott (2006), *Making Comics: Storytelling Secrets of Comics, Manga and Graphic Novels*, New York: Harper.

McGuire, Richard (2014), *Here*, New York: Pantheon.

McFarlane, Todd, and Bob Wiacek (1988), cover art, *The Incredible Hulk,* No. 340, New York: Marvel.

McKean, Dave (2016), *Black Dog: The Dreams of Paul Nash*, Milwaukie, OR: Dark Horse.

McKean, Dave (2016), *Cages*, Milwaukie, OR: Dark Horse.

McMillen, Stuart (2019), "My signature trademark: visual scenes broken into panels," stuartmcmillen.com, May. Available online: https://www.stuartmcmillen.com/blog/visual-trademark-broken-into-panels/.

Madden, Matt (2005), *99 Ways to Tell a Story: Exercises in Style*, New York: Chamberlain Bros.

Mag Uidhir, Christy (2013), "How to Frame Serial Art," *Journal of Aesthetics and Art Criticis*, Vol. 71, No. 3, pp. 261–5.

Mag Uidhir, Christy (2014), "Comics and Collective Authorship," Aaron Meskin and Roy T. Cook (eds.), *The Art of Comics: A Philosophical Approach*, Oxford: Wiley-Blackwell.

Mantlo, Bill, Butch Guice, Rick Magyar, Carl Gafford, and Rick Parker (1983), *The Avengers Annuals* #12 (November), New York: Marvel.

Marble, Annie Russell (2004), "The Reign of the Spectacular," Jeet Heer and Kent Worcester (eds.), *Arguing Comics: Literary Masters on a Popular Medium*, Jackson: University of Mississippi Press, pp. 7–8.

Marchetto, Marisa Acocella (2006), *CancerVixen*, New York: Pantheon.

Maroh, Julie (2010), *Blue is the Warmest Color*, Vancouver: Arsenal Pulp Press.

Masereel, Frans (1989), *The City, The Sun, Landscapes and Voices*, and *Hamburg*, Berlin: Schocken.

Mateu-Mestre, Marcos (2010), *Framed Ink: Drawing and Composition for Visual Storytelling*, Culver City, CA: Design Studio Press.

Mather, David (2016), "Analogies," Caroline A. Jones, David Mather and Rebecca Uchill (eds.), *Experience: Culture, Cognition, and the Common Sense*, Cambridge, MA: MIT Press, pp. 56–71.

Matisse, Henri (1985), *Jazz*, New York: George Braziller.

Medley, Stuart (2010), "Discerning pictures: how we look at and understand images in comics," *Studies in Comics*, Vol. 1, No. 1, pp. 53–70.

Mendelsund, Peter (2014), *What We See When We Read*, New York: Vintage.

Meskin, Aaron (2007), "Defining Comics?" *Journal of Aesthetics and Art Criticism*, Vol. 65, No. 4, pp. 369–79.

Meskin, Aaron (2014), "The Ontology of Comics," Aaron Meskin and Roy T. Cook (eds.), *The Art of Comics: A Philosophical Approach*, Oxford: Wiley-Blackwell, pp. 31–46.

Mikkonen, Kai (2017), *The Narratology of Comic Art*, New York: Routledge.

Mikkonen, Kai, and Olli Philippe Lautenbacher (2019), "Global Attention in Reading Comics: Eye-movement Indications of Interplay between Narrative Content and Layout," *ImageTexT: Interdisciplinary Comics Studies*, Vol. 10, No. 2. Available online: imagetext.english.ufl.edu/archives/v10_2/mikkonen/).

Miller, Ann (2007), *Reading Bande Dessinée: Critical Approaches to French-Language Comic Strip,* Bristol: Intellect Books.

Miller, Frank, and Bill Sienkiewicz (2012), *Elektra: Assassin*, New York: Marvel.

Mitchell, W. T. J. (1994), *Picture Theory: Essays on Verbal and Visual Representation*, Chicago: The University of Chicago Press.

Miodrag, Hannah (2010), "Fragmented Text: The Spatial Arrangement of Words in Comics," *International Journal of Comic Art*, Vol. 12, No. 2/3, pp. 309–27.

Miodrag, Hannah (2013), *Comics and Language: Reimagining Critical Discourse on the Form*, Jackson: University Press of Mississippi.

Molotiu, Andrei (2009), *Abstract Comics*, Seattle: Fantagraphics.

Molotiu, Andrei (2012), "Abstract Form: Sequential Dynamism and Iconostatis in Abstract Comics and Steve Ditko's *Amazing Spider-Man*," Matthew J. Smith and Randy Duncan (eds.), *Critical Approaches to Comics*, New York: Routledge.

Moore, Alan (2008), *Alan Moore's Writing for Comics*, Rantoul, IL: Avatar.

Moore, Alan, and Dave Gibbons (1987), *Watchmen*, New York: DC.

Moore, Alan, and Eddie Campbell (2001), *From Hell*, Paddington, Australia: Eddie Campbell Comics.

Mulvey, Laura (1999), "Visual Pleasure and Narrative Cinema," Leo Braudy and Marshall Cohen (eds.), *Film Theory and Criticism: Introductory Readings*, Oxford: Oxford University Press, pp. 833–44.

Murel, Jake (2019), "Belonging: A German Reckons with History and Home," *The Comics Journal*, November 19.

Muth, Jon J., Kent Williams, Walter Simonson, and Louise Simonson (1988), *Havok & Wolverine—Meltdown* #1, New York: Epic.

Nattiez, Jean-Jacques, and Katharine Ellis (1990), "Can One Speak of Narrativity in Music?" *Journal of the Royal Musical Association*, Vol. 115, No. 2, pp. 240–57.

Newtson, Darren, and Gretchen Engquist (1976), "The perceptual organization of ongoing behavior," *Journal of Experimental Social Psychology*, Vol. 12, No. 5, pp. 436–50.

Newtson, Darren, Gretchen Engquist, and Joyce Bios (1977), "The Objective Basis of Behavior Units," *Journal of Personality and Social Psychology*, Vol. 35, No. 12, pp. 847–62.

Nikolajeva, Maria, and Carole Scott (2016), *How Picture Books Work*, New York: Routledge.

Nguyen, Nhu-Hoa (2006), "The Rhetoric of Omission in Comic Art," *International Journal of Comic Art*, Vol. 8, No. 1, pp. 283–300.

Newman, Samuel P. (1827), *A Practical System of Rhetoric*, Portland, OR: William Hyde.

O'Neil, Dennis (2001), *The DC Comics Guide to Writing Comics*, New York: DC.

Oravetz, Kenneth (2019), "The Comics Lens: Madeleine Witt as an Exempla of New Modes of Comics Thought," Comics Studies Society Conference, University of Illinois at Urbana-Champaign, August 2018.

Oyola, Osvaldo (2012), "Who is Peter Parker?" *The Middle Spaces*, July 16. Available online: https://themiddlespaces.com/2012/07/16/who-is-peter-parker/.

Palahniuk, Chuck, and Cameron Stewart (2015), *Fight Club II*, Milwaukie, OR: Dark Horse.

Pederson, Kaitlin, and Neil Cohn (2016), "The changing pages of comics: Page layouts across eight decades of American superhero comics," *Studies in Comics*, Vol. 7, No. 1, pp. 7–28.

Pedri, Nancy (2015), "What's the Matter of Seeing in Graphic Memoir?" *South Central Review*, Vol. 32, No. 3, pp. 8–29.

Peeters, Benoît (2007), "Four Conceptions of the Page," trans. Jesse Cohn, *ImageTexT: Interdisciplinary Comics Studies*, Vol. 3, No. 3. Available online: http://imagetext.english. ufl.edu/archives/v3_3/peeters/.

Peirce, Charles Sanders (1984), *The Writings of Charles S. Peirce*, Volume 2: 1867–1871, Edward C. Moore (ed.), Peirce Edition Project. Bloomington: Indiana University Press.

Percy, Benjamin (2016), "Superpowered Storytelling: What I've Learned from Writing Comics," *Poets & Writers*, Vol. 44, No. 4, pp. 25–8.

Pérez, George, and John Costanza (1988), *Wonder Woman #20* (September), New York: DC.

Postema, Barbara (2013), *Narrative Structure in Comics: Making Sense of Fragments*, Rochester: RIT Press.

Pratt, Henry John (2009), "Narrative in Comics," *Journal of Aesthetics and Art Criticism*, Vol. 67, No. 1, pp. 107–17.

Pyle, Kevin (2012), *Take What You Can Carry*, New York: Square Fish.

Radvansky, Gabriel A., and Jeffrey M. Zacks (2014), *Event Cognition*, Oxford: Oxford University Press.

Ramsey, Luke (2015), *Intelligent Sentient?*, Montreal: Drawn & Quarterly.

Reed, Brian (2004), "'Eden or Ebb of the Sea': Susan Howe's Word Squares and Postlinear Poetics," *Postmodern Culture*. Available online: http://pmc.iath.virginia.edu/ issue.104/14.2reed.html.

Rifkind, Candida, Brandon Christopher, and Alice RL (2019), *How Comics Work*, Winnipeg: Department of English, University of Winnipeg. Available online: https:// www.uwinnipeg.ca/1b19/docs/how-comics-work-web-cc-by-nc-nd.pdf

Roberts, Keiler (2018), *Chlorine Gardens*, Toronto: Koyoma Press.

Rogers, Sean (2017), "Review: GG's *I'm Not Here*," *The Globe and Mail*, September 15. Available online: https://www.theglobeandmail.com/arts/books-and-media/book-reviews/review-ggs-im-not-here-gary-panters-songy-of-paradise-and-mimi-ponds-the-customer-is-always-wrong/article36275951/.

Rucka, Greg, and J. H. Williams III (2010), *Batwoman: Elegy*, New York: DC.

Rust, Martha (2016), "Circles, Lines, and Coils: Picturing Life Stories in Medieval Manuscripts and Rolls," New York Comics & Picture-story Symposium, The New School, September 20, 2016.

Sabin, Roger (1996), *Comics, Comix & Graphic Novels: A History of Comic Art*, London: Phaidon.

Samson, Jacques (2014), "Modern Pictorial Enunciative Strategies," Ann Miller and Bart Beaty (eds.), *The French Comics Theory Reader*, Leuven: Leuven University Press, pp. 157–62.

Sanford, Anthony J., and Patrick Sturt (2002), "Depth of processing in language comprehension: Not noticing the evidence," *Trends in Cognitive Sciences*, Vol. 6, No. 9, pp. 382–86.

Santoro, Frank (2019), *Pittsburgh*, New York: New York Review Comics.

Saraceni, Mario (2003), *The Language of Comics*, New York: Routledge.

Saraceni, Mario (2016), "Relatedness: Aspects of Textual Connectivity in Comics," Neil Cohn (ed.), *The Visual Narrative Reader*, London: Bloomsbury, pp. 115–28.

Sayim, Bilge, and Patrick Cavanagh (2011), "What line drawings reveal about the visual brain," *Frontiers in Human Neuroscience*, Vol. 5, Article 115, pp. 1–4.

Schell, Jonathan (2004), "Invitation to a Degraded World," *Final Edition*, Vol. 1, No. 1. Available online: https://www.motherjones.com/politics/2004/10/invitation-degraded-world/.

Schwarcz, Joseph H. (1982), *Ways of the Illustrator: Visual Communication in Children's Literature*, Chicago: American Library Association.

Seth (2007), "Afterword," George A. Walker (ed.), *Graphic Witness: Four Wordless Graphic Novels*, Buffalo: Firefly.

Seth (2004), *It's a Good Life, If You Don't Weaken*, Montreal: Drawn & Quarterly.

Severini, Gino (2009), "Plastic Analogies of Dynamism: Futurist Manifesto," Lawrence Rainey, Christine Poggi, and Laura Wittman (eds.), *Futurism: An Anthology*, New Haven: Yale University Press, pp. 165–168.

Shapton, Leanne (2016), *Was She Pretty?* Montreal: Drawn & Quarterly.

Shklovsky, V. (1970), "Sterne's *Tristram Shandy*: Stylistic Commentary," L. T. Lemon and M. J. Reis (eds., trans.), *Russian Formalist Criticism: Four Essays,* Lincoln, NE: University of Nebraska Press, pp. 25–57.

Shooter, Jim, and John Byrne (1977), *The Avengers*, #166, New York: Marvel.

Shooter, Jim, David D. Michelinie, Sal Buscema, and D. Hands (1978), *The Avengers* #173, July, New York: Marvel.

Siciliano, Gina (2019), *I Know What I Am*, Seattle: Fantagraphics.

Siegel, Jerry, and Joe Shuster (2006), *The Superman Chronicles*, Vol. 1, New York: DC.

Sienkiewicz, Bill (1984), *The New Mutants*, #21, New York: Marvel.

Sienkiewicz, Bill (2019), *Revolution*, Houston: Six Foot Press.

Smith, Andrew A. (2011), "Comics: Neal Adams overview illustrates his lasting impact," *Seattle Times*, June 29. Available online: http://www.seattletimes.com/entertainment/books/comics-neal-adams-overview-illustrateshis-lasting-impact/.

Smolderen, Thierry (2014). *The Origins of Comics: From William Hogarth to Winsor McCay*, trans. Bart Beaty and Nick Ngyen. Jackson: University of Mississippi Press.

Spiegelman, Art (2010), "Reading Pictures," *Lynd Ward*, New York: The Library of America, pp. ix–xxv.

Stainbrook, Eric (2003), *Reading Comics: A Theoretical Analysis of Textuality and Discourse in the Comics Medium*, Dissertation, Pennsylvania: Indiana University of Pennsylvania.

Stainbrook, Eric (2016), "'A Little Cohesion between Friends; Or, We're Just Exploring Our Textuality: Reconciling Cohesion in Written Language and Visual Language," Neil Cohn (ed.), *The Visual Narrative Reader*, London: Bloomsbury, pp.129–54.

Steranko, Jim (2013), *S.H.I.E.L.D by Steranko: The Complete Collection*, New York: Marvel.

Sterckx, Pierre (2014), "The Magnifying Glass or the Sponge," Ann Miller and Bart Beaty (eds.), *The French Comics Theory Reader*, Leuven: Leuven University Press, pp. 139–46.

Sousanis, Nick (2015), *Unflattening*, Cambridge, MA: Harvard University Press.

Szawerna, Michael (2012), "Toward a cognitive approach to analyzing comics: The contrasting construals of comics in similarity-based theories of conceptual representation," Zdzisław Wąsik (ed.), *Alternate Construals in Language and Linguistics*. *Philologica Wratislaviensia: Acta et Studia*, Wroclaw: Philological School of Higher Education, pp. 59–74.

Tabachnick, Stephen (2011), "Autobiography as Discovery in *Epileptic*," Michael A. Chaney (ed.), *Graphic Subjects: Critical Essays on Autobiography and Graphic Novels*, Madison: University of Wisconsin Press, pp.101–66.

Tabachnick, Stephen E. (2017), "From Comics to the Graphic Novel: William Hogarth to Will Eisner," *The Cambridge Companion to the Graphic Novel*, Cambridge: Cambridge University Press, pp. 26–40.

Tabulo, Kym (2014), "Abstract Sequential Art," *Journal of Graphic Novels and Comics*, Vol. 5, No. 1, pp. 29–41.

Talbot, Bryan (2007), *Alice in Sunderland: An Entertainment*, Milwaukie, OR: Dark Horse.

Tamaki, Jillian (2015), *SuperMutantMagic Academy*, Montreal: Drawn & Quarterly.

Tanaka, Veronique (2008), *Metronome*, New York: NBM.

Therriault, D. J., M. Rinck, and R. A. Zwaan (2006), "Assessing the Influence of Dimensional Focus during Situation Model Construction," *Memory Cognition*, Vol. 34, No. 1, pp. 78–89.

Todorov, Tzvetan (1969), "Structural Analysis of Narrative," trans. Arnold Weinstein, *NOVEL: A Forum on Fiction*, Vol. 3, No. 1, pp. 70–6.

Tomine, Adrian (2015), *Killing and Dying*, Montreal: Drawn & Quarterly.

Tversky, Barbara (2010), "Visualizing Thought," *Topics in Cognitive Science*, Vol. 3, pp. 499–535.

Tversky, Barbara, Jeffrey M. Zacks, and Bridgette Martin Hard (2007), "The Structure of Experience," Thomas F. Shipley and Jeffrey M. Zacks (eds.), *Understanding Events: From Perception to Action*, Oxford: Oxford University Press.

Ulin, David L. (2014), "Lena Finkle's *Magic Barrel* conjures a new literary form," *Los Angeles Times*, December 21. Available online: http://www.latimes.com/books/jacketcopy/la-ca-jc-anya-ulinich-20140720-story.html.

Ulinich, Anya (2014), *Lena Finkle's Magic Barrel*, New York: Penguin.

Varnum, Robin, and Christina T. Gibbons (2001), "Introduction," Robin Varnum and Christina T. Gibbons (eds.), *The Language of Comics: Word and Image*, Jackson: University Press of Mississippi.

Versaci, Roco (2007), *This Book Contains Graphic Language: Comics as Literature*, New York: Continuum.

Villadsen, Rikke (2018), *The Sea*, Seattle: Fantagraphics.

Walden, Tillie (2017), *Spinning*, New York: First Second.

Waldman, Ayelet (2014), "Unmasters of Sex," *The New York Times*, August 8. Available online: https://www.nytimes.com/2014/08/10/books/review/lena-finkles-magic-barrel-by-anya-ulinich.html.

Walker, Mort (2000), *The Lexicon of Comicana*, Lincoln, NE: Authors Guild.

Walker, George A. (2007), "Introduction," George A. Walker (ed.), *Graphic Witness: Four Wordless Graphic Novels*, Buffalo: Firefly.

Walton, Kendall L. (1990), *Mimesis as Make-Believe: On the Foundations of the Representational Arts*, Cambridge, MA: Harvard University Press.

Ward, Lynd (2010), *Vertigo*, New York: The Library of America.

Ware, Chris (2000), *Jimmy Corrigan, the Smartest Kid on Earth*, New York: Pantheon.

Warhol, Robyn (2011), "The Space Between: A Narrative Approach to Alison Bechdel's *Fun Home*," *College Literature*, Vol. 38, No. 3, pp. 1–20.

Wartenberg, Thomas E. (2012), "Wordy Pictures: Theorizing the Relationship between Image and Text in Comics," Aaron Meskin and Roy T. Cook (eds.), *The Art of Comics: A Philosophical Approach*, Oxford: Wiley-Blackwell, pp. 87–104.

Waugh, Coulton (1947), *The Comics*, Jackson: University Press of Mississippi.

Wershler, Darren, Kalervo Sinervo, and Shannon Tien (2013), "A Network Archeology of Unauthorized Comic Book Scans," *Amodern*, October. Available online: amodern.net/article/a-network-archaeology-of-unauthorized-comic-book-scans/.

Westwell, Chantry (2014), "Medieval Comics." British Library, Medieval manuscripts blog, June 5.

Whalen, D. H., Lisa Zunshine, and Michael Holquist (2012), "Theory of Mind and embedding of perspective: A psychological test of a literary 'sweet spot,'" *Scientific Study of Literature*, Vol. 2, No. 2, pp. 301–15.

Wheeler, Lesley (2020), *The State She's In*, Red Wing, MN: Tinderbox Editions.

Willats, John (2006), "Ambiguity in Drawing," TRACEY, September. Available online: https://www.lboro.ac.uk/microsites/sota/tracey/journal/ambi/images/Willats.pdf.

Wilson, Andrew (2005), "My Likeness, My Brother: A powerful autobiographical work from a prizewinning creator of comics in France," *Books & Culture: A Christian Review*, March. Available online: https://www.booksandculture.com/articles/webexclusives/2005/March/050307.html?paging=off.

Witek, Joseph (1989), *Comic Books as History: The Narrative Art of Jack Jackson, Art Spiegelman, and Harvey Pekar*, Jackson: University Press of Mississippi.

Witek, Joseph (2009), "The Arrow and the Grid," Jeet Heer and Kent Worcester (eds.), *A Comics Studies Reader*, Jackson: University Press of Mississippi.

Witek, Joseph (2012), "Comics Modes: Caricature and Illustration in the Crumb Family's *Dirty Laundry*," Matthew J. Smith and Randy Duncan (eds.), *Critical Approaches to Comics*, New York: Routledge.

Wolk, Douglas (2007), *Reading Comics: How Graphic Novels Work and What They Mean*, Cambridge, MA: Da Capo Press.

Wollheim, Richard (1987), *Painting as an Art*, Princeton: Princeton University Press.

Wolterstorff, Nicholas (1980), *Works and Worlds of Art*, Oxford: Clarendon Press.

Woo, Benjamin (2019), "What Kind of Studies is Comics Studies?" Frederick Luis Aldama (ed.), *The Oxford Handbook of Comic Book Studies*, Oxford: Oxford University Press.

Wordsworth, William (1908), *The Poems of Williams Wordsworth*, London: Methuen.

Yslaire and Balac (2016), *Sambre, #1*, Grenoble: Glénat.

Zacks, Jeffrey M., and Barbara Tversky (2001), "Event Structure in Perception and Conception," *Psychological Bulletin*, Vol. 127, No. 1, pp. 3–21.

Zub, Jim, and Steve Cummings (2015), *Wayward*, Portland, OR: Image.

Zucchi, Cino (2011), "(S)love(n)ly Art," Michael Dumontier and Neil Farber, *Constructive Abandonment*, Montreal: Drawn & Quarterly.

Zunshine, Lisa (2011), "What to Expect When You Pick Up a Graphic Novel," *SubStance*, Vol. 40, No. 1, pp. 114–34.

Index

Note: Illustrations are indicated by '*ill.*'